Fullness of Faith

ISAAC HECKER STUDIES
IN RELIGION AND AMERICAN CULTURE

FULLNESS OF FAITH

The Public Significance of Theology

Michael J. Himes
&
Kenneth R. Himes, OFM

Paulist Press
New York/Mahwah, New Jersey

Cover Photo: United Press International

Library of Congress Cataloging-in-Publication Data

Himes, Michael J.
    Fullness of faith: the public significance of theology/Michael J. Himes & Kenneth R. Himes.
    p.   cm.—(Isaac Hecker studies in religion and American culture)
    Includes bibliographical references.
    ISBN 0-8091-3372-5 (pbk.)
    1. Sociology, Christian (Catholic)   2. Christian ethics—Catholic authors.   3. Catholic Church—Doctrines.   4. Church and social problems —United States.   5. Church and social problems—Catholic Church.
I. Himes, Kenneth R., 1950–   . II. Title.   III. Series.
BX1753.H575   1993
230′.2—dc20   92-36140
                                                                         CIP

Published by Paulist Press
997 Macarthur Boulevard
Mahwah, NJ 07430

Printed and bound in the
United States of America

Table of Contents

Acknowledgments

Many of our intellectual debts are cited in the endnotes after each chapter. There are, however, others we wish to acknowledge. Kenneth would like to express thanks to Professor Daniel Hardy and the staff at the Center of Theological Inquiry in Princeton, New Jersey. The opportunity to be a member of the Center during the first half of 1991 enabled him to do much of his writing. Kenneth is indebted also to the Franciscan community at Siena College in Loudonville, New York, who provided a home away from home during the second half of 1991 when the rest of his work was done. In particular, Stephen Lynch, OFM, John Mahon, OFM and William McConville, OFM made his stay enjoyable and productive. Finally, Kenneth would like to thank Vincent Cushing, OFM, President of the Washington Theological Union, James Coriden, Academic Dean of the WTU, and the trustees of the school for granting him the sabbatical leave to work on this book.

Michael wishes to express gratitude to the staff and residents of Moreau Seminary at the University of Notre Dame, and to the administration and faculty of the Seminary of the Immaculate Conception in Huntington, New York, for their hospitality during the writing of this book.

Parts of chapter five were given as a lecture at the Joan B. Kroc Institute for International Peace Studies at the University of Notre Dame and as a John Courtney Murray Lecture at the University of Toledo; part of chapter six was included in the 1992 Thomas Aquinas Lecture at the Aquinas Institute of St. Louis University. We both wish to acknowledge the editors of *America, Commonweal* and *Worship,* who first published material we drew upon for this volume. Parts of chapters two, three and five first appeared in *Commonweal* (9/22/88, 3/14/86, 1/26/90, respectively). Material from *America* (5/9/87) is found in chapter four and from *Worship* (5/88) in chapter seven. The editors at *Commonweal* gave us the impetus to collaborate on this volume by publishing the first three essays we wrote together.

Finally, we wish to acknowledge the support of family and friends, not only in this project, but for the gift of faith they have passed on to us. We know well the debt we owe to others for our calling as priests and theologians.

Dedication

It is to our mother,
Mary V. Himes,
whose rich and lively faith has inspired us,
that we dedicate this book.

1

The Public Church and Public Theology

More than a decade ago Martin Marty wrote a slim volume entitled *The Public Church*.[1] For Marty the expression "public church" was descriptive of those "churches which are especially sensitive to the *res publica*, the public order that surrounds and includes people of faith."[2] In Marty's understanding the public church "is a communion of communions, each of which lives its life partly in response to its separate tradition and partly to the calls for a common Christian vocation."[3] This public church is composed of believers from mainstream Protestant, evangelical Protestant and Catholic traditions. Not every member of the communions represented within those headings is part of the public church, for it is more a movement than a formal institution, a zone of shared concerns and beliefs among Christians of different communions. What unites those who belong to the public church is the desire to move religious belief away from a narrow concern with personal life which effectively has undercut the church's mission to the wider realm of social existence.

The public church is an ecumenical model which envisions "Catholics, evangelicals and mainline Protestants in symbiotic relations." Quoting Johannes Althusius, Marty explains that members of a public church are "*symbiotes* who 'pledge themselves each to the other, *by explicit or tacit agreement*, to mutual communication of whatever is useful and necessary for the harmonious exercise of social life,' or now, in this case, Christian life."[4] The commitment of different communions of Christian believers to come together as a public church already exists. "The public church," Marty argues, "does not await invention but discovery."[5] It is "a partial Christian embodiment within public religion." Benjamin Franklin's term, "public religion," is preferable to "civil religion" because the idea of public religion takes "into account the particularities of the faiths that would not disappear or lightly merge to please other

1

founders of the nation." Public religion describes the way that the various churches and other forms of religious polity "contribute out of their separate resources to public virtue and the common weal."[6] The public church, then, is a specifically Christian witness within public religion.

Marty's expression "public church" became popular although, as so often happens, it has come to mean somewhat different things to different people. We use "public church" to mean a community whose social mission is characterized by three things: 1) respect for the legitimate autonomy of other social institutions, i.e. the public church cannot be the hegemonic institution of Christendom but must respect the reality of secularization; 2) acceptance of some responsibility for the well-being of the wider society, i.e. the public church cannot be sectarian, focused solely on the spiritual well-being of its membership; and 3) commitment to work with other social institutions in shaping the common good of the society, i.e. the public church must be broadly ecumenical, working not only with other Christian believers but with all people of good will—believers of all types and non-believers as well.

The Societal Context of the Public Church

The public church illustrates a possible response by believers to a phenomenon which has bedeviled modern Christianity—privatization, the assumption that religion may be an important dimension of people's lives without having any impact on society. Enough studies have been done to dispel the legend of the "secular" person.[7] Despite earlier theories about the inevitable decline of religion in a modern society, the power of religion remains and seems to be growing in its appeal to many. Advocates of the public church do not fear an age without faith but an age of faith without social meaning.

Privatization refers to the tendency to restrict religious faith to the category of the individual while ruling out any engagement of religion with society. Religion then no longer serves as an integrating element in a person's worldview and identity. Instead, life is fragmented into various compartments with religion being one area alongside others with little interaction among the fragments. Fragmentation results because privatization allows the individual to separate religious faith from many areas of life and reduces religion's scope to the areas that are non-relational and asocial. Religious concerns may be real, and religious convictions may be held, but such convictions have no necessary effect upon work, political events, civic associations or economic activities.

Privatization must be distinguished from secularization and secularism. Privatized religion creates a bifurcation between faith and social existence, ruling out any role for religion in social life. It is clearly a major obstacle to vital religious communities. Secularization designates the fact of the removal of many areas of social life—the arts, education, law, government, economic institutions—from the control of religious bodies. Secularism is an ideological denial of the reality of transcendence. Secularization, the decline of the Christian religion's hegemony in many areas of human existence in the west, has been largely beneficial. Science, medicine, business and commerce, education, high and popular culture, would not have developed as they have if autonomy from the churches in Europe and the Americas had not been achieved. Religious believers can acknowledge and welcome these developments. Although privatization has been a by-product of secularization, believers need not oppose secularization in their battle with privatization. Secularization has, however, altered the landscape on which the contest with privatization must be fought. Privatization cannot be overcome by a return to an outmoded and discredited model of church-world engagement such as Christendom. In our secularized context the church must be engaged with but not seek to control society. This new situation for the church has required a decades-long process of adaptation and led to the search for an appropriate strategy of church engagement.

Throughout the twentieth century Catholicism has struggled to define the church's place in society. Although the "siege mentality" of the mid-nineteenth century gave way to a less hostile, but still uneasy, relationship of dialogue with secular society, the mission of the church to the wider world remained unclear. To some it seemed that the task was to bring society into the church. For others the romantic dream of Christendom remained potent. A more common approach in this country was the selective engagement of the Catholic Church with society through the mediation of church-controlled institutions—hospitals, schools, cultural organizations. With Vatican II things changed noticeably. John XXIII's aggiornamento entailed an embrace of the world that may have bordered on being uncritical; certainly it was a posture different from what had preceded it. If modern society had been viewed as an environment hostile to the church, it was now seen as a locus of grace. Grace and nature were no longer oil and water but realities that intermingled, and the human being was to be celebrated, not only converted. The church perceived the need to examine contemporary social existence with a new sense of respect for the many non-religious institutions that contribute to the well-being of humanity. New strategies for the church's activity within a pluralistic, secularized society had to be found.[8]

The public church is a pointer for such a new strategy. It attempts to combat privatization without denying the legitimate autonomy of social institutions from the church. The public church's direct task, however, is not to oppose privatization but to build up the public life of a people. By making reasoned and sound contributions to the way American society understands and organizes itself, the public church demonstrates the trap of privatization and the benefit of a public faith. Thus, privatization is overcome indirectly through the demonstrated value of religious communities to public life. For this reason, the public church is interested in working with others and not standing alone. If the aim is to contribute to the well-being of society, then other groups and individuals in the society should welcome the endeavors of the public church. At the very least, they should be willing to judge the church on the merits of its performance rather than assume *a priori* that any role for the church in public life is a threat to the common good or a slippery slope to religious domination of the public square.

A Public Theology

As believers reflect upon and analyze the experience of a church that is engaged in the nation's public life, a theology emerges which seeks to make sense of the ecclesial experience. Public theology has been defined as "the effort to discover and communicate the socially significant meanings of Christian symbols and tradition."[9] It is a manner of theological reflection which examines the resources latent within the Christian tradition for understanding the church's public role.

Initial intellectual responses to privatization by believers can be found in the development of political theology which was in its early stages a largely European formulation of public theology.[10] It demonstrated that, to attain its mission, the public church must develop a theology which makes the profoundly public import of religious commitment apparent to those who espouse such commitment. Public theology, therefore, serves the church as well as society. It is an attempt to analyze and disseminate the social meaning of a given church's creed to those who profess that creed. Thus, public theology is not primarily apologetic. Its task is hermeneutical, seeking to interpret basic Christian symbols in such a way that believers can discover the full meaning of those symbols.

The assumption of public theology is that the symbols of religious faith carry public meanings. Uncovering these public meanings is one of theology's and theologians' primary tasks. Attention to this task is not mere theological trendiness. It arises from the church's need to balance an existentialist theology that rightly emphasizes the radically personal meanings of religious symbols. Far from being a reductionist method which claims that religious language is disguised social, political, or economic discourse, public theology insists that the full significance of religious language be recognized. Public theology takes William James' pragmatic principle with utmost seriousness, that if something is true, it makes a difference to someone, somewhere, somewhen.[11] Public theology requires us to examine the full range of the consequences of claiming that a religious symbol is true. The someone, the somewhere, and the somewhen which are affected by the symbol's being true or not are human beings engaged in multiple relationships at particular times and in particular places. Thus religious symbols not only resonate within the sanctuaries of souls; they also give shape to and insight into persons acting publicly with others in the real world.

In short, we share the conviction of Martin Marty "that purely private faith is incomplete."[12] Public theology wants to bring the wisdom of the Christian tradition into public conversation to contribute to the well-being of the society. But public theology also aims at rendering an account of Christian belief that articulates what it means to be a member of the church. An interpretation of the Christian creed that ignores the social dimension of human existence falls far short of the fullness of faith.

The Societal Context of Public Theology

The call for the development of a public theology comes at a moment of crisis in American life. Richard Bernstein has noted that the uneasiness with which people discuss the state of public life is not limited to the United States. The reason, Bernstein suggests, is the gradual reduction of reason to what Max Weber called *Zweckrationalität*, instrumental rationality. Public discussion centers on how best to achieve pre-given ends, and "the only concept of 'action' that seems to make sense is the technical application of scientific knowledge."[13] This narrowing of the meaning of reason to one type of rationality is the dark side of the enlightenment legacy. We are left with "a loss of confidence and a deep skepticism about the very possibility of a rational deliberation of the ends and norms that ought to govern our lives. . . ."[14] And so we settle for discussion of the means to ends since science cannot address the questions "How shall we live?" and "For what shall we live?" When reason is defined narrowly as instrumental rationality, there is no hope of reasoned discussion and debate in public about questions of ends. Instead each member of the society is left to make choices in private, justified only to oneself. Fear arises that others will impinge upon individual freedom by imposing social goods which cannot be debated rationally, only enacted by force. This is the state of public life, according to Bernstein: nothing is left to discuss in public.

One finds similar foreboding about the crisis of public life in the analysis offered by Robert Bellah and his colleagues in *Habits of the Heart*.[15] The authors cite what they consider to be a significant problem in the public life of the nation, the inability of people to find a language, a moral tradition, which adequately conveys the nature of social existence. The authors note that Americans experience social relationships of considerable depth and complexity but "have difficulty articulating the richness of their commitments."[16] In the language Americans use, the moral context in which they think, their lives seem more impoverished than they are in fact. Bellah and his associates identify three ongoing cultural conversations since the nation was founded: the "biblical," the "republican," and the "individualist." These three perspectives shape the themes of American life—like success, freedom, fulfillment, justice—in significantly different ways.

The biblical focus, beginning in early Puritan colonial life, develops the theme of a covenanted community transferred to civic and social life. Freedom, within this perspective, has a strong ethical component. Religion and morality are intimately bound together, and the distinction between public and private is not a boundary between religio-ethical concerns and a world divorced from such sensibilities.

The republican tradition, exemplified in Thomas Jefferson or James Madison, draws upon the classical tradition of Greco-Roman political ideals and emphasizes the virtues of public life. The admirable ideal is a life devoted to the betterment of the *polis*. What Jefferson and other American thinkers added to this was the notion of a republic in which everyone participates. Precisely because citizens are equal, they can share in the responsibilities which civic life entails.[17] This republican tradition has a strong ethical component, although its linkage with religion is different from the Puritan model since it provides for religious freedom within the public realm.

The third cultural language, individualism, takes two forms—utilitarian and expressive. Benjamin Franklin represents utilitarian individualism which advocates ambition and self-improvement. Expressive individualism, typified by Walt Whitman, is not so much interested in material well-being as in self-improvement. Freedom and success are measured by the individual's ability to promote his or her emotional as well as intellectual life. According to the authors of *Habits of the Heart*, the individualist tradition in its two forms is dominant in our culture. It is the "first language" of Americans, while the biblical or republican traditions have been relegated to the status of alternative or "second languages."[18] In our private lives expressive individualism is most common while utilitarian individualism rules public life.

The present dilemma is that the dominance of individualism over other cultural "languages" renders us unable to draw upon richer and more communitarian understandings of life. Bellah and his colleagues offer a poignant illustration. Married Americans have more commitment to one another, a greater sense of selfless devotion, than the language of expressive individualism allows them to name adequately. Amid painful moments and demands for self-sacrifice, it is not easy to explain why maintaining a shared life is valuable and concern for the marital relationship important, if all one has to fall back on is talk of self-fulfillment.[19]

As with marriage, so too with citizenship. While people seek more than a life of economic competition and interest group politics, they are tongue-tied when called upon to describe the kind of society sought. The language of individualism makes it difficult for Americans "to think about what a more cooperative, just and equal social order might look like" because the context within which we discuss ideals like freedom, justice and success is skewed by individualism.[20] The description given of one of the persons interviewed by the authors of *Habits of the Heart* is applicable to many, that his "ability to shape a vision of a good life or a good society with others, to debate that vision, and to come to some sort of consensus, is precluded in part by the very definition of freedom" he held, since freedom in the individualist tradition is equated with non-interference.[21]

Bellah and his colleagues are not concerned with a simple gap between our ideals and our practice; that has always been there. Rather, the gulf is between how we act and our ability to articulate our self-understanding. Our ethical discourse cannot carry the freight of our moral lives; we have more commitments to persons and groups, more loyalties to traditions, than we seem able to admit or explain in a cultural conversation limited by the language of individualism. Public discourse, the ability to reason and debate with others, has broken down due to the loss of our other "languages." Utilitarian individualism, like Weber's instrumental rationality, avoids discussion of ends or purposes in favor of means, while expressive individualism reduces ends to personal desires and interests which are outside the realm of public deliberation.

The solution proposed by the writers of *Habits of the Heart* is to retrieve the neglected strands of American public conversation, those of biblical and republican languages, in order to supplement the now dominant individualism. These second languages of public life must be given renewed prominence in the way that Americans talk and think. Renewing the life of "communities of memory"[22] in which the language of civic virtue and biblical morality are sustained is a vital element in the repair of public life. Among the major examples of communities of memory the authors cite religious institutions. In gatherings such as churches people

learn how to relate their experience to that of others and are schooled in a
moral framework which helps them see the connections between the
actions of individuals and the building up of the common good.[23]

This role for the Christian churches and other religious groups
resonates with Bernstein's solution to the crisis of public life. He
wonders "where in our society one can find the vestiges of community
that might still play a role in fostering the type of public life" needed for a
democracy. He continues, "The town meeting, the neighborhood, the
local community council are either destroyed or deformed in our society. . . . It is from this perspective, that I want to raise the question of the
possible role of religion in the future of American public life."[24] Religion's role in public life, according to Bernstein, is not to be yet another
interest group pressing a particular agenda on a pluralist society. Rather,
it is to open a communal space between the individual's private life and
the "impersonal abstractions of society and state."[25] What is needed for
the good of public life is the cultivation of

> those types of public spaces in which individuals can come
> together and debate; can encounter each other in the formation,
> clarification, and testing of opinions; where judgment, delibera-
> tion and *phronesis* can flourish; where individuals become
> aware of the creative power that springs up among them; where
> there is a tangible experience of overcoming the privatization,
> subjectivization, and the narcissistic tendencies so pervasive in
> our daily lives.[26]

For Bernstein the churches hold out hope despite their internal difficulties because vestiges of a communal life and communal bonds still survive
within their confines. Thus, to use the terminology of the authors of
Habits of the Heart, the practices of such communities of memory can be
a way to reawaken the second languages of our public life.

A Roman Catholic Perspective

In the diagnosis of American public life offered by observers like
Bernstein and Bellah and his colleagues, there are striking similarities to
the observations of another figure who wrote decades earlier: John
Courtney Murray. Murray remains a major figure in American Catholic
intellectual history. While best known for his work on the issue of
religious liberty and the question of church-state relations, his interests
were broader. For Murray the controversy over the United States' constitutional arrangement of separation of church and state was a holdover

from the nineteenth century. The development in the Catholic position, championed by Murray and eventually accepted at Vatican II, merely brought Catholic thought into accord with modern democratic political theory. In the twentieth century, Murray maintained, the great issue is not "church and state" but "church and world." How should the church act in relation to a society which is pluralist and secularized? What is the church's contribution to public life in such an environment? The difficulty was that any answer had first to address a problem confronting American society. Murray's analysis of that problem, as well as his proposed response, correlates with much of what is now offered by Bellah and Bernstein and others who perceive a critical problem in American public life.

The claim that freedom is the basis of American society once seemed self-evident, whereas now, Murray observed, it seems problematic. Yet, "the immediate question is not whether the free society is really free," but "whether American society is properly civil." To answer that immediate question one had to establish a clear standard of civility. "The specifying note of political association is its rational deliberative quality, its dependence for its permanent cohesiveness on argument among men."[27] Or again, "the distinctive bond of the civil multitude is reason, or more exactly, that exercise of reason which is argument."[28] For argument to occur one must be clear what the argument is about. Murray posited three themes for public argument that make for civil society.

> First, the argument is about public affairs, the *res publica*, . . . which call for public decision and action by government. . . . Second, the public argument concerns the affairs of the commonwealth. . . . [These are] affairs that fall, at least in decisive part, beyond the limited scope of government. . . . They go beyond the necessities of the public order as such; they bear upon the quality of the common life [e.g. education and the advancement of knowledge].[29]

Murray thought the third theme both the most difficult and the most important element of public argument. "It concerns the constitutional consensus whereby the people acquires its identity as a people and the society is endowed with its vital form . . . its sense of purpose as a collectivity." This consensus was, therefore, necessary for there to be a constitutional order. "This consensus is the intuitional a priori of all the rationalities and technicalities of constitutional and statutory law."[30] Without such a consensus, argument is not really possible. If everything is in doubt, there can be no real disagreement, merely discord and confusion. "There can be no argument except on the premise, and within a context, of agreement."[31]

The great danger to the *juris consensus* is what Murray referred to as "the barbarian." The barbarian does not appear in "bearskins with a club in hand"; the modern barbarian might "wear a Brooks Brothers suit and carry a ball-point pen."[32] The modern barbarian is identified by his or her acts.

> This is perennially the work of the barbarian, to undermine rational standards of judgment, to corrupt the inherited intuitive wisdom by which the people have always lived, and to do this not by spreading new beliefs but by creating a climate of doubt and bewilderment in which clarity about the larger aims of life is dimmed and the self-confidence of the people is destroyed. . . . Today the barbarian is the man who makes open and explicit rejection of the traditional role of reason and logic in human affairs. He is the man who reduces all spiritual and moral questions to the test of practical results or to an analysis of language or to decision in terms of individual subjective feeling.[33]

This description of the barbarian demonstrates Murray's worry about the state of public discourse in the nation. Too many people had come to doubt the fundamental truths on which the nation was founded. Public discourse in a democracy required some commonly held convictions about the nature and foundations of social life so that there could be intelligent communication. Without agreement on some foundational issues no argument was possible, for people would talk past one another, speaking at different levels with different assumptions.

Further complicating the situation was the reality of pluralism. The United States at the mid-point of the twentieth century was neither Puritan New England nor the colonial America of the founders of the republic. The religious or philosophic unity of these societies was gone, and the mark of public life had become its pluralism. People lacked not only a shared universe of discourse but a shared history. Our experiences are so different that "they create not sympathies but alienations" among people.[34]

Looking at America, Murray saw four great communities, conspiracies as he termed them, which offered people a coherent consensual world of meaning, language and opinion. These he identified as Protestant, Catholic, Jewish and secularist. His hope was "somehow to make the four great conspiracies among us conspire into one conspiracy that will be American society—civil, just, free, peaceful, one."[35] The work of the conspirators would be to renew the public philosophy of the nation. Murray agreed that many doubted the existence of such a consensus within the America of his day. But that did not deny the need for such a shared philosophy. The framework for such a project was the natural law tradition. It was Murray's belief that the Catholic Church had an important contribution to make in this regard since it was one of the institutions in American life, possibly the principal institution, which had preserved the philosophical legacy of natural law.[36]

A Public Philosophy

As with many Catholic thinkers who were educated in the heyday of the Thomistic revival, Murray was confident that human reason could know the truths necessary for sound social life (public philosophy) and that reasonable people could achieve agreement on the matter (public consensus). Without such a philosophy and consensus Murray did not think intelligent discourse could be carried on in the political order.

For Murray, public philosophy was a framework for politico-moral conversation rather than a set of moral injunctions. But this did not mean that the public philosophy was purely procedural and without content. Indeed, the argument that the public philosophy was simply a procedure for decision-making was a viewpoint Murray lamented.[37] He maintained that the public philosophy's "focal concept is the idea of law."

> We hold in common a concept of the nature of law and its relationships to reason and will, to social fact and to political purpose. We understand the complex relationship between law and freedom. We have an idea of the relation between the order of law and the order of morals. We also have an idea of the uses of force in support of law. We have criteria of good law, norms of jurisprudence that judge the necessity of law and determine the limits of its usefulness. We have an idea of justice, which is at once the basis of law and its goal. We have an ideal of social equality and of social unity and of the value of law for the achievement of both. We believe in the principle of consent, in terms of which the order of coercive law makes contact with the freedom of the public conscience. We distinguish between state and society, between the relatively narrow order of law as such and the wider order of the total public good. We understand the relation between law and social progress; we grasp the notion of law as a force for orderly change as well as for social stability. We understand the value of law as a

means of educating the public conscience to higher viewpoints on matters of public morality.[38]

Murray was convinced of the necessity of public philosophy if there was to be vitality in the American democratic experience. Civil discourse required public philosophy, for it provided the agreed upon parameters within which genuine argument could occur.[39] Public philosophy had a threefold purpose. Its first function was "to determine the broad purposes of our nation, as a political unity organized for action in history." Secondly, it supplied "the standards according to which judgment is to be passed on the means the nation adopts to further its purposes." Finally, the existence of a public philosophy "furnishes the basis of communication between government and the people and among the people themselves."[40]

Murray saw that America had reached a point of crisis, for the nation no longer operated with a public consensus. This had to be rebuilt through the conspiracy of the four great traditions to bring about a shared public philosophy. This same worry has been given recent expression in *Habits of the Heart* whose authors suggest that the three moral traditions or languages—biblical religion, civic republicanism, and individualism—were the original "conspirators" (to use Murray's term) which gave rise to a public philosophy and nurtured a public consensus. In recent times the public philosophy of the nation has come to be so dominated by individualism that the richness of American public philosophy has been lost. This constriction of public philosophy to but one tradition has imperiled the ability of Americans to make sense of their social experience. While Murray feared the simple demise of public philosophy, Bellah and his colleagues bemoan the impoverished nature of our public philosophy with its excessively individualist premises. What they propose as a remedy is something akin to his project: the renovation of our public life through a retrieval of a rich and broad moral framework. Where the two proposals differ, however, is in the details of the remedy.

Murray's project was focused on the vitality of the natural law tradition for American public philosophy. Bellah and his associates see a more complex mosaic consisting of the three primary traditions which they suggest were present at the outset of the nation's history and which remain necessary today for an adequate public consensus. The difference between the two positions is important. Murray was convinced that the public discourse could have none of the religious imagery and warrants that might be found in the biblical tradition identified by the more contemporary proponents of a renewal in public discourse.[41] While his own natural law approach was more beholden to religious convictions than he acknowledged or at least cared to admit, there was in his stated proposal no room for theology to inform the public discourse of the nation.[42]

Beyond Murray

A number of sympathetic critics of Murray have raised the question of the ability of theology to contribute to the public discourse of the nation. Three elements can be identified which have occasioned the renewed interest in a public theology to supplement a public philosophy. First, our present public discourse seems inadequate to the task of renewing the public life of the nation. Second, the emergence of political and liberation theologies has "heightened awareness of the political dimensions of the whole theological enterprise." Finally, there is an "increased understanding of the social power of religious symbols and beliefs."[43] Religion has reasserted its public role despite the claims of secularism.

John Coleman appreciates the strengths in Murray's advocacy of a public philosophy. One manifest strength is the provision of rules of argument "which, in principle, apply equally to Catholics, Protestants, Jews, and secularists." A second plus is Murray's "frank recognition" of the "extraordinary symbolic pluralism in American life." This acknowledgement of pluralism helps avoid any one "particularistic self-understanding of America" from becoming the dominating force in society.[44] But Coleman also cites three weaknesses with Murray's approach. The bias of individualism within the regnant public discourse is to favor liberty and undercut social justice. Murray was not indifferent to justice but, without appeal to the biblical tradition, he was left with only the republican tradition as a resource to counteract the excesses of an unchecked individualism. In Coleman's opinion the civic republican tradition is too weak in its hold on the American imagination adequately to temper the troublesome aspects of liberal individualism. It is the biblical tradition that holds out the best hope of resurrecting communitarian and social justice components within an American public philosophy. Neglect of this resource "skews Murray's writings on public issues too strongly in the direction of liberal individualism, despite his own intentions."[45] Coleman's second reservation about Murray's work is that the latter did not admit the implicit theological bases for his natural law philosophy. "Were Murray to have made explicit the theological premises about revelation and reason, nature and grace, which ground his own understanding of natural law" it would have "undercut claims for a neutral, objective ground for discourse in a pluralist society."[46] The third criticism pertains to the symbols Murray uses in his public philosophy. Relying on studies of symbol and ritual done by cultural anthropologists

Victor Turner and Mary Douglass, Coleman points out the "thin" nature of the symbol system available to Enlightenment thought. The emphasis on "conceptual clarity and analytic rigor" in modern secular thought is not able to match the "rich, polyvalent power of religious symbolism" in its ability to "command commitments of emotional depth." In its attempt to be universal, secular public discourse becomes "chaste, sober and thin," unable to "stir human hearts and minds to sacrifice, service, and deep love of the community."[47] Coleman concludes that, despite the risks deriving from its tendency to narrowness and intolerance, absent a revival of civic republican theory, the tradition of biblical religion is needed to overcome the failures of liberal individualism. Unless Murray's public philosophy is supplemented with a public theology the "sense of drift in American identity and purpose" which Murray so deftly analyzed will continue.[48]

Like Coleman, Robin Lovin appreciates Murray's achievement but believes that the emphasis on public philosophy has led to an under-appreciation of the contribution which public theology can make. As an illustration he suggests that the biblical image of covenant is an important statement about the responsibility persons have for promoting common life and it is a useful antidote to the insufficient development of the commonweal in social contract theory. While it is clear that the ideal of covenant is biblical in origin, it has become part of the wider patrimony of American social thought. For Lovin "a public theology that builds on the moral aspiration for a covenanted community clearly does not seek to impose alien or sectarian norms on our national life."[49] Instead, public theology makes clear the theological foundations of much of our constitutional system. Murray knew this, Lovin maintains, but was reluctant to point out the religious roots of our legal-political order.

Lovin notes Murray's important distinction between society and state. Clarity on this distinction was central to Murray's social theory, for through it the problem of religious liberty could be resolved. Religious truth is a social good, but adjudication of competing religious truths is beyond the competence of a limited state. The restricted range of the state had to be asserted if totalitarianism was to be avoided. The state is not co-terminous with society, for this broader reality includes other institutions, such as the church, with a legitimate sphere of freedom from the state. Any intelligible human rights theory requires the society-state distinction. Human rights are founded on human dignity as this is experienced in community with others. Human rights ought to be recognized by the state but are not its creation. Yet the need for clarity about distinguishing the two as Murray does "must not obscure the actual interpenetration of society and state in contemporary life."[50]

While explicit religious discourse cannot be used in the jurisprudence of the nation or become the language of public policy, we should not imagine that no interaction between society and state occurs. And "just as society and state are increasingly interpenetrating, so must the Christian vision be woven into the fabric of policy and jurisprudence." That is done not through religious lobbies promoting institutional self-interest, but by the way religion shapes and influences the minds and hearts of the public.

Using the powerful rhetoric of biblical and religious imagery, appealing to people's religious conscience, challenging the self-understanding of the nation through biblical metaphors—all these tactics were used during the civil rights campaigns of the 1950s and 1960s. In the same way, today it is possible to imagine the judicious use of public theology for the building of a public consensus on social matters. The state cannot rely upon religious argument, but people in American society can and do look to religion as a source for moral insight and formation. Public theology can maximize the impact that religious belief has by making the social implications of religious commitment clear. "Murray's unfinished agenda, then, includes a rethinking of the distinction between society and state, and thus the roles of the Church and the theologian in the social-political sphere."[51]

Reflections such as these have led David Hollenbach to call for American Catholics to "move beyond an approach to public questions based on Murray's version of the public philosophy." What is needed today, Hollenbach writes, is a "public theology which attempts to illuminate the urgent moral questions of our time through explicit use of the great symbols and doctrines of the Christian faith."[52] There are difficulties in responding to Hollenbach's call, but we agree with him that a public church which serves society must "develop a theology whose roots in the biblical symbolic vision are evident, and which then seeks to interpret the contemporary meaning and significance of these symbols in a rigorous and critical way." What public theology must do is to "combine symbol and creative critical interpretation" so that the power of religious symbols once again shapes public life.[53]

Theology as Public Discourse

How can Christian theology, with all its historical particularism, be accepted as public discourse in a pluralist America? To answer this question we must examine the nature of "public-ness."

In his typically careful and creative manner, David Tracy has discussed the question of whether a particularist religious tradition can have public resources. He suggests as a working definition of "public" that which is "available to all intelligent, reasonable and responsible members of that culture despite their otherwise crucial differences in belief and practice." Like Murray, Tracy holds that the public realm must have the "possibility of discussion (argument, conversation) among various participants."[54] This public discussion must be based on reason. In our own age the reasonableness of religion is challenged by many. But the larger issue for our post-modern culture is that what counts as "reason" is itself in dispute.

Recent years have seen growing attention paid to the narrative-based nature of knowledge. Knowledge is social and the knower comes to know through participation in an historically rooted community which has its own metaphors, symbols and stories that allow the person to make sense of experience.[55] In theology this movement has had significant influence, but it throws into question the very possibility of theology being public since the particularist nature of the Christian community's narrative renders it unreasonable unless one happens to share the community's worldview.[56] The consequence is, therefore, that "there is no authentic public realm where a public, shared reason can rule; there are only particular traditions which can either witness to their truth, make temporary coalitions with other traditions, or become . . . merely particularist 'interest groups.' "[57] Without dismissing the value of recent work on narrative, Tracy proposes that we "shift the major focus of the debate away from 'origins' to 'effects.' " While the proposition that all models of reason have communal and historical origins may be true, there is no need to conclude that the effects of such particular traditions "are as non-public, non-shareable as their origins."[58] The question, he suggests, can be put: "Is it or is it not the case that, however particular in origin and expression any classic work of art or religion may be, its effects are nonetheless public?" Tracy answers this question. "The effects of a classic work of art or a classic religious tradition are public as providing disclosive and transformative possibilities for all persons."[59]

In his response to the question Tracy is relying on his previous writing on the idea of a "classic."[60] In his use of the word, a classic is a "phenomenon whose excess and permanence of meaning resists definitive interpretation."[61] What happens when a person seriously engages a classic in "conversation," i.e. opens himself or herself to the power of a classic of art or religion? The possibility of a disclosive-transformative event occurs.[62] The range of reaction to such an event is wide. One extreme is a "tentative sense of resonance," while the other end of the spectrum can be "appropriately described as a 'shock of recognition.' " In *every* case along the whole spectrum, however, *some* disclosure-transformation, and thereby some truth, is in fact present—and present as communicable, shareable, public."[63]

This is both extremely important for society and a crucial task for theology. If theology does not address its interpretation of religious classics to the society in a communicable, shareable, public fashion, it furthers the divide between "facts" and "values" and implicitly justifies the surrender of the "objective" public world to instrumental reason and the confinement to the "subjective" private domain of all judgments of what is good, beautiful, and true. Tracy has distinguished three "publics"—the society at large (embracing the realms of techno-economic structures, polity and culture), the academy, and the church—which theology must address.[64] Failure to do so may reduce religion to irrelevance and deliver society over to idolatry. Religion cannot advance claims regarding ultimate values and simultaneously admit that it has nothing to say about the world in which men and women are educated, choose professions, make money, educate their children, decide issues of peace and war, make budgets, pass laws, and carry on the vast majority of their waking hours. Any religion which does is simply incredible. And those important social activities will, in fact, not be carried forward without decisions made, usually unreflectively and implicitly, on the basis of values which are taken for granted. Those values—"common sense," "what everyone knows and does," "what is obviously the case," "the way we have always done it"—then become the absolute standards, the sacred norms, by which the society is conformed to what it uncritically takes as ultimate. The evacuation of the public square by religion in the misguided notion that pluralism will thus be protected frequently produces a vacuum which is gradually filled by bigoted social self-idolatry. Theologians are obligated "to fight against the privatizing forces which separate the realm of culture from the realm of polity."[65]

A theology which acquiesces in its segregation from the issues of society (and of Tracy's second public, the academy) necessarily distorts the religious believer's self-understanding. The decision for religious belief is, of course, profoundly personal. But "personal" does not mean "private." The person is constituted by the communities of which he or she is a member. A genuinely personal decision is also public, in that it is the act of one who emerges from various communal contexts and who affects others by his or her act. The relegation of religion to the private sphere while claiming that it is profoundly personal furthers the impoverishment of the meaning of "person."

While not all theology is public theology in the sense in which we are using the term, all theologians are engaged in a public enterprise.

Indeed, the drive to genuine publicness is not an idiosyncratic program of some theologians. Rather it is incumbent upon every theologian, no matter which public any single theologian principally addresses. Of course, it is not the case that every theologian must make the issue of publicness the principal, explicit focus of theology. Yet it is the case that some theologians must address this question explicitly and systematically on behalf of all. The social complexity is there. The theological complexity will not go away by attempts to ignore it. Those theologians who emphasize the public of the larger society, either through prophetic protest and critique or through integrative theologies of culture, are either purely private visionaries or they should command a public hearing. If the latter is the case, they are making public statements to the society and should be held accountable for the plausibility or implausibility of their advice.[66]

Public statements to the society must follow certain procedures, however. There are standards for public conversation. Criteria of intelligibility (coherence), truthfulness (provision of warrants and evidence), rightness (moral integrity) and equality (mutual reciprocity) are norms for genuine public discourse. Granted that the response to the disclosive power of a classic is highly personal, once we seek to express that response, to communicate the truth disclosed, we are acting in public and bound to the standards of public discourse. Tracy admits that it is unlikely that the same response to a religious classic will be found among adherents and outsiders to a given tradition. "But if the religious classics of any particular tradition are genuine classics, then they will also provide public, disclosive possibilities to all."[67] It will be up to the wider public with which the knowledge is shared, a community of inquiry and interpretation, to assess which claims about a classic are best, better, inadequate. This means that "truth in the public realm will be fundamentally a matter of consensus." But it is precisely the use of a criterion for public truth which is different from that which would be used to interpret one's own tradition which allows public theology to avoid being seen as the imposition of the claims of a religious group upon the society.

The public theologian searches for a way to make truth claims which can be tested by the public without the public having to assent to everything that the theologian believes. So Martin Luther King, Jr. made arguments about social justice that were rooted in his biblical theology without presupposing that his hearers had to accept the entire belief system of Southern Baptists. Religion, no less than art, can be a source of publicly accessible insight. Religious classics need be no less public in their effects than other classics despite their particularist origins. Tracy offers Reinhold Niebuhr as an exemplar of public religion in modern American culture.[68] Despite his heavy reliance on biblical themes and symbols Niebuhr was able to communicate with a secular and pluralist nation. His skill at interpreting basic Christian symbols was a resource for public understanding of our common life even for those who did not assent to Niebuhr's biblical faith.[69] The phenomenon of what has been called "atheists for Niebuhr" shows that the public nature of Niebuhr's use of classic religious symbols allowed the disclosive-transformative power of those symbols to be appropriated by Christians and non-Christians alike.

Theology in the Public Forum

Although public theology seeks to influence the societal order it does not pose constitutional problems. The setting for public theology is wider than the narrow concern of the first amendment with church-state relations. True, in some contexts the word "public" refers to government as when we distinguish the private from the public sector. But, as others have noted, the idea of "public" ever since the eighteenth century has taken on another meaning which is *contrasted* to government. In this sense "public" has come to mean "the citizenry who reflect on matters of common concern, engage in deliberation together, and choose their representatives to constitute the government, whose powers are limited by a constitution. Religious bodies are very much part of *this* meaning of the public."[70] It is in this second sense of the word public that we use it as a modifier of both church and theology. Our advocacy of public theology is in keeping with the history of the American experience. It is evident to any student of that history that "there has not been a major issue in the history of the United States on which religious bodies did not speak out, publicly and vociferously. . . ."[71] Despite the occasional sound of alarm by one or another critic, this activity has never imperiled our constitutional order, for the framers of the constitution opposed state endorsement of religion but never meant for this to entail the exclusion of the churches from public life. "The founders of the American republic were quite clear on the public place of religion in this latter sense. They believed that religious belief made an essential contribution to the formation of a responsible citizenry capable of sustaining a democratic republic."[72]

Properly understood, therefore, public theology is an issue of religion and society, not church and state. Useful descriptions of the former pair of terms are provided by Richard McBrien. He defines religion "as

the whole complexus of attitudes, convictions, emotions, gestures, rituals, symbols, beliefs, and institutions by which persons come to terms
with, and express, their personal and/or communal relationships with
ultimate Reality (God and everything that pertains to God)."[73] When
explaining the meaning of society, McBrien emphasizes what distinguishes a society is not size but its systemic character. Society is "a
system of interaction." It is a gathering of various communities that are
ordered for cooperation and communication so as to enhance human
well-being. "Society is composed of many diverse communities and
groups: families, voluntary associations, colleges and universities, small
businesses, corporations, labor unions, religious organizations and communities, and even governmental agencies."[74] It is evident in this framework that the state is but one part of society. The state is the institution
which is charged with the responsibility of maintaining public order
within society. Public order is a part of the common good of society but
does not comprise the entirety of that good.[75] All the various elements of
society bear a measure of responsibility for fostering the common good.
The state has its proper sphere but is not competent to address all dimensions of societal well-being. Other components of society, the churches
for example, have their role to play in achieving the common good.

Public theology is one of the ways that religious institutions can
contribute to societal existence. The implications of religious belief for
social life are developed through public theology. Explaining and defending the overall vision of society which a church holds is an exercise
in public theology. Such public speech is held to the same norms governing other public discourse.

Public theology is an example of the politics of persuasion, not
coercion. The claims of a religious vision can be unpersuasive or uncon-
vincing by standards of public discourse but there is no reason to presume they will be so in every case. Far from presenting an infringement
of the first amendment on the matter of church-state relations, public
theology is an exercise of speech protected by the first amendment to the
constitution.

Public Theology and Civil Religion

In 1967 Robert Bellah wrote a paper "Civil Religion in America"
which sparked a good deal of interest in the idea of a civil religion.[76]
Bellah was concerned with how the nation could preserve certain traditional democratic values and ideals in the cultural upheaval of the 1960s.
He surveyed presidential inaugural addresses and found there a variety of
convictions which he labeled civil religion. While the Protestant ethos of
the nation contributed to this civil religion, it could not be said that civil

religion was identical with any particular interpretation of Christianity. Bellah proposed a reading of American history—our charter documents, key personages, sense of purpose, national celebrations, wars—that highlighted a set of beliefs, prophets and priests, symbols and rituals, which constitute our civil religion.

What a civil religion provides, argued Bellah, is a common frame of reference for the nation. It is an effort to look at the nation's public life for signs of transcendent meaning. In Bellah's careful and subtle formulation of American civil religion, those signals of transcendence are pointers toward values *in* American life but *not* limited *to* American life. Those values can therefore stand as norms of judgment *over* America. In Bellah's words, "the American civil religion is not the worship of the American nation but an understanding of the American experience in the light of ultimate and universal reality."[77] Positively, civil religion resists the tendency toward privatizing religious symbols. It also reflects a concern for pluralism and tolerance while still seeking common ground on which to shape a national ethos. Thus, civil religion's value is that it offers cultural support to those values and practices necessary for the well-being of the republic.

There are problems with civil religion, however. One is that civil religion can become a national idolatry. Although Bellah himself was careful to speak of the prophetic element of civil religion and the role that transcendent elements play in moving people beyond simple loyalty to the nation, the risk of idolatry remains. The risk is chiefly due to the fact that civil religion focuses so strongly on the nation itself. The referents for civil religion are too national, too localized, to avoid idolatry completely. The risk remains that what "is" becomes enshrined and blessed as what "ought to be." Civil religion can vest the status quo with an aura of sacredness that hinders social criticism and change. A second difficulty is that the particularity of civil religion is not found in the religious traditions that it resembles but in the civic life it sacralizes. The religious emphasis of civil religion is on a bland deism which avoids more particularist religious traditions for the sake of tolerance. Ultimately such an approach for relating religion to public life cannot satisfy those with commitments to a specific religious tradition. Civil religion will not have the depth of true religion even if it admirably strives for a breadth that is respectful of pluralistic national life.

Public theology can learn from the aims of civil religion while resisting its deficiencies. Like civil religion, public theology combats the privatizing of religion; it opposes both a secularism which sees no place for religion in public affairs and a sectarianism which denies the responsibility to make religious belief accessible. But public theology differs from civil religion in two significant ways. First, it reverses the method of civil religion. Whereas civil religion examines public life in the United States for signs of transcendence or ultimate concern, public theology begins by looking at the Christian tradition for its public significance.[78] Second, civil religion, because of its concern for pluralism, devalues the particularist traditions of religious belief whereas public theology is a serious retrieval of what is accessible to all within a particular religion.[79] Public theology does not shy away from drawing upon a particular religious tradition. Thus, by its rootedness within a religious tradition and not the national experience, public theology is less prone to the idolatry of culture than civil religion. Public theology's engagement with a particular religious tradition which makes universal claims about revelation provides resources for moving beyond the historical experience of the nation-state.

This articulation of a given religious heritage, however, does not undercut public theology's demurrer about domination of the public square. In accord with civil religion's concern for tolerance and pluralism, public theology asks for no acceptance from people beyond what truth it can illuminate and make persuasive through public conversation and argument. Despite the pluralism of our society, we believe that public theology can work within the symbol system of a religious community such as Roman Catholicism.

The Difference Public Theology Can Make

Alexis de Tocqueville has written, "Every religion has some political opinion linked to it by affinity. The spirit of man, left to follow its bent, will regulate society and the City of God in uniform fashion; it will, if I dare put it so, seek to *harmonize* earth with heaven."[80] Public theology attempts to explicate the affinities between a religious tradition and a political opinion. This does not mean, however, that one moves immediately from theology to public policy.

Theology must be mediated by social ethics before it makes specific judgments about action. It is simplistic politically and fundamentalistic theologically to ignore the mediating role of social ethics. While the God of the Hebrew and Christian scriptures has concern for the poor, the weak and the exile, that claim is hardly sufficient in itself for determining the details of taxation, welfare reform, regulation of private property or other societal policies. Rather, one's basic orienting attitudes toward public life are shaped by one's theological stance. These fundamental attitudes must then be informed by a social ethic—e.g. theories of justice, the state, and freedom—before the morality of public policy can be debated.

What de Tocqueville understood was that political judgments arise out of a deeply held set of convictions about the nature of the person, society and the world. Any philosophical or theological worldview is value-laden and shapes the orientation one has toward more particular judgments. Public theology, as we practice it, is an articulation of the Roman Catholic tradition's worldview or background theory which informs a social ethic and consequent public policy choices.

The discipline of Catholic social ethics has paid insufficient attention to this theological foundation. In the admirable effort to bring the moral wisdom of the tradition to bear on policy choices, social ethicists have become learned in weapons analysis, agricultural economics and prison reform. What has sometimes been ignored is the distinctively theological underpinning for moral choices. For the church, one of the benefits of public theology is that it makes explicit the theological component of social ethics so that believers can understand and test the coherence of their religious beliefs with their public policy decisions.

Suggesting that public theology is several steps removed from public policy does not diminish its import for society. The power of ideas can be slighted in a culture as pragmatic as our own. While headlines are devoted to the decisions of presidents and premiers, corporate executives and bankers, theoretical discussions, if mentioned at all, are relegated to the back pages. But behind the everyday decisions of political and economic life are a set of basic ideas. These ideas "comprise a view of human nature, of how people behave as citizens. They also reflect a view of social improvement, of why we think that society is better in one state than another."[81] To leave such fundamental ideas unexamined is to ensure that public policy discussion is played out within the narrow confines of the conventional wisdom.

One of the roles of a public church is "to provide the public with alternative visions of what is desirable and possible, to stimulate deliberation about them, provoke a reexamination of premises and values, and thus to broaden the range of potential responses and deepen society's understanding of itself."[82] A public church cannot accomplish this task unless it gives birth to a public theology that examines and formulates ideas which can be discussed in public. In the presentation and discussion of publicly significant ideas the public church can make a great contribution to national life. By joining the public debate, a public theology contributes to the vitality of a democratic society. In such a society "persuasion, not violence or manipulation, is the quintessence of public life," and public theology offers ideas for public clarification, testing and purification to see if they may prove persuasive.[83]

Public theology, like other ideas, can be important to and powerful within national life today for three reasons.[84] First, many actions and policy proposals cannot be explained by present assumptions about human nature, society or the world. Second, a fair number of our most successful politicians are men and women who have crafted not just policies but visions for American life. Whether or not the prophet was right that, without a vision, the people perish, it seems clear that, without a vision, the people complain about the void. Finally, public discussion is often dominated by the initial framing of the question. The very way an issue comes before the public for discussion can determine the outcome. A public theology can suggest alternative ways of thinking by holding up elements of a tradition which may be neglected in America's culture of liberal individualism. Our hope, at least, is that theology can contribute to public conversation and that the broadening of the conversation to include theology might provide a stimulus to rethink aspects of our public life.

While convinced that public theology is a needed element in the renewal of democratic life, we reemphasize the importance of a public theology for the church. Recent decades have witnessed a resurgence of interest in the social mission of the churches. A wide variety of topics have been addressed by church bodies and leaders. But many believers differ with the conclusions reached by their church spokespersons. The title of Paul Ramsey's book *Who Speaks for the Church?*[85] poses a general question, and his polemic against the World Council of Churches could well be extended to include other religious institutions. On what basis does a group or individual issue a statement on political matters which claims the support of the church? Clearly, a Catholic bishop or a church convention can cite canon law or church polity as the formal basis for public pronouncements or actions. The issue, however, is not juridical but political. Power *de jure* is not always power *de facto*. A statement by a bishop may be an accurate and well-reasoned formulation of the church's social teaching as it pertains to some matter, but it may not be received by the church community. In what sense, then, is it a pronouncement of the church?

Part of the difficulty is illustrated by a complaint recounted by the authors of *Habits of the Heart* in their second volume. They tell the tale of a theologian who found church activists uninterested in discussing the theological foundation for their lobbying on a number of issues.[86] The activists wanted to move right to matters of strategy and tactics for implementation. The theologian, who was sympathetic to the cause, complained, "That's part of their problem, of course, particularly the poli-sci types. They're so theologically inarticulate that they can't persuade anybody in the churches who doesn't already agree with them, and even then they come across as political partisans, not as reflective Christians." The authors agree with this assessment that too often the social concerns of the church are not expressed in ways that reveal the deep biblical and theological roots of the concern. "Perhaps in the process of learning the state's languages of legal rights, cost-benefit utilities, and justice as due process, they have forgotten the language of covenant and communion." Within Roman Catholicism we are not convinced that the situation depicted is as extreme as that portrayed, but there is enough resonance within our experience to elicit concern. A public theology helps to avoid the neglect of our biblical and theological tradition when we move to matters of social life. It provides the rich foundation available to the church for taking on the task of building a just and peaceful world.

There is an even more serious obstacle to the effectiveness of the church's social mission. Sometimes opposition to a church pronouncement comes not from those who differ with the conclusions but from those who question the propriety of any church involvement in political matters. Privatized religion should be a deeper and more pressing concern for the Catholic Church than internal criticism or dissent. How can persons be nurtured in a religious community where there is preaching, ritual, teaching, and action based on the gospel and remain uncomprehending of the social significance of religious faith? We maintain that basic creedal symbols and statements of Christianity have public meaning. Public theology makes the linkage between the faith we profess and how we live in society. Whether the interpretations we offer are persuasive is not as important as that the reader see the essentially public nature of religious belief. We propose a public theology because we are convinced a religion cannot be true that is simply private. Such faith is erroneous not so much in what it affirms as in what it ignores. Only an interpretation of the Christian tradition which accords a central place to public theology can provide an account of the tradition that embraces the fullness of faith.

The Plan of this Volume

In this book we have tried to do public theology by discussing the social implications, the public significance, of central symbols within the Catholic tradition. We agree with David Tracy that Reinhold Niebuhr has been the most successful proponent of public theology in this century. The starting point for much of his thought, as a child of the reformation, was human sinfulness. We believe that this is the wrong starting point for public theology, at least within the Catholic tradition. But the influence of Niebuhr demands that we tackle the topic of sin at the outset. Thus, the next chapter takes up the theological symbol of original sin and explores its secularized consequence for the development of the political philosophy of liberalism. We shall attempt to reorient the emphasis Niebuhr gave to sin by offering an alternative reading of the doctrine of original sin. That alternative reading will introduce the theme which dominates this volume, the essentially communitarian character of the Catholic imagination. In subsequent chapters we then take up a series of theological symbols all of which have great importance for the Catholic tradition. Chapter three treats *the* theological subject, the reality of God and the divine nature. Our conviction is that the symbol of the Trinity reminds believers of something central to a theocentric view of the nature of reality: it is grounded in the loving communion of the Godhead. We believe this is the right context for discussing that theme so dear to liberalism—rights. Liberalism's infatuation with rights is not simply misguided. There is much good in the rights-language of western liberalism. But a flaw of liberalism is the context, the regnant individualism of our culture, within which people situate rights. Our reflection on the Trinity suggests another way of viewing the matter.

When the loving God seeks to communicate something of the divine, what theologians have referred to as *Deus pro nobis* or God *ad extra*, as distinct from God *ad intra*, the inner life of God, we have the experience of grace. Chapter four is an exploration of how the theology of grace points us toward a public policy of defending human life. The defense of life is grounded in the sacramental vision of grace which informs Catholic theology's understanding of the human person and the created order.

Chapter five focuses at greater length on the symbol of creation. After a long period of neglect the problem of the environment now has drawn the attention of many. As with many social movements, alliances are forged which bring people of various viewpoints together for the sake of achieving practical social change. It is our belief that the practical changes sought are more likely to succeed if appeal can be made to an underlying set of ideas which give the necessary changes depth and consistency. Changing the way we think is often a prelude to changing the way we act. A theology of creation can inform an environmental ethic which will guide social activism.

Within the Christian tradition the central historical event is the life and ministry of Jesus of Nazareth. Grasping the significance of what it means to claim that God entered into history through a definite person at a certain time in a specific place leads to a reflection on the meaning of the particular. We, too, are flesh and bone, temporally and historically located. How does that fact condition how we live, whom we love and what we value? We live in a world that is trumpeted as the global village, as being on the threshold of a new world order. Yet the persistence of local attachments, the permanence of elements within human life that outlast all the new world orders announced, requires that we think critically about the nature of human loyalty and what part it plays in political life. Chapter six reflects on the significance of the incarnation for an understanding of true patriotism.

Our final chapter addresses the somewhat neglected theological symbol of the communion of saints. Although professed in the Nicene Creed every Sunday at Catholic liturgies, the meaning of being in communion with others across time and space is insufficiently appreciated for the audacious challenge it presents to the American mind-set. Individualism deprives people of history, for it denies the way that persons exist within the history of communities. Belief in the communion of saints calls us to attend to the bonds that tie us together and that, in turn, occasions a need for an ethical vision which respects the responsibilities and duties of our diverse relations.

In his brilliant but idiosyncratic volume *Theology and Social Theory*, John Milbank has suggested that there are finally two competing renditions of what reality is like.[87] There is a story of peace, Milbank claims,   and he cites Augustine as a pre-eminent exemplar of this view. Alternatively, there is a story of violence as told by Nietzsche. Certainly the choice is stark when reduced to these options. Milbank suggests that theology has difficulty with modern social theory, for the latter relies on a story of violence for its fundamental orientation. Whether that is so in every case, we believe that liberalism as it evolved from Thomas Hobbes is derived from a story of violence. This book demonstrates that the Catholic theological tradition tells a story of peace. Perhaps if we and others tell the story well, the significance of theology for reforming our public life will be made evident.

2 | Original Sin and the Myth of Self-Interest

During the presidential election debate in 1980, then candidate Ronald Reagan asked voters the question, "Are you better off now than you were four years ago?" Political pundits at the time agreed it was a clever and pointed way of evoking the dissatisfaction of voters with Jimmy Carter's administration. The assumption behind the question was simple: Americans vote in their economic self-interest. The fact behind the question was that the inflation of the late 1970s had hurt a great many people. Ergo, Reagan's question was a useful debate tactic.

Ronald Reagan's assumption was and is the conventional wisdom in politics: voters are economically self-interested, and the state of the economy goes a long way toward determining the election results. We have no quibble with the second half of the conventional wisdom. The economy is a powerful political issue. But concerning the first half we have our doubts. Our skepticism is based on studies by several political scientists who question how much economic self-interest influences voting.[1]

If self-interest were uniquely powerful, then there should be clear and direct correlations between how a person votes and how his or her economic standing has changed between elections. As Harvard political scientist Steven Kelman reports, no such correlations appear in the recent empirical studies of social scientists. Correlations do appear, however, between voting behavior and how an individual perceives the economy in general. In other words, there is evidence that citizens vote not with an eye focused primarily on their own pocket but on the state of the economy as a whole.[2] These studies on the effect of self-interest on voting are supported by other studies on self-interest and policy views. On a range of issues both foreign and domestic, Kelman cites evidence that political ideology is a better indicator than self-interest of what policy a person will support. The prevailing assumption of political and

28

economic self-interest is an unreliable one if these recent studies are correct. But this assumption is so often accepted as self-evident that even to question it seems bizarre. Why should this be so?

Theological Anthropology and Social Thought

It was Reinhold Niebuhr who quipped that original sin was the one empirically verifiable Christian tenet. All one had to do, maintained Niebuhr, was observe one's neighbor. For the great Protestant theologian and his followers, original sin was the religious symbol cited to explain self-interest in politics. Within the school of "Christian realism" the fall is used not only to explain but to justify political and economic arrangements premised on self-interest. Anything else would be open to the charge of naiveté, the worst failing of non-realists.

Political and economic systems always embody an understanding of the human. Liberalism and capitalism, with their emphasis on self-interest, are founded ultimately upon a theological anthropology quite different from that which grounds a model of political economy which stresses community. The term "liberalism" is, of course, not used here in the constricted partisan meaning which it has in contemporary American politics. In its traditional sense, liberalism refers to a perspective in political philosophy, especially within the English-speaking world, which abstracts the person from community, sets individual freedom and rights at odds with the community, and correspondingly stresses contractual theories of society. This meaning of "liberalism" encompasses political philosophers as different as Robert Nozick and John Rawls.[3] The divergence between liberalism and communitarianism is based on which theological symbol one emphasizes, original sin or the Trinity, when discussing what has happened to the image and likeness of God in human nature.

In the next chapter we will discuss the import of the Trinity as a political symbol. Here we wish to take up the doctrine of original sin in the context of a Catholic public theology. By no means do we intend to suggest that a theological doctrine can determine or explain the political and economic history of a nation. We simply suggest that a particular theological position may be in accord with one political or economic theory and not with another. To ignore original sin is naive indeed, and the communitarian vision found in Catholic social teaching certainly does not do so. But how one "unpacks" that great religious symbol is crucial for the social ethic one endorses. Liberalism assumes that people act on self-interest. Communitarian approaches do not deny self-interest but think it possible to transcend it on occasion with proper support.

Reformation Theology of Human Nature

The reformation debates on grace and justification necessarily entailed some description of humanity "in the state of nature," i.e. deprived of grace after the fall. However much the reformers differed among themselves on issues such as eucharistic theology and ecclesial polity, they agreed on the utter corruption of the human person as a result of the sin of Adam. Luther's description of the human being as "turned in on himself" expressed the conviction that the fall had destroyed the capacity for genuine other-directedness. The Formula of Concord (1576) held original sin to be "so profound a corruption of human nature as to leave nothing sound, nothing uncorrupt in the body or soul of man, or in his mental or bodily powers."[4] In 1619 the Synod of Dort, which set the main lines of Calvinist orthodoxy, taught that after the fall the human being was left in "blindness of mind, horrible darkness, vanity, and perverseness of judgment; became wicked, rebellious, and obdurate in heart and will, and impure in all his affections."[5] Although some glimmers of natural light remain by which humanity has some knowledge of God, natural things and morality, human beings pollute this light and are incapable of using it correctly "even in things natural and civil." This is echoed in the Westminster Confession's declaration that fallen human beings are "dead in sin and wholly defiled in all the faculties and parts of soul and body,"[6] and have become "utterly indisposed, disabled, and made opposite to all good, and wholly inclined to all evil."[7] The individual, radically turned in on himself or herself and closed to any possibility of agapic community, is locked into selfishness.

Obviously this doctrine of total depravity as a result of the fall has been much developed in the course of the four hundred years which separates us from the classical Protestantism of the sixteenth century reformers. But it is that theological anthropology which, in its secularized form, found eloquent voice in Thomas Hobbes. David Carlin has referred to Hobbesian anthropology as a secularized version of the Augustinian anthropology.[8] In fact, that is but partially true. The anthropology which undergirds Hobbes' social ethics was Augustine read through lenses ground by the reformers.

Secular Versions of Reformation Theology:
Hobbes and Smith

Probably Hobbes' most often quoted statement is his characterization in *Leviathan* of life in the state of nature as "solitary, poor, nasty, brutish, and short."[9] He undergirded that dark description by appeal to seventeenth century physics. "Life itself is but motion," and "when a thing is in motion, it will eternally be in motion, unless somewhat else stay it."[10] What stays the motion of human life is the competing motion of another human life. The equality of human beings inevitably generates competition which, fueled by greed, the desire for security, or the hope of glory, produces the natural state of human beings: "they are in that condition which is called Warre; and such a warre, as is of every man, against every man."[11] Entry into civil society is necessary to control the worst excesses of this war of all against each. Membership in civil community allows each person to acquire and enjoy the secure possession of goods both physical ("gain") and intellectual ("glory"). Because it is to the individual's advantage to enter into community with others, the basis of human community is not love but self-interest. "All society therefore is either for gain, or for glory; that is not so much for love of our fellows, as for love of ourselves."[12] If society is merely the controlled war of each against each, no *common* good exists, only a collection of competing individual goods, some of which may from time to time coincide.

A century and a quarter after *Leviathan*, Adam Smith attempted to introduce the idea of the common good into the Hobbesian vision of society as barely controlled war. In this effort, he was one of many social ethicians in England, Scotland, and France who had sought escape from the gloomy picture drawn by Hobbes. Some, like Bishop Cumberland, argued that self-interest is prevented from driving individuals to the universal civil war which Hobbes had described as the state of nature by the balanced design of the universe.[13] Others, like the Earl of Shaftesbury, traced that balance within the human being and claimed that self-interest, mighty power though it be, is counterpoised by other human passions.[14] And others, like Pierre Nicole, maintained that *enlightened* self-interest, through the exchange of services, produced an earthly society so just and equable that it is indistinguishable from the community of saints, save that it lacks the infusion of charity.[15] Smith turned the problem into the solution: self-interest could be relied upon to check itself because of the common human desire for a correspondence of feeling with others or what he termed "sympathy."

Smith had no doubt that human beings are motivated by self-interest. "It is not from the benevolence of the butcher, the brewer, or the baker, that we expect our dinner, but from their regard to their own interest," he wrote in *An Inquiry into the Nature and Causes of the Wealth of Nations*. "We address ourselves, not to their humanity but to their self-love, and never talk to them of our own necessities but of their advantages."[16] But the interests of the self are not only material; each person requires for his or her well-being some sense of self-worth which comes from seeing the feelings of others in harmony with one's own. In *The Theory of Moral Sentiments*, Smith acknowledged that, to achieve that sympathy which the individual requires for his or her own good, one may even "humble the arrogance of his self-love, and bring it down to something which other men can go along with."[17] Thus self-interest, pursued with a sufficiently deep understanding of what the self is and what its full range of interests embraces, serves the common good.

Nothing so effectively furthers sympathy, the ability to share others' perceptions of themselves and of oneself, as the need—Smith would say the drive—to "truck, barter, and exchange one thing for another."[18] Thus the freedom of trade for which Smith strenuously argued in *The Wealth of Nations* is necessary for the achievement of human community, because through it sympathy among human beings is accomplished. His advocacy of free trade was a moral stance, and his economic work was an outgrowth of his social ethics.

The "invisible hand" of the free marketplace is the mechanism of this transmutation of self-interest into the service of the common good.

> Every individual is continually exerting himself to find out the most advantageous employment for whatever capital he can command. It is his own advantage, indeed, and not that of the society, which he has in view. But the study of his own advantage naturally, or rather necessarily leads him to prefer that employment which is most advantageous to the society.[19]

Smith's treatise on economics can be read correctly only in conjunction with his theory of social ethics. His concern was to resolve the problem of the common good within the Hobbesian framework which postulated self-interest as the sole human motivation.

Thus the denial of the possibility of altruism as a motive in human affairs was tacitly accepted even by those who rejected the social and political consequences which Hobbes drew from it. Behind and below Hobbes' denial of that possibility lies a secularized doctrine of the effects of original sin. But the form of that doctrine had been rejected by Roman Catholicism.

Another Theological Anthropology: Roman Catholicism

Catholic doctrine acknowledged the tragic consequences of Adam's sin but insisted that the human being remained essentially intact after the fall. Adam lost "the holiness and justice in which he had been constituted" and "incurred the wrath and indignation of God" and "was changed in body and soul for the worse," the Council of Trent taught.[20] But human beings are not utterly corrupted and "free will, weakened as it was in its powers and downward bent, was by no means extinguished in them."[21] Indeed, Trent specifically condemned the opinion that all human works done "before justification" (Hobbes' "state of nature") are sinful, that is, purely self-interested.[22] Later in the sixteenth century, disputes about the sovereignty of grace and the status of human freedom led to the teaching that the original justice and holiness of Adam were "accidental," not intrinsic to the human person as human. This original justice and holiness were lost as a result of original sin, but since they were accidental qualities, human nature remained essentially unimpaired. As some counter-reformation Catholic theologians phrased the point, the human person, created in the image and likeness of God, might lose that likeness, consisting in original justice and holiness, but retained the image of God. Beneath these counter-reformation statements lies an important claim about the meaning of human existence.

Deeply ingrained in the western Christian tradition is the Augustinian insight that, as creatures who exist solely to be the recipients of the divine self-gift, our hearts are restless until they rest in God. This insight was echoed in the central point of Thomas Aquinas' theological vision, that at the core of human existence is a natural desire to see God. Thus there is a connaturality between nature and grace; nature has an aptitude for grace. Extinguish this restlessness, this desire for the beatific vision, and what remains is no longer a *human* being. Original sin may have distorted this restlessness, it may have skewed the direction of this desire, but it has not undone God's creation: humanity remains *human*. The longing for agape is experienced in the call to be agapic, the call to give oneself away. Consequently, Catholic doctrine has insisted in opposition to the darker views of the reformers that the human being, made in the image of God who is agape, remains in that image even after the fall and so is capable, even if with great difficulty, of genuine other-directedness.

The secularized theological anthropology which underlies Hobbes' social philosophy and which Smith accepted is classically Protestant. If one were to develop a secularized theological anthropology of the Catholic view of original sin, what social theory emerges? We do not claim to be able to construct a complete political and economic ethic reflective of the theological anthropology of the Catholic tradition. What we shall offer here are several comments which serve as pointers toward what a social theory in accord with a Catholic theology of original sin might look like.

Catholicism and Communitarianism

Unlike Hobbes, a Catholic-inspired model of society will acknowledge not only a need to minimize and restrain the evil of self-interest but also a challenge to maximize the good of self-giving. Because Catholics believe that the most important word we say about the the human is grace, not sin, strategies for community must be given priority over concern for limiting or channeling self-interest. That is why Roman Catholic social thought has traditionally posited that humanity is social by nature. In the words of the economics pastoral, human dignity is "realized in community with others."[23] Thus, a fundamental characteristic of Catholic social theory is its stress on the necessity for persons to express their social nature through the institutions they create to order their lives. Political and economic institutions premised on the primacy of self-interest can never embody the theological vision of a good society in the Catholic tradition.

Catholicism's criticism of the classical liberal philosophy of society shares many elements with other communitarian critiques of liberalism. In general, communitarians oppose the ahistorical, asocial, disembodied view of rational agency in liberalism. For liberals, the unencumbered self—lacking the "dense networks of overlapping commitments, relationships, loyalties, involvements"—is understood to possess rights before society.[24] Therefore, a community, political or otherwise, can only be voluntarily contracted between atomistic individuals who join together to protect and advance their rights. It is this picture of human nature and human society which communitarians oppose.

A difficulty for those committed to a communitarian vision is that many Americans have an idealized portrait of what constitutes community. Images of Currier and Ives' prints and Norman Rockwell's paintings tend to dominate the imagination of many people when the topic of community arises. It is America as the peaceful village, the gathering of the similar on the village green, where everyone knows everyone else by name. There is a powerful temptation to lapse into nostalgic thinking whenever discussion turns to community. This approach cannot lead to the serious rethinking of American public life needed today. If the people portrayed in the Rockwell paintings ever did truly reflect the reality of the warm relations of small town America, such experience cannot serve as an image for our present reality of large urban centers surrounded by the booming edge cities of a transformed suburbia.

It must be admitted that Roman Catholicism has not entirely escaped an element of nostalgia in its regard for a medieval "golden age."[25] There is within Catholic social teaching, especially in the writing of Leo XIII and Pius XI, an appeal to a romanticized vision of economic relations, political order and communal life as these supposedly existed in the era of Christendom. This sort of yearning for a pre-industrial society unaware of mass communications, urban sprawl, easy transportation and

huge pluralistic populations cannot serve as a blueprint for the communitarian thinker in our time. But the vision behind the blueprint retains
value. The societal vision inspired by the medieval legacy is of a society
marked by fraternal and sororal relations. It is this vision which stands
behind the modern views of Catholic social teaching even if the tradition
has had to adapt its understanding of the norms of justice and the make-
up of political and economic institutions to reflect modern reality.

What is needed for contemporary communitarian theory is a political rather than sentimental concept of community. Freeing ourselves
from the "cult of little communities" requires abandonment of the idea
that face to face communication is of the essence of all community.
Equally important is the need to avoid a bland conformism in which all
must have the same values if community is to be deemed true. These
approaches cannot form the basis for political community in large, pluralistic societies.[26]

Political Community Today

What is needed for a political concept of community is a renewed
appreciation of the centrality of public discourse. Hannah Arendt reminds us that it was public conversation which was prized in the now
idealized democracy of the Greek *polis*.

> When . . . we read in Aristotle that philia, friendship among
> citizens, is one of the fundamental requirements for the well-
> being of the City, we tend to think he was speaking of no more
> than the absence of factions and civil war within it. But for the
> Greeks the essence of friendship consisted in discourse. They
> held that only the constant interchange of talk united citizens in
> a polis. . . . However much we are affected by the things of the
> world, however deeply they may stir and stimulate us, they
> become human for us only when we can discuss them with our
> fellows.[27]

Political discourse stands at the center of modern communitarian theory.
What we need is shared discourse, not an identity of interests or personal
intimacy, for political community. Friendship, in its political expression,
consists in the regular participation of people in the ongoing conversation of a society about its aims, ideals, and practices. Christopher Lasch
proposes that what is needed is "a conversational relationship with the
past, one that seeks neither to deny the past nor to achieve an imaginative
restoration of the past but to enter into a dialogue with the traditions that

still shape our view of the world. . . ."[28] Liberal individualism, as experienced in American society, too often is guilty of denial of the past whereas a sentimental communitarianism, offered by some critics of American society, too often longs to recreate a past. We will suggest in a later chapter that a social theory informed by the doctrine of the communion of saints reminds us of the need to be in conversation with our past while allowing us the freedom to discern the pattern of faithfulness to the tradition today. In this and in other ways theology can be a part of the shared discourse of society. Critical theology is an effort to enter into dialogue with a religious tradition that shapes the view of the world held by many Americans. The use of theology in public, as explained in chapter one, need not be seen as an imposition of one tradition upon all, but simply the enriching of our societal conversation by finding room for religious traditions that continue to shape the imagination and form the convictions of millions.

Liberalism, according to communitarians, has failed in five significant ways: 1) it has led to the decline of civic virtue, the practices encouraged by what has been called the tradition of republicanism or civic republicanism; 2) liberalism fosters a political community that speaks of an individual citizen's rights but downplays civic duties; 3) there has been a disappearance of public space where common life can occur; 4) there is a marked lack of participation in the political activities necessary for democracy to flourish; 5) endemic to liberalism is a failure to acknowledge that social life is constitutive of the human person resulting in the neglect of important social institutions.[29]

Communitarianism, however, should not be defined merely by its opposition to liberalism. It is important to put positively what communitarianism is about. At this point, as might be expected, various theorists part company. In this book we will utilize various themes of Catholic social teaching to describe one brand of communitarian thought, recognizing that the communitarian critics of liberalism are a diverse group, many of whom would differ with our approach. Our primary interest in what follows is to suggest that flowing from the theological commitments of the Catholic tradition are orientations in social thought which stand opposed to the foundational theory of classical liberalism.

Roman Catholic Social Theory

For a long time Roman Catholicism spoke of a "third way" between the individualism of laissez-faire capitalism and the collectivist schemes of more radical socialist theories. Some saw in the solidarism or corporatism of Pius XI a blueprint for this third or middle way. Of late, however, there has been a growing alliance between Catholic social thought and many of the structures of liberal democracy. Undoubtedly it was the church's bitter experience in the 1930s and 1940s of totalitarian regimes on both the right and the left which led to its reconsideration of the benefits of democratic politics. Jacques Maritain and Yves Simon were among those twentieth century theorists who began to emphasize the "special affinity" that existed between Catholic social theory and liberal democracy.[30]

Yet, while the structures of democratic life—civil liberties, a limited constitutional state, pluralistic government—are appealing to the Catholic mind, the commonly held social philosophy underlying these features in Anglo-American politics remains problematic. And so Catholicism has looked within its own tradition for intellectual resources that might provide an alternative foundation for democratic politics. The quest has been for a Catholic social theory which can support and enrich liberal democracy yet oppose the individualism and myth of self-interest which historically has undergirded liberal institutions.

In developing its alternative theory Catholic teaching hearkens back to the classical period of western political thought. For Aristotle the human was a *zoon politikon*, a political animal. For Cicero and the Roman Stoics the noble life was one dedicated to the *res publica*, that is, public matters. Within the classical western imagination an ethical framework developed which reflected this view of human nature and the good life. This ethical viewpoint was taken up and translated by Aquinas for the society of medieval Christendom.

Aquinas accepted the idea of Aristotle that society was an order which existed for the mutual exchange of human activities all in service of the common good. The image which frequently has been used by Catholic thinkers to describe this traditional perspective is that of society as an organism. Conceiving of society as an organism or body enables Catholicism to talk about the distinctiveness of each part while at the same time emphasizing the need for each part to contribute to the well-being of the whole.

A popular text in pre-conciliar Catholic social teaching explained the import of remembering the analogical nature of the claim that society is an organism. An organism, be it plant, animal or human, is a "substantial, corporeal whole" with an inner life which directs all its parts to the purposes of the whole. Society, however, is not a physical unity and thus not an organism. The parts—human persons—cannot simply be subordinated to the whole. Yet society does have its own principle of activity, the common good. Through their correspondence of action toward the common good individual persons form a social unity. Perhaps the better image, according to J. Messner, is to see society as an "organism of social organisms" having a common end.[31] We are reminded by the author that losing sight of the analogical nature of the language leads to collectivism and statism.

Principles of Catholic Social Theory

Lurking within this description of the Catholic outlook on society can be found what Andrew Greeley has called the "three cardinal principles of Catholic social theory": personalism, subsidiarity and pluralism.[32] By personalism is meant the conviction that the human person possesses a dignity which cannot be reduced or denied in the name of some collective good. It is to maintain that "the goal of the society is to develop and enrich the individual human person." The personalist refuses to subordinate any human being to the collectivity.

Subsidiarity holds that "no organization should be bigger than necessary and that nothing should be done by a larger and higher social unit than can be done effectively by a lower and smaller unit." There is a bias toward the grassroots, the local setting, when discussing societal organization. This is not to be understood in a way that opposes the state or other large social entities, for these are both necessary and natural. Subsidiarity, in effect, establishes a criterion that intervention by the larger social unit must be justified and can be so only by the inability or unwillingness of the smaller unit to accomplish a social task.

The third of the cardinal principles is pluralism, which affirms that "a healthy society is characterized by a wide variety of intermediate groups freely flourishing between the individual and the state." Within society there needs to be a plethora of organizations which allow for social interaction and promote the individual's participation in group activity. A good society fosters such mediating structures so that public life is not equated with the state or governmental life.[33]

These three "cardinal principles" along with the tradition's understanding of human nature work to forge a communitarian outlook in Catholic social theory. Catholicism's optimism regarding the person's ability to act on motives other than self-interest means that in creating a social order institutions can rely upon human dispositions toward cooperation and self-giving, not just competition. The benign view of human nature found in Catholic theology leads toward a more benign view of human society in Catholic social thought. Unlike Hobbes, the Catholic view does not accept that the state is necessarily oppressive, even if coercive measures are sometimes needed for social order. The state, like other societal institutions, arises naturally from the interaction of persons who create a variety of organizational mechanisms so that shared activities are encouraged and shared goods can be obtained.

The Common Good: A New Foundation

Fundamental for this communitarian framework is a dedication to, and promotion of, the priority of the common good. It is this theme that further distinguishes the communitarian approach from a liberal individualism which sees society as merely the interplay (contractual or coerced) of individual interests. Any social theory that does not focus on the common good is missing an elemental fact about society according to the Catholic tradition, for the purpose of social life is the attainment of the common good.

Traditionally, the common good has been explained in Catholic teaching through the method of natural law philosophy. More recent church teaching has utilized the biblical witness.[34] Yet characteristic of Catholic interpretations of the biblical material is the emphasis placed on the communal and social dimensions of God's way with humanity. We are called to be a people, and when specific individuals in the biblical narratives are called it is always for the sake of the people.

Greater reliance upon the biblical basis for the theory of the common good is reflective of a number of changes that have occurred in Catholic thought on this topic. When Leo XIII formulated *Rerum Novarum*, the first great document of modern Catholic social teaching, he relied heavily upon Thomistic ideas. In this tradition the common good was, according to Dennis McCann, "self-evidently substantive, objectively knowable, and indivisible."[35] But more recent Catholic social teaching reflects several significant shifts in outlook, and these have redounded to the way the common good must be understood in the tradition.

Charles Curran has summarized many of the profound changes in Catholic social teaching under the heading of "changing anthropological bases."[36] Essentially, what Curran spotlights within the tradition is how the recurring theme of personalism has forced the church to consider again the nature of human dignity, the fundamental value which any social construct must serve. In doing so, several new emphases in Catholic social teaching have become important. These new emphases are freedom, equality and participation.

Regarding the first of these emphases, it is no secret that Leo XIII was fearful of human freedom and held the masses in low esteem with regard to their ability to exercise political freedom responsibly. It was the duty of the ruler to care for the great majority of the population who could not be entrusted with self-determination. The papal position was elitist and paternalistic. Democracy was suspect as a political system after the upheavals of the earlier part of the nineteenth century. By the papacy of Pius XII, however, democracy was viewed more kindly, and in subsequent pontificates there regularly appear statements of approval regarding democracy.

Leo disapproved of many modern civil liberties. He was reluctant to embrace freedom of the press or speech out of fear that truth would be lost amidst errors disseminated with legal protection. Freedom of religion, of course, was especially insidious since it relegated revelation to a secondary authority below personal conscience. Behind Leo's fear of liberty was his deep mistrust of liberalism "which in his mind was the root cause of all the problems of the modern day."[37] For Leo, liberalism represented an exaltation of the individual over all norms including divine truth. Seen through papal eyes liberalism was a doctrine of license that was not true liberty. While sensitive to the abuses of much of nineteenth century liberal thought Leo was not as discerning regarding the beneficial elements of the liberal agenda. His response to the movement was to advocate a social order that was paternalistic and authoritarian.

Still Leo saw enough of the power of liberalism to realize that a continuation of Pius IX's strategy of a church divorced from the world would not be a successful pastoral strategy. And so, in his attempt to articulate an agenda that placed the church on the side of social reform, he began a dialogue with modernity which allowed the better aspects of the modern age to influence the papacy. Subsequent popes continued the conversation so that by the pontificates of John XXIII and Paul VI things had changed to such a degree that the essential freedom of the person was trumpeted in conciliar decrees and subsequent papal teaching.[38]

Equality was also opposed in early papal social teaching because it seemed to undermine the organic nature of society. Within the organic model there was stress on each person performing the duties appropriate to his or her station in life. Talk of equality made such stable role definitions more difficult to accept. It heightened expectations of social change and undercut a culture of inherited privilege. For Leo class divisions were natural and accepted. He saw no difficulty with inequality based on lineage or social position. To follow a hierarchical ordering in society was simply part of the heritage of medieval Christianity which Leo accepted uncritically. Societal hierachies reflected the chain of being which scholastic metaphysics saw as the divine plan. In this perspective it was possible to conceive of a fairly stable set of relations and roles which an individual could see as divinely sanctioned.

Equality in dignity was accepted by the papacy, but this concept was not effectively translated into ideas about political, social or economic equality. So when he wrote *Rerum Novarum* in 1891, Leo did not see egalitarian justice as the social norm but stressed distributive justice which provided a minimum for all. As decades passed, however, the church came to an awareness that equality in dignity needed to be incarnated in social policies and structures. Thus, contemporary Catholic social teaching, while not embracing a strict egalitarianism, has shown increased sensitivity to the relative nature of wealth and poverty with a concomitant interest in narrowing the gaps between rich and poor, workers and management, agricultural and industrial laborers.[39]

The theme of participation has also become more important in modern papal social thought. While the value of active community involvement is a staple of the tradition, hence subsidiarity and pluralism, this insight was not always developed consistently to include all social structures. At present, however, there is greater recognition that the participatory nature of genuine communities favors democratic political structures so as to allow for the exercise of self-determination. The paternalistic state of Leo has given way to an appreciation of democracy.

Another indication of the importance given to participation in Catholic social teaching is seen in the treatment of economic life. In the first draft of the pastoral letter issued by the American episcopacy on the U.S. economy the bishops asked two questions: "What does the economy do to people, and what does it do for people?" In later drafts and in the final version a third question was added: "How do people participate in the economy?"[40] Participation is not a political ideal alone but touches upon economic matters as well. It is a criterion for assessing the moral soundness of an economic system.

This call for active participation implies subsidiarity and pluralism. What is needed for healthy social life is that an abundance of human associations and groups be allowed to flourish so that persons will be able to find a wide array of institutions that give form and structure to participatory community in the various realms of human existence. Furthermore, the bias is toward the grassroots when deciding at what level decision-making should occur in an organized group. This is to insure that even a well-meaning paternalism does not eviscerate the participation of people in the life of the community.

Participation as a moral ideal underscores that the common good requires more than liberal self-interest. A devotion to the well-being of others, what might be called solidarity, is an essential disposition of persons in community. For other-directedness to be encouraged there must be occasions and places where such self-giving is evoked and endorsed. A communitarian spirit need not be created: it is there. But we must find ways to institutionalize and express it. People must be called, and enabled, to participate in the life of the community so that they can contribute to the common good and thereby give expression to their social nature. In sum, participation plays a key role in any communitarian social theory, Catholic or otherwise.

The Common Good: Related Issues

The topics of freedom, equality and participation are all related to the experience of human dignity. If the common good aims to protect and promote human dignity, then, as our understanding of the elements of that dignity develop, our thinking regarding the common good must also be open to development. Use of the common good in Catholic social theory should reflect an appreciation for and commitment to a rightful freedom, equal regard and broad participation in the way we organize society. Within this transformed context, Catholic social teaching has taken up anew questions which touch upon the common good. In what follows three illustrations will be presented of how freedom, equality and participation have caused a revision of the meaning of the common good in Catholic thought.

A dramatic change in Catholic teaching on religious freedom provides an example of how the common good has been recast. Traditionally seen as an outgrowth of indifferentism, religious liberty was inimical to Catholicism. If religious liberty was ever to be approved by the church it would have to be demonstrated that the granting of such liberty was not on the basis of indifference toward religious truth. Through the work of many individuals and movements, Vatican II acknowledged an alternative foundation for the right of religious liberty, a right grounded not on religious indifference but on the theory of the limited state and a differentiated common good.

In the conciliar view, religious truth is an important element in human well-being and thus part of the full common good. This is not indifferentism, for the the value of religious truth did not change in Catholic teaching. Rather, the church recognized that the common good consists of both spiritual and temporal elements. With an Augustinian appreciation for the limitations of what can be hoped for in the human city within history the church acknowledged that the city of God cannot be identified with any society. While all societies must aim toward achievement of the common good, the temporal common good is all that can be assumed to be possible in history. Further, as the principle of pluralism maintains, the constitutionally limited state is not to be equated with society. Its responsibilities are more narrow.

Discerning precisely what the responsibilities of the state are can be better done if the distinction is made between the common good and public order which is an element of the common good. While the purpose of society is the achievement of the common good, the narrower purpose of the state is to create and maintain public order. This latter expression encompasses an order of public peace, an order of public morality and an order of justice. Serving those elements of the common good required for public order, while leaving to others the achievement of dimensions of the common good beyond this task, explains the conciliar approval of the separation of church and state and religious freedom.

It is not that religious truth is unimportant for the common good or that a believer must not hold firm to the truth of his or her tradition. Rather, it is that the state has a limited role to play in achieving the full common good which includes the promotion of religious truth. Catholic social thought has come to an appreciation of the complexity of the common good and an acceptance of its different levels as well as the responsibilities they generate. The temporal element of the common good to be promoted by the state is public order. It is up to other societal bodies to promote additional dimensions of the common good such as the spiritual. But this effort on the part of others must be done without resort to the coercive power of the state. This means that considerable freedom of belief and activity, an arena of civil liberties, is beyond governmental intrusion even in a society with a communitarian rather than liberal understanding of the role of the state.[41]

Rethinking the importance of equality for understanding human dignity has led to a focus in post-conciliar teaching on how inequality has become "the central social problem of our time" which must be attacked through policies that lessen the gaps between groups and nations in our world.[42] Briefly, this conclusion has been reached in four steps. 1) The basis for equality is seen in the common origin and destiny of the human family. 2) This foundation grounds a moral norm calling for a lessening of inequality. 3) Additional support for the moral norm comes from an assessment of the harm caused to the social order by inequality. 4) Backing for the norm is garnered through assessment of the harmful consequences of inequality in the international order. At the heart of these assessments is a sense of the divisiveness which inequality creates. Community is impossible with significant inequality.[43]

In order to foster a shared common quality of life, a variety of duties have been distilled. Characteristic of each of these duties of solidarity is the aim of restricting inequalities which block "common sharing in a full human life."[44] Differences due to training, temperament, skill, etc. will continue but must be regulated so that legitimate differences are those which do not stand in the way of people relating to one another in a manner of genuine concern and regard.

In such a framework the common good "is no longer an abstract principle of adjustment for competing principles of justice; it is the image of familial sharing in the banquet of life. . . ."[45] There is a clear vision, in other words, of what efforts to attain the common good are aiming toward—a world where people experience mutual concern, shared economic well-being and commitment of sacrifice in order to close divisions between peoples.

The theme of participation in the Catholic understanding of personal dignity also lends itself to reconceiving the common good in Catholic social teaching. Dennis McCann has proposed a procedural, as distinct from substantive, definition of the common good open to determination through the processes of public conversation and debate. Even the results of this open process must be seen as "inevitably partial and perspectival" since it would reflect the consensus of a society that is historically and culturally limited.[46] But widespread participation in the determination of the content of the common good will serve as a check against too self-serving a description of the common good by an elite who claim to speak for those marginalized from the processes of public life. Also various social movements have arisen which have challenged the harmonious vision of society that stemmed from the organic model. The sense of conflict and the reality of power has caused the Catholic tradition to incorporate elements of conflictual models of society into its predominantly cooperative vision. Whether the roots of conflict are seen as sin, or simply the inevitable consequence of pluralism and useful competition, the need is there for an understanding of the common good which is not unduly optimistic about how society is ordered and reformed. Cooperation is possible, but the element of conflict cannot be denied.

McCann makes an important point when he notes that Catholic social theory, loyal to the common-good tradition, accepted the Thomistic vision and the presumption of a unanimity in society which is unknown today. Early papal social encyclicals also presumed a social unity that appears at odds with the stubborn pluralism of modern life. Contemporary descriptions of the common good must take account of the variety of options available to the modern person in choosing a life plan. What is sought are cooperative endeavors in pursuit of purposes, some of which are shared. The common good must not be seen as so specific in detail that diversity within society is repressed. What must be sought instead is an open, informed, civil discussion by citizens so that consensus on what Murray called the orders of justice, peace and morality in public life might be attained through persuasion, not coercion. Such a societal experiment requires structures that encourage participation in the public conversation rather than exclusion. Pluralism in society is best protected if participation in public life is widespread and the common good reflects the consensus of more rather than fewer citizens.

This approach to the question of the common good finds support in Murray's notion of the United States as "a pattern of interacting conspiracies."[47] The four conspiracies—Protestant, Catholic, Jewish and secularist—had to be brought together in public discussion so that a public consensus could be forged. The outcome of such conspiring was Murray's hoped for reestablishment of a public philosophy to guide public affairs. It may be, however, that Murray believed in a core within the public consensus that was less historically conditioned than McCann's procedural definition of the common good as being the good we pursue in common.[48] In either case, however, it is not possible to think of the common good in a manner that simply ignores the historically conditioned nature of the idea. Once one acknowledges the manifold changes concerning the Catholic view of the common good, McCann concludes, attempts at universal, ahistorical, substantive definitions of this key concept must be suspect.[49]

To sum up, the anthropological shift in Catholic social teaching cited by Curran has pointed out how freedom, equality and participation have become major themes in the church's understanding of the human person. This shift has, in turn, occasioned a reconceptualization of the nature of the common good in Catholic social thought.

The Common Good and Human Rights

In a recent effort at such reconceptualization, David Hollenbach has suggested that we view the common good of civil society as that "measure of the communion of persons that is achievable in society."[50] We seek, therefore, in our public deliberation to establish consensus on the policies which encourage the "communion of persons."

One aspect of the common good which has achieved consensus status in American society is that the common good is intimately related to human rights. No definition of the common good is likely to gain a hearing if it does not include an understanding of the import of human rights. It is true that the Catholic Church was slow in coming to an endorsement of the rights-language of western democracies. Yet in recent decades it has become a major proponent of human rights in its social teaching.[51]

Consequently, Catholicism's communitarianism with its insistence on the reality of human rights should be classified, in Allen Buchanan's terminology, as a moderate form of communitarianism. Radical communitarianism denies the existence of individual rights in the name of the common good while moderate versions of communitarian theory accept the existence of individual rights but challenge the priority which liberalism accords such moral claims.[52] Unlike the radical communitarian approach, Catholic social theory's advocacy of personalism prevents the suppression or denial of individual human rights. But stress on the social nature of the person moves the Catholic tradition a) to contextualize rights within a community and b) to embrace a wider array of human rights than the standard liberal account of civil and political liberties. Catholic human rights theory with its endorsement of both economic and social rights along with civil and political liberties is grounded upon a personalist rather than liberal foundation. Granting rights of empowerment or enablement through social and economic goods like housing, food and health care illustrates the Catholic concern for a person's ability to enter into the life of a community rather than an individualistic concern for self-development apart from social relations.

Emphasis given to the value of participation helps to explain the increased attention to rights-language in Catholic social theory. Unless people are able to enter into the life of the group in a meaningful way there are reduced opportunities for self-donation. Human rights, be they political, economic or social, are statements about the conditions needed for participatory community to be realized. Human rights in Catholic teaching are moral claims which ought to have legal standing because they are claims to goods which are necessary for the person to participate with dignity in the communal life of a society. This is what distinguishes the Catholic tradition on human rights from the individualism of liberalism's appeal to rights. In Catholic theory, rights-language is contextualized by the moral imperative of participatory community.

Implications for Public Life and Policies

If one accepts that a communitarian vision of society is preferable to liberal individualism as the foundation for democratic society, the question remains about the practical effects. What difference would it make if society were to think in terms more akin to Catholic social theory than liberalism? What are the practical implications of a communitarian theory? While it is not possible to offer detailed responses to this concern, especially since the intellectual ferment out of which new directions develop has only begun, several orientations for public life can be cited which indicate the direction in which a communitarian commitment leads. In employing Catholic social thought we are aware that the tradition is composed of basic insights and assumptions about human nature, not blueprints for creating the good society. We do not presume that our proposals can claim to be *the* Catholic position on social action and policy. Ours is but an attempt to prod our collective societal imagination by suggesting some ideas about public life that are derived from a communitarian rather than liberal perspective.

1. *Community Rights:* We are familiar with the idea of certain collective rights claimed by groups, for example political self-determination or territorial sovereignty. A communitarian view would highlight the fact that many groups in addition to nations have plausible rights-claims that deserve consideration and respect. The principles of subsidiarity and pluralism in Catholic social theory reflect the tradition's appreciation for natural communities like families, neighborhoods, and ethnic groups.[53] A communitarian approach to rights would seek to protect and foster such social realities. Advocacy of the rights of the individual without balancing these alongside concerns for preserving the fabric and ethos of a community is one consequence of the individualism of our society.

Communitarians draw attention to what might be called the "principle of reciprocal obligation." Society, acting through its institutions, has a responsibility toward the individual but the person also has obligations toward society. Student loan programs, the G.I. Bill, and job training programs are all examples of how society can offer assistance to a person in need while the individual incurs a responsibility to perform certain acts in return. There is also a need for the person to accept the responsibilities which derive from social roles like parent, teacher, citizen, consumer. A good society entrusts men and women with social standing and provides support for good performance within these roles. It is fair to expect reasonable efforts on the part of each individual to meet the duties incumbent on those who fill social roles. As Maryann Glendon has shown, we have as a society and as individuals not done well by children after the break-up of marriages.[54] Communitarianism also seeks to encourage appropriate moral restraint so that the confusion between one's right to do something and what it is right for one to do is lessened. Raising up community rights and the need for responsibility on the part of each person toward society is an educative task important to the communitarian project.

2. *Economics:* In economic life several issues arise. First, perhaps, is the reality of interdependence and how liberal market mechanisms pay insufficient attention to this reality. Classic market theory presumes agents acting for self-interest and remaining independent except when engaged in market transactions. The common good is obtained serendipitously through the sum of private transactions performed by self-interested agents. What this ignores is that in an interdependent society there are unintended public results of private transactions and these can

be positive or negative. The public consequences are what economists call "externalities," for they are not seen as intrinsic to the action of the individuals exchanging goods and services in the market.[55]

Yet it is the unintended negative consequences of market decisions which haunt our society—crime, drug abuse, homelessness, pollution are all externalities at least partially generated by persons acting in a market system that presumes rationality is the seeking of private self-interest. For example, as Garret Hardin demonstrated in his oft-cited essay "The Tragedy of the Commons," the logic of self-interest drives individuals to ignore the social costs of their "private" acts.[56] If a producer can lower costs of production by dumping smoke and fumes into the atmosphere it makes sense to do so. If society decides to improve air quality everyone will pay for the cost of the clean-up but the producer alone gains the benefit of pollution, lower production costs. Thus, the entire benefit is private while the cost, the externality, is socially borne. A self-interested person will be encouraged by the norms of a self-interested market philosophy to pollute if he or she can benefit.

The net effect of externalities is the failure of liberal market economics for "the market system underproduces private goods with social benefits and it overproduces private goods with social costs." And, as Charles Wilber notes, when "social costs and benefits diverge from private costs and benefits, what is best for each individual is not what is best for society."[57] A clearer focus on interdependence and a better understanding of how the common good cannot simply be equated with the sum of individual goods would be one element of a communitarian approach to economics.

3. *Public Services:* One of the important tasks for any society is the organization of its services. Not just that education is provided but how children are educated; not just that the sick are cared for but how they are cared for; not just that social welfare is available but how the indigent receive assistance—these are crucial issues for the well-being of any society. A criticism of public services is not meant to denigrate the hard work and good will of many who provide such services in our nation. But it would be unrealistic to ignore the large amount of dissatisfaction which exists concerning the delivery of services in the United States. Welfare recipients complain about the demeaning nature of the system. Parents are near desperation in many locales over the state of their children's school system. The list of complaints is seemingly without end.

A communitarian critique of present delivery of public services immediately focuses upon the bureaucratic nature of so many of the organizations which are meant to provide service. Too many people find the present bureaucracies of public service hopelessly impenetrable and unresponsive. The structures of public life have lost their human scale and the resulting impersonalism and inefficiency stymie the delivery of services.

In Catholic social thought the principle of subsidiarity challenges existing social services to reconsider the usefulness of neighborhood and voluntary organizations. There is no reason, given the present unhappy state of public service, that the state should control what the city can do and no reason for the city to maintain power over services best provided at borough or neighborhood levels. It is important for government to have oversight and review in a structured manner so as to avoid local corruption and test performance, but processes to establish accountability should flow both ways. Ultimately the persons served by a social agency should be able to review its performance. In our large bureaucratic organizations there is little if any way that the individual's voice is heard or, if heard, acknowledged. Reconfiguring public services along lines that utilize community-based organizations is a venture that might enable individuals to have greater voice in the design and assessment of public service agencies.[58]

4. *Family Life:* The basic community in any society is the family. It is vital to society that there be healthy family units which are supported by the economic and political policies of the culture. While arguments for intervention in family life can be justified, the presumption for Catholic social theory is that as much freedom and power ought to be invested at this level as possible. In this respect, certain present practices of U.S. society require examination. Two examples of the kinds of policies that a communitarian perspective might advocate deal with education of children and the work of parents.

Many families have little control over the education of children. It is clear that there is a near monopoly exercised by the state over primary education. Furthermore, it is apparent that American education is experiencing something of a crisis. Entrenched forces battle for control of education while comparative studies show the U.S. slipping behind other nations in the task of preparing young people for the scientifically and technically sophisticated world that awaits them.

In our existing situation it is useful to consider alternatives to the standard way of addressing the issue. While poor parenting exists, it is reasonable to accept that most parents want what is best for their child and are willing to make sacrifices for their offspring. It is also reasonable to presume that the parent is best situated to know what is, in fact, in the best interests of the child. This does not mean we ought to dismiss the wisdom and knowledge of professional educators, but it does mean that parents should have greater ability to weigh the options created by educators and then have the means to exercise some choices. Participation is key for the life of any community. When authority and power, be it formal or informal, is in the hands of an elite, the risk increases that the community ceases to serve the real interests of persons for the sake of an abstract "people." What really happens is that the elite shape the community's practices to their own advantage.

A variety of reforms might begin to alter that circumstance but few suggestions would change the status quo as quickly and as thoroughly as acceptance of a voucher system. Giving parents or legal guardians the opportunity to spend the tax dollars apportioned for their child's education will move parents back into the center of educational decision-making. Once there are genuine choices available for education there may be genuine reform within the educational system. And giving to families the fundamental decision about which school a child attends is arguably one of the best ways to introduce choice.

Another illustration of support for family life addresses how our present culture permits work to separate family members from each other. The forty hour work week was implemented to protect blue-collar industrial workers from exploitation. Today the group most often found working excessive hours is not the laboring class but professional and managerial workers. In many firms the expectation is that advancement, even retention, depends upon the willingness to spend fifty or sixty hours on the job. The tired white collar commuter lugging an attaché case and straggling home in the dark is not an uncommon sight. Often the hours are worst for young adults who are struggling to make it within the corporation. It is at this time in life, however, that a couple is first adapting to married life, and these are also the years when children are most dependent upon parents. Yet the excessive work regimen of our society makes time spent as a family a good to be enjoyed on weekends only. While our society pays lip service to the value of family, workaday experience is of long hours spent traveling to and from work, longer hours at the workplace and less time with spouses and children.

Faced with this contradiction a communitarian viewpoint will investigate policies that promote sabbaticals from work, parental and maternity leave policies, work-week laws for all classes of labor, and other measures which will facilitate family members having the possibility of more time together.[59]

5. *The State:* When Catholic social teaching expounds the responsibility of the state for public order, it includes the idea of social justice. Concern for social justice, in turn, led the church to teach that the state must be willing and able to intervene in public life, especially economic life. As modern society becomes more complex and bureaucratic, the

state is often the only institution capable of checking and remedying the abuses of a free society. While not forgetting the principle of subsidiarity, there is an awareness that an activist state is a necessary condition for attaining justice in society.

When a social theory emphasizes the promotion of the common good as much as the regulation of self-interest, a more positive view of the state is possible. A communitarian vision permits a broader range of government activity since it can argue with consistency that the state may take a more active role in the life of a people. The use of public funds to promote artistic endeavors and to provide tuition assistance for those in private schools are examples of how the state may have a more positive role in society than liberalism admits in theory. If the government has a minimal role, how can it subsidize museums, theater companies, art exhibits or private education? Some citizens may argue that such activities promote the well-being of each citizen and therefore it is correct for liberalism to use tax revenue for the sake of the arts or private education. The difficulty with this position is that large numbers of individuals acknowledge no personal benefit from such state activity and even disavow any interest in supporting such institutions. Such objections strike us as consistent with the creed of liberalism: it is not within the state's purview to promote the arts or education unless it is demonstrable that such activity is in the self-interest of citizens. Calling upon individuals to help finance programs from which they derive no clear and direct benefit is difficult for liberalism to justify as is demonstrated by the attacks upon the welfare state found in the writings of Friedrich Hayek, Milton Friedman, and Robert Nozick. Catholic social teaching, in contrast, by its appeal to the values of participatory community, the common good, and the role of the state in promoting such values, offers a different set of arguments to assess the propriety of state activity in areas like welfare policy, education, or public support of the arts.

6. *Import of Public Life and Leadership:* A communitarian social theory yields a richer understanding of the reasons people act. Self-interest is insufficient to explain public behavior which confounds the logic of self-interest. The Catholic vision of the person, which admits the resiliency of the image of a self-giving God in the human, offers a more adequate basis for social ethics than a univocal emphasis on original sin. Our lives are more complex than the "realists" propose, and self-interest does not do justice to the feelings of loyalty, duty and affection which we experience in social life. These and similar deeply felt motives for action are generated, at least in part, by communal experience.

A multi-dimensional account of motivation in politics and economics points out the importance of cultivating a public philosophy and theology. If self-interest is the irresistible or acceptable norm for social action, then little attention needs to be given to the role of a shared philosophy or theology within a society. And so liberalism allows an agnosticism regarding the common good and is content with various competing forces each trying to attain its own narrowly construed vision of the good. The role of government is simply to guarantee that the rules of competition are fair. A communitarian model, on the other hand, suggests that a central task of society is to search for shared understanding of the social good and for policy judgments to be made about good and bad choices according to some agreed-upon standards of right and wrong action. A shared public philosophy and theology forged through public debate is a vital social good. Self-interest cannot foster substantive public debate, for it must presuppose that all such conversation would be merely a smoke screen for individual self-aggrandizement. Liberalism not only denigrates the import of a philosophy of the common good but legitimates self-interest politically while capitalism celebrates it economically.

The task of the public leader in a communitarian model entails the promotion of debate so that a people can be galvanized behind ideas. This approach to political economy gives a central place to the influence of public ideas. There really are very few things in a democracy more powerful than an idea whose time has come. To be able to articulate an idea that resonates with a people's commitment to the common good is one of the most significant gifts a leader can bring to public life. To contribute to the development of a philosophy of the common good, however, is not the leader's task alone.

7. *The Church:* There is a vital role for voluntary associations such as the church in a communitarian model of society. Within the experience of voluntary associations two dimensions stand out: 1) the experience of solidarity by which a person identifies with a group; and 2) the experience of a symbol system which offers an interpretive value framework. Individuals have "reference groups" which provide a sense of belonging and identity. Loyalty to such a group will permit a person to overcome economic self-interest if the group's interest is at stake. In the same way, the presence of certain basic values may draw people away from self-interest if the value system adopted is oriented toward self-giving. Again, a number of studies mentioned by Kelman and Gary Orren have shown how factors other than self-interest determine political and economic activity.[60]

With regard to the first motivational source, a person can identify with poor reference groups as readily as with good ones. One of the aims of a church which is truly catholic is the creation of moral communities that stretch our particular loyalties to more universal concerns. This is an important goal, for we are always tempted to identify with more restrictive definitions of self that limit our concerns to family, neighborhood, nation, class, race, etc. One of the weaknesses of liberalism has been the way that too often people join groups not for the experience of broadening loyalties but for the sake of more effectively advancing self-interest. Interest-group liberalism has promoted two consequences which are injurious to the common good. First, the creation of interest-groups allows a person to withdraw from public life rather than enter it. The group now becomes the advocate of one's interests and looks out for the individual so one need not involve oneself in public life. Second, the interest-group is bound to promote the self-interest of its members and so takes the lowest common denominator of self-interest on each occasion even though, when confronted with a matter where self-interest is involved, the individual can balance self-interest and other interests to resolve the matter more appropriately. Public life is diminished by the prevalence of interest-groups because through such groups self-interest comes to dominate public life, on occasion even beyond the wishes of members of the interest-group.

On the second matter, the formation and adoption of a core values-framework, the experience of community is an originating source of these values. The religious community plays a vital educative role in the shaping of a person's core values through its rituals, narratives, and symbols. Furthermore, it reinforces an individual's commitment to certain values by clarification of the connection between moral experience and deeply held convictions regarding the meaning and nature of God, creation and human history. In its creedal and liturgical discourse the church provides a foundation for public morality so that political-moral choice can express one's self-understanding.

What an experience of church membership allows, therefore, is the process of identification with a given community so that one's interests expand beyond self-interest narrowly construed. Participation in a voluntary association like the church can also offer a set of values which claim our devotion and protection. Within the Catholic understanding this role for the church makes sense, given the shaping of public life by a wide array of forces, positive and negative.

Hobbes and Smith, embracing the minimalist view of the state held by the reformers, also undercut the public role of the church. Because neither gave a central role to altruism in social life, neither saw a positive role for the state. Why should the state encourage self-giving in social life when such behavior is either impossible, as with Hobbes, or unnecessary, as with Smith? If either of these views be true, then what need for the church to cultivate a communal ethos that calls people to self-giving and solidarity? In short, public life premised on self-interest as the sole engine of human action makes much of the church's ministry unnecessary to successful societies. By contrast, a communitarian theory such as Catholicism places great weight on the place of the church as a school for virtues, qualities needed if society is to be transformed into a more humane reality.

In a communitarian framework the church should make a further contribution to the political life of a nation through the way it educates participants in the task of civic discourse. The church's political influence would not be that of a voting bloc or religiously motivated interest group. By shaping the public values and ideas of a people, the church could help to create the moral climate within which policy issues are framed and debated. And as a reference group that challenges individuals to replace self-interest with self-giving, the church ought to enlarge the role that reasoned discourse is able to play in the life of the political body.

Conclusion

Communitarian philosophies in general and Catholic social theory in particular are marked by a fundamental conviction that human life cannot achieve its fullness without a lively involvement in public life. This contrasts with liberal notions that see public life as an artificial construct made for the convenience of essentially atomistic individuals. Public life in the liberal vision comes about due to the inevitable frustrations and conflicts born of the individualistic competition found in the state of nature. Politics may be necessary but only functionally necessary. It is secondary to the natural state of economic competition and exists to enforce the rules of the free market. Government is, in this account, a conflict-manager.

This stands in stark contrast to the communitarian view that politics is about our common life and that the institutions and practices of public life are meant to improve the quality of our life together.[61] The myth of self-interest as the sole or, at least, always dominant motive in human action remains a cornerstone of liberal social and economic theory. That myth is rooted in a vision of human action which arises, we have argued, from a particular theological anthropology. A fundamental but often overlooked reason for the Catholic tradition's uneasiness with and criticism of liberalism is that Catholicism disagrees with that theological anthropology. What is at stake is not only a series of prudential judgments concerning social and economic policy but an understanding of what it is to be human.

3 | The Trinity and Human Rights

The Catholic Church was slow in coming to an endorsement of the rights that were promoted by the European revolutions of the nineteenth century. It was not until 1963 in *Pacem in Terris* that Pope John XXIII enumerated those human rights that the church endorsed.[1] Once the idea of human rights took hold, however, it became central to the social teaching of Roman Catholicism. David Hollenbach has suggested that the cause of human rights is now the "prime focus" of the "ethical teaching and pastoral strategy" of the papacy in the realm of justice and peace.[2]

Like other aspects of its teaching, the human rights position of the Catholic hierarchy is subject to critical scrutiny. In the case of social pronouncements, politically conservative voices have frequently been raised in dissent. One of the more serious reservations voiced about recent Catholic statements on social questions concerns its use of the language of "rights" to discuss economic goods like food, shelter, employment, and minimum income. During the early years of the Reagan administration there was a particularly intense attack on the idea of "entitlement rights" which were claimed by the poor. The challenge to the idea of economic and social rights was also pressed within the American Catholic community during the writing of the bishops' pastoral letter "Economic Justice for All."[3]

We believe that the criticism of this dimension of Catholic human rights theory is misguided but understandable, given the inadequate manner in which the church has developed this teaching. The biggest problem is that the church has not shown how its approach to human rights is derived from its understanding of reality and the human person. Here is one of the prime services that can be rendered by a foundational political theology.

The Trinitarian God

No belief is more central to the Christian tradition than the Trinity. It has not been merely an element in creedal statements, but classically the very form of such statements, the organizing principle of Christian faith since the fourth century. And yet, since the time of the Protestant and Catholic reformations, the Trinity has gone largely untreated and unexplored: when the theological agenda is determined by polemics, what is accepted by everyone is discussed by no one. When the Trinity is presented in preaching and catechesis as information—odd but authoritative—about the inner life of God, the central Christian symbol is robbed of its depth and transformative power.

The doctrine of the Trinity is an elaborate spelling-out of the most basic Christian metaphor for God, represented in numerous ways in the synoptic gospels and by Paul, and finally given simple but classic expression in the Johannine documents: God is agape (1 Jn 4:8, 16). "God," i.e. the mystery which grounds and surrounds all existence, is pure self-gift. This is the extraordinary claim which undergirds the synoptic gospels' linking of the commandments to love God and to love the neighbor as being exactly equivalent, and allows the fourth gospel to collapse the two into one new commandment: "Love one another; just as I have loved you, you also must love one another" (Jn 3:34). We are urged to "be perfect as your heavenly Father is perfect," and when we discover in the preceding verses that the Father's perfection consists in his not making a distinction between the good and the wicked, on both of whom he makes the sun shine and the rain fall (Mt 5:43–48), the purity of the self-gift which is named "God" is significantly revealed. As Augustine argued again and again, God loves because that is the divine nature, not because creation deserves it. In parable after parable, statement after statement, the meaning of "God" is revealed as the one who is perfectly self-giving.

The classic doctrine of the Trinity is an attempt to understand the freedom of that self-gift. If God is agape, then some recipient of the divine self-gift is necessary. If that recipient is other than God, a creature, then creation is necessary for God to be God. But such a position is not only incipiently pantheistic, it ends by making God less than agape. The foundation of created being would then have to be divine eros, for God's love would necessarily seek fulfillment in creating. But if God is agape, and the nature of agape is to be entirely free, God, being God, must be pure self-gift, without any necessary reference to creation. God must eternally be giver and receiver and gift. "God" is the name of the relationship of an endless perfect mutual self-gift: in our traditional imagery, the Father gives himself totally to the Son, the Son gives himself totally to the Father, and the Spirit, proceeding from both, is the bond of that pure agapic love. In frequently used patristic imagery, God is the lover, the beloved, and the love between them.[4] "God" is the name of a relationship and the poles of the relationship. God is not a person, if by that we mean one pole of a relationship. God is the very fullness of relatedness.

This is the central Christian insight: "to be" and "to love" are synonymous. To hold onto life is to lose it; to give it away is to see it become everlasting life. This is not an ethical ideal. Rather, the oft-repeated statement of the synoptic gospels is a description, a corollary of the claim that being and loving are identical. This is the heart of the doctrine of the Trinity and the deepest claim which Christianity makes about being, including human being.

The claim advanced here founds the argument of this book, for it is the deep ground of a communitarian ethics and politics. To exist is to be in a network of relationships, a network whose dimensions are, in fact, co-terminous with the universe spatially and temporally. Existence, as we experience it, is to be somewhere sometime. But to be somewhere is to be near to, far from, above, below, right of, left of, in front of, behind everything else. Likewise, to be sometime is to be before, contemporary with, or after everything else. To be is to be in relation to every other being. This is true of human and non-human being. What characterizes the human is the capacity to know and will its relatedness. The more we grasp the immensity of our relationships and the more we choose them, i.e. love them, the more fully we exist. To limit one's acknowledgement of relatedness (for we cannot limit the fact of our universal relatedness) and one's acceptance of those relationships is to diminish one's existence. To deny relationality and to reject relationships are to hover on the edge of non-being.

Thus the notion of personhood owes much to trinitarian reflection. When Augustine defended the Latin use of *persona* in speaking of the Trinity, he did so by insisting that a person does not exist *ad semetipsum*, "as directed to self," but *ad invicem*, "as directed to others."[5] The very meaning of personhood is relatedness to others. Consistent with his position that terms predicated of God and creatures are done so properly of God and only by extension of creatures, Thomas Aquinas taught that "person" applies preeminently to God.[6] This is because, in God, relation is not an accident, but is the divine essence itself.[7] One becomes more fully the person one is, therefore, by entering ever more fully into ever more relationships. For example, one knows who one is by consciously appropriating the almost infinite array of one's relationships. As someone comes to a wider and deeper understanding of history and appreciates the relatedness of the here and now to countless theres and thens, one simultaneously becomes more fully *this* one and no other. It is a corollary of the Trinity that selfhood is in direct proportion to relatedness.

Revelation has been well described by Rowan Williams as "a questioning attention to our present life in the light of a particular past—a past seen as 'generative.' "[8] Williams refers to Norman Gottwald's claim that the doctrine of God in the Hebrew scriptures is unintelligible unless it is seen to be intimately related to the social organization of ancient Israel.[9] The distinctiveness of Yahweh is that he is the God of Israel, a people structured in a particular way. As Williams notes, this coincides with Paul Ricoeur's analysis of revelation as "the process whereby a community takes cognizance of its own distinctive identity."[10] The community "constitutes a concept of God for itself by asking what it is that constitutes itself. To be able to answer the question about our roots, our context, what it is that has formed us, is at least to begin to deal with the question of the meaning of 'God.' "[11]

The Christian community, however, claims to be (ultimately) inclusive of the whole of humanity. It, therefore, holds that its account of human experience is, at least potentially, a universal account. This certainly does not mean that Christians can claim as a result of their experience at present to have a universally adequate account of the experience of all people living at all times and places (and those Christians who do so claim may well have cause to examine their consciences on the score of idolatry). But the insistence that Christian life is life "in Christ" and that Christ is " the new Adam" is a claim that life reinterpreted in light of the life, death, and destiny of Jesus of Nazareth yields a description of human experience potentially and ultimately applicable to all persons, since in Christ "there is neither Jew nor Greek, neither slave nor free, neither male nor female" (Gal 3:28).

Trinitarian doctrine interprets the Christian experience of human life. This is not to say that the doctrine "really" refers to human experience and has been arbitrarily extrapolated to a transcendent ground called "God." Rather, the doctrine developed because Christians found it the necessary description of their experience of shared life. Christian *praxis* led to the formal expression of Christian *doxa*. Living in a particular way shapes our experience of ourselves and others in a particular way. We talk about our experience and, in doing so, refine our way of talking about it. Gradually we establish a standard vocabulary, system of grammar and set of metaphors. Walter Kasper has described the doctrine of the Trinity as the "grammar and summation" of creation and salvation.[12] But "creation" and "salvation" are not categories descriptive only of things as a whole; *we* are created and saved, and so the Trinity is the summary grammar of our most fundamental experience of ourselves. Basic to that experience is that we know ourselves as social, as communal in the very structure of our being, as essentially political. The Christian claim that one exists to the degree that one enters into relationship with others, specifically the relationship of self-gift, is both grounded in and explicated by the doctrine of the Trinity. Thus the doctrine of the Trinity is an essentially and radically political statement: it maintains that not only is human existence social but that the ground of all being is relationship.

The Trinity's Public Significance

A public theology grounded in the Trinity provides the deepest foundation possible within the Christian tradition for the rejection of the individualistic bias which can distort the ethic of human rights as it is commonly understood. In order to draw out the public meaning of the Trinity, two consequences of the doctrine must be noted.

First, if being and loving agapically are identical, as the trinitarian doctrine claims, then existence does not precede entry into relationship. It *is* relationship. Being *is* being related. Coming into communion with others is not subsequent to existence. Being at all is being with. So central is this to the Christian tradition that the principle is both derived from and elevated into the meaning of "God." For God is not the one, the absolute, the alone. "God" is community, relationship, Trinity, agape. Aristotle observed that the human person is intrinsically political.[13] In this sense, Christianity teaches that so is God.

Second, the *imago Dei* motif, which is often employed as the theological base for the use of rights-language in contemporary Catholic social thought,[14] is transformed by bringing it into connection with the central Christian insight given metaphorical expression in 1 John 4:8.16, and theological elaboration in the doctrine of the Trinity. For if God is triune, if God is the perfect relationship of the lover and the beloved and the love which unites them, then to maintain that the human being is created in the image of God is to proclaim the human being capable of self-gift. The human person is the point at which creation is able to respond by giving oneself in return. The fundamental human right is the right to give oneself away to another and ultimately to the Other.

> Indeed, the Lord Jesus, when He prayed to the Father, 'that all may be one ... as we are one' (John 17:21–22), opened up broad vistas closed to human reason. For He implied a certain likeness between the union of the divine Persons, and in the union of God's sons in truth and charity. This likeness reveals

that man, who is the only creature on earth which God willed for itself, cannot fully find himself except through a sincere gift of himself.[15]

Christian revelation thus sheds a broad and dazzling light on the true nature of humanity, precisely by its understanding of the nature of God in whose image we are made. Unless we recover the import of the Trinity for thinking about God, we will not think wisely about the human person.

A man is alienated if he refuses to transcend himself and to live the experience of self-giving and of the formation of an authentic human community oriented towards his final destiny. A society is alienated if its forms of social organization, production and consumption make it more difficult to offer this gift of self and to establish this solidarity between people.[16]

How far this Christian understanding of the human person is from the enlightenment understanding of human nature. In the Hobbesian war of all against each, the goal of human life is the achievement of sovereign independence. Entry into any relationship, save that of dominance, lessens one's independence and so undermines one's humanity. Rights are the primitive property of the individual and must be preserved from society's encroachment. To protect the most important rights, one may have to sacrifice certain of one's freedoms by entering into a social contract clearly determining the relationships which will exist between the individuals forming the society. At least in theory, however, the perfectly free, fully human being will be totally independent and absolutely self-determining. The "God" who undergirds such an ethic is the sovereign individual. Whatever the "God" of the enlightenment might have been, he was clearly not triune. Throughout the eighteenth century, the defenders of what was, on the one hand, presumed to be orthodoxy emphasized divine sovereignty in order to defend God's independence, while religious liberals like the deists, on the other hand, in order to defend the universe's independence, stressed God's non-intervention in the smooth-running mechanism of creation. Both accepted God as removed and largely uninvolved. It was an era of religious individualism, and strikingly unitarian.

The Christian trinitarian understanding, in contrast, is communitarian, both theologically and politically. The individual does not precede the community. The individual and the community give life to one another: as the individual is more truly intelligent and free, more truly human and so more completely self-gift, the network of relationships in which the individual exists is furthered and enriched. Thus, humanity and relatedness are directly proportional; the broader and deeper that network of relationships, the more truly human the community and the individual. For humanity requires free and intelligent participation in being, and according to the Christian tradition, the ground of being is perfect relatedness. Each relationship brings with it responsibilities. In order to carry out responsibilities, rights arise. The fundamental responsibility is to give oneself away as perfectly as possible. The fundamental right is the right to do so.

Any accounting of human rights that stresses, as its foundation, freedom as non-interference rather than freedom for self-gift in relationship, freedom for participation in community, is a skewed understanding of the ground of human rights. The mistaken grounding of rights by Hobbes, Locke, and others, highly significant in the making of a particularly American mind-set, is understandable, given liberalism's agnosticism on the nature of the human good. But Christianity acknowledges no such agnosticism. It stresses the necessity of community for humans to grow in the image of God, to engage in acts of self-giving that can become truly reciprocal. The liberal tradition starts with the individual; here is the significance of the observation that liberalism is the political equivalent of unitarianism. In contrast, a trinitarian vision sees the individual and community as co-existent. There is no being apart from relatedness; God is the One only because God is the Three. A political theory shaped by the Christian tradition can only understand the person as an individual in community. The most fundamental human right is the right to exercise the power of self-giving, the opportunity for entrance into relationship, for deeper participation in the life of the human community.

All other rights are derivative. All consequent rights are claims to the pre-conditions for community, the locus of self-giving. Denying instrumental rights that secure necessary conditions for human community seriously weakens the opportunity to exercise the fundamental right of self-giving which is the expression of our nature and dignity.

Using Rights-Language

Important to distinguish in the discussion of human rights is the difference between legal and moral rights. A legal right is a right which is sanctioned by civil law; a person can appeal to the state for its enforcement. Such rights, moreover, may be constitutional or statutory: a constitutional right is one that is protected by existing constitutional law; a statutory right is one which is guaranteed by legislation, usually on the federal or state level. In order to have legal rights, the subject of such a claim must belong to the given political or legal community.

Moral rights are rights which are warranted by appeal to convincing ethical reasoning and argument. These rights can be, and often are, implemented as legal rights; but the two categories (legal and moral) are not perfectly congruent and can even be in conflict. Indeed, moral rights can at times be violated by existing legal rights. For example, if there is, as many would contend, a human right to bodily integrity, then that right would be violated by a country that gives police the right to torture prisoners in the name of national security. Or in another case, the human right to freedom was violated by those countries which had legally institutionalized slavery. In sum, moral rights may be embodied in legal systems and often are, but whether they are or not, they are still rights that are grounded on ethical argument rather than positive law.

Because human rights have their warrant in ethical theory, all human rights are moral rights; but only some human rights are legal rights. Human rights constitute a class of moral rights, and the subject of such rights need not belong to any particular political or legal community but only to the human community. Failure to keep clear the distinction between moral and legal rights results in considerable confusion when arguing for a right because the term "right" means different things to different people.

> In the mouth of the lawyer, the sociologist or historian, it [a right] is quasi-descriptive, i.e., it means that there is an established rule, whether legal or conventional, which accords the rights. But in the mouth of the reformer and moralist, it must necessarily mean "I believe (for reasons I am prepared to give) that X ought to have R if he wants it. . . ."[17]

Lawyers customarily appeal to existing law to establish the validity of a particular rights-claim when we are in the realm of legal rights. But the matter of human rights entails another kind of appeal. While it is true that some human rights are protected by law, the primary basis of any human right is not law *qua se* but a moral argument.

This does not mean that social reformers are indifferent about the legal institutionalization of human rights. Rather, that is a chief aim of human rights advocates, for legal recognition provides a strong sanction to human rights claims. But, it must be remembered, the moral and legal standing of human rights are not identical. Our interest is the theological basis for the moral argument in favor of a broad human rights agenda. In order to safeguard and enhance the foundational human right of self-giving, it is necessary to develop strategies which protect and foster human community.

Human Rights in Catholic Social Thought

While the language of rights has never been absent from the writings of the papacy in the modern era, the central role that human rights have assumed in Catholic social teaching is of recent vintage. The chief reason for this is that the language of human rights allows a central teaching office to address a pluralistic world, a universal church which recognizes the distinctiveness of local churches.[18] Perhaps this acceptance of pluralism within the church's teaching is most marked in the conciliar Declaration on Religious Freedom.[19] Whereas before the Second Vatican Council it was taught that there was one ideal arrangement in church-state relations, the council's teaching on the right to religious liberty acknowledged that state establishment of Catholicism is but one way of organizing civil society. The influence of the American church was significant in this area for moving the discussion of church-state relations away from a focus on the European experience.

Just as the church-state issue was resolved by acknowledging the reality of pluralism, other issues have been reconsidered in light of pluralism. Karl Rahner suggested that Vatican II was the initial experience of a truly world church after centuries of a European church that had missionary outposts.[20] The growing strength and voice of the church in other parts of the globe brought home to the papacy an awareness of the diverse cultures within which the gospel has taken root. In his letter commemorating the eightieth anniversary of *Rerum Novarum*, Paul VI expressly acknowledged that the pluralism of the world prevented any single solution being offered by the church in its social teaching: "In the face of such widely varying situations it is difficult for us to utter a unified message and to put forward a solution which has universal validity. Such is not our ambition, nor is it our mission."[21] The Synod of Bishops held in 1971 illustrated the impact of the new voices of third world bishops in the church, giving further evidence of Rahner's claim.[22] Henceforth, when the social message of the church was to be proclaimed, it had to be done in a way that was cognizant of the pluralistic context of the modern world.

What all this meant was that the papacy had to discover a way to teach within the world-church. By relying on the language of human rights the church found a way to speak a universal message that was respectful of a pluralistic world. There is no claim in post-conciliar social teaching that there is one Catholic position on the proper ordering of society. Instead, the variety of political, economic and cultural institutions is accepted. But the church holds up the moral imperative of human rights as minimal social conditions which all nations must respect. It is not for the church to devise a blueprint for society. Yet the church calls upon all people to protect and promote human rights irrespective of the way that a community is structured. Human rights are the moral parameters within which a social order must be organized.

In effect, Roman Catholicism has employed the language of human rights to articulate the framework within which a just strategy for establishing community must operate. "Catholic social teaching spells out the basic demands of justice in greater detail in the human rights of every person. These fundamental rights are prerequisites for a dignified life in community."[23] The moral weight of any human rights claim, then, is contingent upon the relation of the good that is sought to human community, the historical locus and creative expression of self-giving persons. That community fosters and sustains the distinct but interrelated levels of human personhood—the physical, intellectual, aesthetic, moral, religious—which interact to constitute the human person. Serious deprivation on any one of these levels can threaten the integrity of human community. Thus the list of goods that can be appealed to as an appropriate object of human rights claims is extensive. It must be acknowledged, however, that not everything necessary for human community can be put into the language and thought form of human rights.[24]

Understanding Human Rights

A human right cannot be an unlimited claim. We do not have a moral claim to everything and anything. "What is in question is the advancement of persons, not just the multiplying of things that people can use."[25] There is a need to distinguish between those goods which are basic conditions for the possibility of a community composed of self-giving persons, and those goods which are less pressing, less directly related to the fundamental right of participation in the life of self-giving.

In making such necessary distinctions, a serious danger to be avoided is modern society's inclination to utilize the state with its authorized political authority to adjudicate truth-claims about human fulfillment. While we believe liberalism is at fault for its neglect of the common good, there should not be an attempt to use the powers of the state to impose too detailed a plan for society's end. The pluralism of our culture must be respected, and no one group should presume that its vision will be perfectly translated into public policy.

One way of addressing the matter might be to rely on Barrington Moore's thesis of "the unity of misery and the diversity of happiness."[26] Briefly put, those evils which threaten human community are more easily agreed upon than enumerating those goods which foster human happiness. Consequently, rights to overcome, or protect against, the sources of misery can be the legitimate concern of government with less controversy than if the state were to define a person's life plan. Hunger, disease, physical violence, excessive control of free expression, association and movement, and other such human miseries can be warded off or limited by the establishment of certain rights. While liberalism can encourage concern for the other, and the acknowledgement of our obligation to play a part in the communal life of a people, Catholic social theory provides a stronger basis than liberalism for such a stance.

The Christian tradition provides a communitarian critique of liberal ideology. Liberalism sees the end of politics as focusing on the free individual, but freedom is too narrowly defined in this perspective. The communitarian vision offers an outlook where the basic idea is that people accept their interdependence as both empirically and normatively true, thereby enhancing a shared sympathy and purpose, and accepting responsibility for the well-being of one another and the community.[27] The Christian grounding of rights-language seeks to avoid the individualist bias of liberal dogma by placing rights in the context of community. This is achieved by recognizing that self-giving arises from and creates a setting of communal relations.

Yet the use of rights-language preserves Catholic social thought from collectivism. In the name of the group we must not remove personal liberty. The collectivist would view the human person as existing for the state. A person's appeal to rights is meant to check any such ideology. The communitarian holds that human rights arise from the fundamental conditions for communal life. But there is also the conviction that the most fundamental right, that of self-giving, is one that arises from the nature of the person created in the image of the trinitarian God. A communitarian rendering of rights-language seeks to avoid the individualist bias of liberal dogma by placing rights in the context of community. This is achieved by recognition that exercise of the fundamental human right is only possible within community. At the same time, the *raison d'être* of the community is the enrichment of the person. Collectivism is checked because society has the responsibility to provide for each person the opportunity to be self-giving.

In this framework, there is an acknowledgement of true mutuality. Not only is one diminished by the denial of his or her rights but all others are likewise lessened because of the absence of full participation in communal life. If a person or group is hindered in entering deeply into the life of the community, then all the other members of the community are hindered in actualizing their humanity. Our relational nature, therefore, constitutes both a promise and a threat. It is a promise in that the possibility of true communion is congruent with the nature of our being, indeed with the nature of all being, subsisting as it does in the triune God. But it is a threat insofar as failure to establish community entails a diminution of human life, not only for the marginalized, but for those who prevent the inclusion of all persons in participatory community. This is the profoundly theological reason why liberation theology, like all public theologies, should underscore that the ending of oppression is for the sake of both the oppressor as well as the oppressed. This emphasis on community flows from the theology of the Trinity. Human rights have a social dimension because self-giving leads to mutually enriching communal relationships. Human rights are claims to those goods which allow people to act upon the responsibility to be self-gift. There is no convincing reason why in themselves economic goods should be ruled out *a priori* as legitimate objects of human rights claims.

Criticism of the Human Rights Agenda

There are a number of objections to the theory of social and economic rights as human rights. English philosopher Maurice Cranston ranks among the most persistent of the critics who oppose an expanded roster of human rights beyond traditional civil liberties. He has summarized the major complaints against the "new" human rights in his writings. Cranston proposes a threefold test for evaluating a human rights claim. He believes that the customary civil and political rights pass each test, while the newer social and economic rights do not. The three tests are practicability, paramount importance, and universality.[28]

(a) *Practicability*

The first test simply makes the point that if it is impossible for a thing to be done, it cannot be claimed as a right. He is not referring to logical impossibility, but physical impossibility, arguing that, in the latter sense, it is not possible for a poor, undeveloped country to guarantee an adequate standard of living for its citizens. Thus, it cannot be a right. Anticipating one possible response to his view, viz. human rights are ideals to be striven for, Cranston rejects the idea that rights are ideals to be pursued but not presently implemented. "An ideal is something to be aimed at, but cannot by definition be immediately realized. A right, on the contrary, is something that can, and from the moral point of view *must*, be respected here and now."[29] This is true regardless of the way one defines right. Even if one accepts the opinion that a right is best understood as a "legitimate claim," the sense is that such a claim is to be actualized in the present, not the unrealized future. In sum, a right cannot be an ideal for a futurist state but must be embodied in existing societal structures. A right pertains to the moral demand incumbent upon people in the present, not some moral ideal toward which they aspire.

In response to Cranston's practicability test there are several remarks to be made. It is true that not every state can satisfy the welfare claims of its inhabitants. But why restrict the guarantor of the claim to the nation-state? "There seems no good reason why we should accept so tough a test of practicability, why we should accept that the social and economic rights in question should not be claimed by all men *against* all men."[30] It does seem plausible that some economic and social rights can be guaranteed if there were a fair sharing of the world's goods. Even if some human rights cannot be met in full, they can be satisfied in part. If that is insufficient to pass Cranston's practicability test, then more than social and economic rights fail. As D.D. Raphael states, "No amount of criminal legislation or of police forces will be able to prevent all homicides; but that is no reason for saying that the right to life should be struck out of our list of human rights as not being universally practicable."[31] After all, certain civil and political liberties which Cranston holds dear are not practical for poor countries, or countries undergoing social upheaval. Trial by peers, voting rights, impartial tribunals—all these are seemingly impractical in some situations. One reason is that the apparatus of a judicial system—courts, police, adminstrative services, legal services, etc.—does not compare all that favorably with the cost of providing for social and economic rights.

Is it true that we simply cannot meet a broad range of social and economic claims? To some extent, the counsel of professionals in various fields, such as health, agriculture, finance, etc., is required to answer this problem. But several words of caution must be raised. While it is true that some of the rights-claims of recent vintage may be excessive, not all are self-evidently so. We should be careful about dismissing certain rights because they call for major reform of the status quo. What may have to give way is not the voice of those denied their rights, but the economic and political structures which make justice "impractical." This is not to settle the nettlesome question of how best to overcome the injustice, but to point out that it is the ethical legitimacy of a claim that makes the struggle to overcome the problem a moral imperative.

In many developing nations today, civil and political liberties are denied in the name of development or national security. Often the rights of a free press or of labor are denied people now, while future generations are supposedly to benefit from the sacrifice of the present generation's rights. This is an ethic of development that is unacceptable to the Christian belief in the equality of all. No generation should have to be pitted against another for basic rights safeguarding a dignity which all share equally. Even if an economy is such that the full panoply of basic human rights cannot be immediately provided for the citizenry, there is good reason to use rights-language in describing the situation.

> . . . [T]here is a real point in insisting that the deprived claimant has a genuine right to the fulfillment of his basic needs even in hopeless conditions of scarcity, for that mode of expression emphasizes that the reason why no other person has a duty to help him has nothing to do with his qualification for the help. He has not failed in any way; rather circumstances have failed him.[32]

We should not be surprised by the idea that rights can be circumscribed for the sake of some higher good or due to pressing circumstances. But in such circumstances we do not say that the rights are non-existent; rather, we call the circumstances extreme. In situations of extreme scarcity, the language of rights reminds us that the reason no one fails in his or her moral duty to help another in distress is not that the deprived person has no claim but that circumstances have prohibited the securing of the right. So if a society, acting through its government, decides that as a result of an exceptional situation—e.g. a drought—the right to food cannot be fully implemented, we should not conclude that the right does not exist. Rather we conclude that the exceptional circumstance is precisely that—exceptional. It is not an acceptable state, and it must be remedied because it is offensive to a human right. We should hesitate, then, before granting too much persuasive power to the practicality argument. The issue of practicality raises a legitimate concern. But it is a caution against excessive rights-language, not a decisive argument opposing human rights which include economic rights.

(b) *Importance*

The second test for a human right is that of paramount importance. Cranston believes that a human right is "something of which no one may be deprived without a grave affront to justice."[33] It hard to see how economic and social rights fail this test. Cranston admits there is a moral duty to relieve great distress. Given the correlativity between rights and duties, which he stresses, there must be a right to relief from great distress. The only way to deny a right to social and economic goods, then, is to deny that social and economic distress is *great* distress. That seems contrary to experience. Importance is, of course, a matter of degree, and preventing abuse of civil liberties like the right to life is of paramount importance. Yet it is simply not the case that civil and political rights should always be accorded greater weight than social and economic rights.[34] Cranston labels the latter "luxuries," and indeed some rights, e.g. some of those proposed in the United Nations' "Universal Declaration of Human Rights," do seem to be so. But housing, food, health care and other goods seem to be of more importance than what we usually mean by luxury items.

(c) *Universality*

A third test which Cranston proposes is that of universality. He denies that the new welfare rights satisfy this test because they are rights of a certain class, not of the human race. Among the examples Cranston cites is unemployment compensation, which he believes can only be claimed by a certain class, the unemployed. It is a right attached to a social role, not humankind.

But is "being employed or unemployed" a social role? David Watson challenges this line of thinking. He takes up the case of the worker who has a right to decent working hours.

> Why should that man enjoy reasonable limitation of his working hours? Because he is in employment. This reply simply will not do as a justification. To be a father is amongst other things to have the right to discipline your children. But to be in employment entails nothing about the limitation of your working hours. The reply we need, I suggest, is "Because he is an employed man." We justify a reasonable limitation of working hours by referring not to the fact that the man is employed, but to the fact that he is a human being. . . . Why should that man be given a fair trial? Because he is accused? No because he is an accused man.[35]

Regarding the third test, universality, it would appear that economic and social rights qualify. At least some of these rights can be grounded upon the dignity of all humanity. Thus, they are rights open to all to claim. Cranston believes that social and economic rights are not universal in scope but restricted to members of a given nation-state, the rights of citizens not humans. Watson's rejoinder is that the referent for the newer rights is the fact that the subject claiming the rights is a human person.

(d) *Novelty*

There is a fourth objection to social and economic rights as human rights, though the charge is not leveled by Cranston. It is the issue of history and the alleged novelty of recent human rights-claims. How is it that these particular rights were unknown to, or unclaimed in, earlier ages? By way of response to this objection, it must first be said that it is not true to say that earlier generations knew nothing of economic rights. Thomas Paine defended the idea of welfare rights such as old-age benefits and child support.[36] Yet even if it were true that no one had claimed such human rights before the twentieth century, that would not be a refutation of the present claims. To call something a right is to say it is necessary for participation in community life. What constitutes the necessary conditions for community is not a fixed agenda. Rather it will vary from age to age, and therefore one should not presume that twentieth century rights-claims will be in full accord with those of the eighteenth century.

Our awareness of human rights, like all knowledge, is subject to historical process. Rights take shape with the passing of time as people pay attention to emerging conditions in society. Thus the right to work was only generally recognized in the industrial era when large numbers of unemployed workers became a consequence of the emerging urban factory economy. We ought not to conclude that the right came to be at that point. "Rather the assertion of the right is rooted in the belief that it is part of man's nature to work and that therefore any situation which deprives him of fulfilling this natural propensity ought to be corrected."[37] A right is a necessary empowerment for people to participate in community. What constitutes necessary social conditions for participation will vary from age to age. Work has been a vital form of such participation. The conditions of work change with time, and the content of a right to work will be shaped accordingly.

In earlier times, the right to health care was limited to such public health measures as quarantine. But today, since society is able to provide considerably more care, thanks to remarkable advances in medicine, personnel and resources, we have altered our understanding of what is the extent of the right to health care. As human effort and resources affect the conditions for participating in community, the instrumental rights themselves undergo change. In medieval Europe, no one would have claimed a right to formal education as necessary for entering into human community; in twentieth century America, however, it is inconceivable that a person could be denied a basic formal education and still be said to have the same ability as others to participate in community.

If one considers the differences between pre- and post-industrial society, one sees reasons that social and economic rights are later claims than civil and political liberties. Social and economic rights were not sought in a time when 1) people felt free to control their social and economic lives once civil and political liberties were granted, and 2) people believed the state to be a threat rather than a means to a free, participatory community. Today we are aware of larger social and economic forces which require countervailing force to secure personal well-being, and we have come to understand that the state can play a more positive role in protecting personal dignity than that of the night-watchman of minimal-state theorists.

Human Rights and Human Duties

Human-rights advocates must delineate the claims we have against others and the community. Any talk of rights leads to a study of duties, for duty is often understood to be a correlative concept to "right." In the case of many rights, the duty is fairly clear-cut, but it is not so obvious when discussing human rights. Rights can be divided into *in personam* and *in rem* rights according to the duties which the right generates. *In personam* rights are those which place duties upon specific, identifiable individuals, for example the rights and duties that result from a contract between an employer and employee. *In rem* rights, on the other hand, refer to legitimate claims that correlate with the duties of persons in general. If I have a right to the privacy of my backyard, then it is everyone's duty to avoid trespassing in my yard. My right is a claim against people in general to be dutiful about respecting my right of privacy. In similar fashion, a human right is an *in rem* right; it generates a duty upon all.

An important problem remains, however. Some human rights do not readily yield the locus or nature of the duty. It is easy to see my duty when talking about private property: one simply should not trespass. This is hardly a burden in normal circumstances. But a human right like the right to food is more problematic. In acknowledging that many in our world are denied this human right, do I personally have the duty to feed them? What burden of moral culpability rests on me for the starving in U.S. society and throughout the globe? How is an individual to understand his duty to respond to the *in rem* right to food which these starving people possess? The duty such a right imposes is not always clear in such cases; if it is clear, it appears to be so onerous that the individual can only fail in his or her duty.[38]

Government's Role

Satisfaction of *in rem* rights requires an organizational response since the scale and complexity of the duties is beyond individual fulfillment. Given the nature of some claims, the government, representing all those in a given society, offers the resources to meet the claims made by individual members of that society. Government ought not to act alone, for it may, and should, acknowledge other groups' rights to act on behalf of the community. The principle of subsidiarity applies in this area also. Yet the magnitude of some human rights-claims, especially when a whole group seems deprived of a specific right, leads us to conclude that the agent for satisfying such claims will frequently be the state or national government. This applies to economic rights as well, because no smaller group can properly respond to the duties generated by the right. There are clearly situations where the response of individuals and even voluntary associations are woefully inadequate to the human-rights violations in question. Only organized, governmental action is an adequate response to the injustice of the human right denied.

Of course, some governments are unwilling to live up to their responsibility, or may simply deny it exists. The human right is not thereby invalidated. The appeal must then go out to the wider community—all fellow persons. The deprived person or group makes claims on other people in the name of shared humanity, and the community of humanity through various international and trans-national agencies can act when the national community fails to meet the duty. This is precisely what has happened in cases of dissidents from oppressive regimes as well as political refugees from abusive governments or starving peoples in impoverished nations. These victims appeal to other nation states, not in the name of citizenship but in the name of humanity. And aid to these people was, and is, not an act of supererogation but simple justice. Human rights are ultimately claims of everyone against everyone for some assistance in the establishment of participatory community. Obligations to meet the duties imposed by a rights claim fall upon those best able to assume them. In most cases the assumption is that the national government is the agent best suited to protect the rights of those living within its territorial borders. This may not always be true; a powerful or wealthy government may be better able to protect some people's rights than the country of citizenship or residence. The usual expectation is reliable, however, as a good rule of thumb.

Individuals trying to understand their responsibility to meet their duty for such *in rem* rights as adequate food, shelter or health care must think in structural as well as individual categories. A person can be expected to support political and economic policies that lead to resolving the ills that frustrate human rights. The individual moral agent can act to meet a duty to fulfill a human rights-claim by conscientious citizenship and active participation in organized activity promoting justice on the national and international levels. In brief, exercising the fundamental right of self-giving through organized communal activity aimed at social justice assists others denied the basic conditions of participatory community. The exercise of one's fundamental human right ought to enable others to exercise that same human right.

Conclusion

Human rights are moral claims to some good which *can* be provided and which *should* be provided in light of the moral ideal of establishing communities which can mirror the trinitarian life of self-giving. Such communities require a basic level of material well-being, and government is the usual means through which each person fulfills part of the duty to safeguard the human rights of his or her brothers and sisters. The extent of a social or economic right can be debated. Just as we debate the extent of the rights to free speech or religious expression, or the right to life itself, so we can debate the extent of a right to food, shelter or health care. But the foundation of such rights-language is theologically strong and the appropriateness of such language in the Catholic tradition is clear.

4 | Grace and a Consistent Ethic of Life

The secularization of the Christian world does not necessarily take the form of a direct denial of the sacred; it comes about indirectly, through a universalization of the sacred. This, by abolishing the distinction between the sacred and the secular, gives the same result. . . . Fearful lest it become relegated to the position of an isolated sect, Christianity seems to be making frenzied efforts at mimicry in order to escape being devoured by its enemies—a reaction that seems defensive, but is in fact self-destructive. In the hope of saving itself, it seems to be assuming the colors of its environment, but the result is that it loses its identity, which depends on just that distinction between the sacred and the profane, and on the conflict that can and often must exist between them.[1]

Leszek Kolakowski here makes two claims, and the seriousness of the one depends upon the accuracy of the other. The first claim is that Christianity, by which he seems to mean the churches, is engaged in a frantic attempt to win a hearing and gain respectability in the modern western world and that this attempt is motivated by fear of loss of persuasiveness and authority. This claim is very grave, indeed, if the second claim is so. For Kolakowski maintains that, since the identity of Christianity is dependent on a distinction between the sacred and the secular and their unavoidable conflict, the churches' efforts are not only futile but suicidal. Thus these "frenzied efforts" at dissolving the boundary between the sacred and the secular will ultimately result in the dissolution of Christianity itself.

Putting aside the question of whether the efforts of the Christian churches in western society are frenzied or not, we should consider two issues. Is the church's involvement in secular concerns motivated by fear? Is the attempt to formulate a public theology actuated by fear—or ambition, or pride, or mere intellectual curiosity, or any one of a host of other motives extrinsic to the gospel itself—or is it intrinsic to the very nature of Christianity? And, second, is the identity of Christianity dependent upon a distinction between the sacred and the secular, a distinction which in fact presupposes hostility between the two domains? Because our answer to the first question is that we believe that the call for public theology arises out of the nature of the Catholic Christian worldview, we must treat the two questions together, since in both we are engaged with the fundamental stance of Catholic Christianity toward the whole of human experience, "the world."

The sacred and the secular are tricky terms when used with reference to Christianity. Any tradition which claims that God has entered history in the person of a human being like us in all things except sin clearly places the sacred in a peculiar relationship to the secular. The New Testament insists that one cannot simply separate the two as distinct and incompatible realms. The story of the question of the coin of tribute and the saying accompanying it, "Give to Caesar what is Caesar's, and to God what is God's" (Mt 22:21b; Mk 12:17; Lk 20:25), is frequently heard as teaching a division between the realms of the sacred and the secular, thus assuring the autonomy of both. In fact, the story seems to be a warning against idolatry, i.e. the identification of a creature, in this case, the Roman emperor, with God. The Christian understanding of the sacred and secular is far more subtle and complex than any simple division of human experience into realms.[2]

Much has been written about secularity and the process of secularization which is supposed to typify the modern western man and woman. Less attention has been paid in the discussion to the meaning of the correlative term. What do we mean by "the sacred"? If we mean a locus of the divine in the otherwise profane world of ordinary experience, then Christianity resolutely denies the existence of the sacred. Any such locus would necessarily be idolatrous. For it places God over against that which is not God, the profane, the merely creaturely. But such antagonism implies comparability, some shared plane on which two opposing realities come into conflict. But there is no shared plane between God and creatures. Creatures can mutually oppose one another so that what is attributed to one cannot be attributed to another. But God and creation cannot compete. This principle is central to the Catholic Christian understanding of grace.

Grace, Freedom and Sin

If we understand by "grace" the self-communication of God outside the Trinity, then the problem of the relationship between grace and nature is in fact the question of how God is related to all finite or creaturely reality. From the perspective of believers in the doctrine of creation, God cannot be an "unmoved mover" standing quite apart from the reality which God has called into being. The existence of finite being is the present creative act of God, not an event which happened "in the beginning" and now has ceased. The issue of God's relation to all creation is heightened when the particular creatures in question are human persons and the social world which they construct. For human beings are capable of accepting or rejecting the self-gift of God. How that is possible has been the key issue of the western Christian debate about nature and grace, sometimes framed in terms of human freedom and divine predestination, ever since Augustine and Pelagius.

Human freedom is created freedom, i.e. the possibility of human freedom, whether understood in the restricted sense of the power of choice or the richer sense of the capacity for spontaneity and creativity, is a free gift of God. Human creativity is rooted in a logically and ontologically prior divine creativity. We are *made* free. If freedom is constitutive of human being, it is good. For the insistence of the Hebrew and Christian traditions is that all creation is good, and humanity is the culmination of creation and, therefore, "very good" (Gen 1:31). Freedom is not a result of sin. The fall of humanity is not a necessary pre-condition for the exercise of human initiative. The fruit of the tree of the knowledge of good and evil does not yield freedom. Indeed, the biblical narrative in Genesis 3 insists that freedom is the pre-condition of sin. Were the man and the woman not possessed of the power of choice, the serpent's temptation would be pointless and the decision to eat the forbidden fruit unreachable. Sin enters the world not with creaturely freedom but with the misuse of that freedom. Sin is the self-distortion of human freedom.

Paradoxical thinking is often merely unclear thinking. But paradox is unavoidable when dealing with evil, for it is that which should not be. The very claim that what should *not* be *is*, is a paradox. And it leads to the further paradox that the exercise of freedom is good even when the object for which it is exercised is evil. Goethe expresses this seeming contradiction in Mephistopheles' first reply to Faust's demand for his identity: "*Ein Teil von jener Kraft der stets das Böse will/ Und stets das Gute schafft*"[3]—"A part of the power which forever wills evil and forever does good." For to will evil, which is non-existence, the denial of the goodness of finite being, as we learn from the demon's second response when Faust dismisses his first reply as "a riddle," necessarily ·affirms the existence of the one willing.[4] Thus, to will one's non-being is an exercise of one's being. Evil negates itself by being itself. Freely to choose to reject the good, which includes oneself since all that exists is good, according to Genesis 1, is to reject one's own capacity to choose. It is the free rejection of freedom. It implicitly affirms what it explicitly denies. Any exercise of human freedom is an affirmation of human being and is therefore good, even if that exercise is the always frustrated denial of the goodness of human being and so of human freedom. It wills evil and does good.

Every act of freedom is an implicit or explicit acceptance of the gift of created freedom. For even the capacity to sin comes from God. The Christian tradition has always asserted that evil is parasitic on goodness. In mythological terms, the devil is a fallen angel, a self-perverted creature of God. In the face of all forms of ontological and ethical dualism, Christianity has insisted that the devil is not the equal opponent of God. Indeed, when the figure of Satan appears late in the Hebrew tradition, he is a member of the heavenly court and so a minister of God's design (Job 1:6–12). Creatures can stand in opposition to other creatures, but no creature can stand in opposition to God, for God is not the name of a being—even a "supreme being"—in a chain of beings. God is the ground and support of all beings, not a being but the act of being, as Thomas Aquinas maintained.[5] The devil is not, therefore, the enemy of God, a notion which implies some sort of equivalence, but "the enemy of human nature," in the words of Ignatius Loyola.[6] Even the devil glorifies God, not by being the devil but by *being*, not by willing evil but by *willing*.

Thus there is no antagonism between grace and freedom. Freedom is grounded in the economy of grace. Every exercise of human freedom is a response, knowingly or not, to God's gracious self-gift. Such a claim does not by any means discount the terrible reality of evil. It does not dismiss evil as non-being but rather understands sin as the free willing of non-being. Sin remains frighteningly real and powerful. But even sin bears reluctant witness to the foundation of all reality, the self-communication of God, i.e. grace. Consequently, a fundamental optimism about creation permeates this strand of the Christian tradition, not a blind optimism which overlooks the fact of evil and the power of sin, but a profoundly realistic optimism which sees that "where there has been much sin, there is even more grace" (Rom 5:20).

Sacred and Secular Revisited

"The sacred," if understood as the realm of grace, cannot then be opposed within the world to "the profane." Rather a new term must be employed, "the secular." As David Tracy has written, "The ordinary is now recognized as extraordinary by being affirmed not as profane but as secular; the 'world,' as in *Gaudium et Spes* of the Second Vatican Council, is truly affirmed without being canonized; the world's real ambiguity

—its possibilities for both good and evil—is recognized on religious grounds."[7] The secular is recognized "on religious grounds"; it is understood by contrast with the sacred, not the other way around. The secular, not only in its capacity for good but even in its possibilities for evil, bears witness to the reality of the sacred which undergirds it. The relation of the sacred and the secular is more complex than simple juxtaposition and is certainly not conflict. A clear danger seems to arise with this statement, however. The achievement of the autonomy of the "secular" domains of science, the state and commerce has been a long and frequently difficult battle in the history of the west. If the sacred cannot be distinguished from the secular, this hard-won autonomy is undercut. The specter of theocratic claims looms out of what had seemed a finally buried past and threatens the legitimacy of most of the institutions of the modern west. In a constitutional republic which prizes its guarantee of the separation of church and state, even the appearance of such claims is a source of anxiety.

But the statement that the sacred and the secular are not and cannot be opposed realms within the world, a statement which seems to follow necessarily from the Catholic doctrine of grace, is not equivalent to the claim that the sacred and secular cannot be distinguished. The issue is the kind of distinction which is appropriate. The Catholic tradition does not know of any substantive distinction between the sacred and the secular, i.e. it does not acknowledge certain actions, events or relationships which are of their nature remote from grace, "secular," and certain other actions, events, and relationships which are by contrast engraced, "sacred." Thomas Aquinas, treating of miracles (which may well appear to fall within the domain of the sacred if any such domain exists), criticized those who ask the question how much of the miraculous event is explicable by natural causes and how much can be explained only by divine action as if any event can be caused *partim a Deo et partim a naturali agente*, partly by God and partly by a natural agent. Rather, he wrote, every event is caused *totus ab utroque secundum alium modum*, completely by both God and natural agencies but in two different ways.[8] The action of God and the natural causal network of creation are distinguished modally, not substantively: certain things are not caused by God and others by natural factors; *everything* is caused by God *one hundred percent* and caused by natural forces within the world *one hundred percent*.

The modal distinction between grace and nature has underlain much of the Catholic ascetical tradition. The long divisive question of the relation between grace and works is the result of the separating and opposing of two elements deeply rooted in the New Testament documents. The Pauline doctrine of the priority of grace over all human initiative (especially Rom 3–8) has been placed over against James' strong assertion of the uselessness of faith which is not embodied in works (Jas 2:14–26). In their extreme manifestations, the insistence on the former has been made a standard of discernment for a "canon within the canon" by which the "true" gospel may be sorted out from the rest of scripture, and the latter has supported a neo-Pelagian fixation on "gaining merit." A far truer statement of the relationship between the two elements recognizes that everything depends on God yet everything depends on oneself—from two different perspectives.

The Sacred and Politics

The distinction between the sacred and the secular is thus a modal distinction. Viewed from one perspective, and correctly so viewed, every event is secular; viewed with equal correctness from another perspective, every event is sacred. The distinction is real but does not divide and oppose the two realms. God's grace undergirds all being, supports every human act, holds in being and gives effectiveness to every choice and undertaking, brings to its conclusion every relationship. It is not confined to certain spheres of activity, certain kinds of acts or relations. The locus of grace is everywhere, not some circumscribed domain of experience. Yet all human acts, private and social, are free human acts truly originating in human beings motivated by their own ends good and evil, agapic and selfish, wise and foolish. Is this the "universalization of the sacred" against which Kolakowski warns? The answer can only be yes and no. Yes, because the sacred is not some part of experience which is severed from the rest—and by far the larger part—of human individual and communal life which is the religiously neutral secular. The sacred embraces human life in all its aspects, contemplative, active, marital, familial, political, economic, aesthetic. But the answer is no, because the sacred is not simply equivalent to the secular. There is a real but modal difference.

And that difference is crucial, not only to protect against the watering down of the sacred which Kolakowski fears, but to guard against the terror of sacralized politics. The unequivocal canonization of a political act or policy because it is the will of God, or the unavoidable destiny written into a nation's character, or the necessary outcome of the dialectics of history, or a step in a people's manifest destiny identifies political choice and action as religiously, because ultimately, grounded. The danger of sacralized politics (and economics, if one is to listen to the claim made for the free market by some of its evangelists) is ever present and has caused enormous misery in the twentieth century. Deified emperors and priest-kings have not disappeared in the modern west; they have been metamorphosed into Führer-figures who embody irresistible national wills, elites and parties which are the vanguard of inevitable revolutions, and politicians and leadership cliques who identify their goals (usually top-secret) and their political survival with "national security." Maintaining the difference between the sacred and the secular without placing them over against one another is essential.

But how might the difference be described? Nicholas Lash offers an insightful suggestion:

> The relationship of Christian memory and proclamation to the human world of which such memory and proclamation forms a part, and in which it occurs and functions, is best expressed *not* in terms of the relationship of "religion" to "secularity" (let alone of "weltanschauung" to "fact") but rather in terms of the relationship of (sacramental) "form" to "matter."[9]

Rather than juxtaposed domains, the sacred is the sacramental form of the secular, i.e. the sacred is the secular in its full depth.

Various forms of that claim have been made by many, at least since Durkheim.[10] Because we are social beings, our sense of identity, our language and the ways of viewing the world which are built into it and therefore into us, our continuity in time with past and future generations, our willingness to give ourselves to tasks which may not see completion in our lifetime, our reception of values and standards of beauty from a cultural tradition, all tie us in to communities. And the survival and well-being of these communities are *our* survival and well-being. The life, the choices, the success and the failure of our community support or threaten us on the deepest level of our being. The full depth of the political life of our communities is so identified with the foundations of our existence as the concrete persons we are that this depth can only be regarded as sacred, as that which gives reality and meaning to us. As Langdon Gilkey has written, "Political experience is thus unavoidably religious and therefore theological. It exists within a horizon of ultimacy. Its actions are engendered by the ultimate concerns of being and meaning; its judgments are grounded in ultimate norms; and its élan is enlivened with an ultimate hope for the future."[11] This religious depth to political action is profoundly ambiguous, however. Any political act, platform or party which claims simple identity with the goodness and truth which undergirds human existence—in other words, which claims to be God—becomes demonic.

> The social myths or ethos that make our common life possible have a religious dimension. This is the source of the community's creativity, courage, and confidence; it is also the ground of the demonic in historical life: of blind fanaticism, of infinite arrogance, of imperial ambition, of unlimited cruelty, and of ultimate violence. Even a "secular" analysis of social existence, therefore, uncovers a religious dimension in historical life. This dimension is as yet vague and undefined, the base alike of a community's creativity and of its demonic possibilities. In such an empirical uncovering, the real source or referent of this religious dimension, its ontological roots, are as yet undiscovered and undelineated. And surely any resolution of its stark ambiguity of creativity and of the satanic is as yet unmanifest. All we know through social inquiry is that the religious dimension is very much there; that it is very important, if not crucial, for the life or being of the community; and that it is clearly the main source of history's capacity for suffering and for nemesis.[12]

While recognizing the religious depth to political action, therefore, a careful "demythologizing" of politics is also necessary. No particular political platform, no matter how inclusive, no decision, however just, no action, whatever the nobility of the motive or the care in execution, is ever the realization of perfect goodness, justice and love. We must constantly remind ourselves and be reminded, sometimes roughly, by others that our best goals, hopes, dreams and plans remain partial, biased and imperfect.[13]

Lash's suggestion that the sacred gives sacramental form to the secular seems to be the kind of modal distinction which is required to unite but distinguish the two aspects of human political experience. If everything which exists is rooted in the gracious self-communication of God, grasping anything in its depth, in the foundations of its being, in the full conditions of its actuality, is the discovery of grace. Every human act, precisely because it is the act of a free and creative human being, is grounded in the free agapic act of God. No domain of human activity, private or public, is secular, if secular means remote from or unrelated to the action of grace, independent of divine action. But every human act can implicitly or explicitly either affirm or deny its rootedness in the freedom of God. When a community acts in such a way as to deny its own contingency and finiteness, when it pretends that its motives are unqualifiedly good, that its ends are unconditionally just, that its purposes are absolute dictates, whether of God, or history, or destiny, or the law of survival, those acts are demonic (in Gilkey's use of the term), self-contradictory, distorted. Thus every act bears within it ultimate issues, although, of course, we as individuals and members of communities are not always aware of and attentive to the dimensions of ultimacy in our deeds. Every experience, every act, every event, *can* be a disclosure of the sacred depth of reality, including human beings, most especially in their freedom. This thoroughly Catholic claim about the relationship of grace and nature is well stated by Karl Rahner:

> This experience of God must not be conceived of as though it were one particular experience *among* others at the same level, as for instance an experience of pain at the psychological level can be regarded as at the same level as the experience of an optical reaction. The experience of God constitutes, rather (though here we should perhaps abstract from certain mystical experiences in the true sense), the ultimate depths and the radical essence of *every* spiritual and personal experience (of love, faithfulness, hope and so on), and thereby precisely constitutes also the ultimate unity and totality of experience, in which the person as spiritual possesses himself and is made over to himself.[14]

Sacraments and the Secular

Our acts and decisions have roots that extend infinitely deeper than our conscious motives as they have consequences that go far beyond our immediate objects. The apostle Paul's proclamation "Now is the acceptable time! Today is the day of salvation!" is accurate: every moment is the moment when the presence of grace can be discovered; every act is engraced (2 Cor 6:2b). The moments when we encounter, usually with a shock, the depth of ultimacy in our acts, whether good or evil, agapic or selfish, are sacramental encounters. Sacraments are experiences which uncover for us the presence of the radical mystery of God's self-gift which is the ground of every experience. Those persons, acts, times, places, objects, which we designate as sacred, are revelatory of the truth of all other persons, acts, times, places and objects. They are the same as everything else, i.e. grounded in grace, but they are experienced as having a mode of their own: they are sacramental.

Sacraments are not intrusions into the secular world; they are points at which the depth of the secular is uncovered and revealed as grounded in grace. Accordingly, any true and just estimation of the secular world is dependent on an appreciation of sacramentality. If one does not have an openness to the sacramental depth of one's everyday actions and choices, one's relationships with others, and the places and things with which one comes into contact on a daily basis, then one fundamentally misunderstands who one is and what the world is like. In turn, those persons, things, events, times and places designated as holy cannot genuinely be sacramental unless they illuminate all other persons, things, events, times and places. As Gilkey has written, "To be alive, religious symbols must provide shape and thematization to the patterns of ordinary life; correspondingly, natural, secular life must receive its fundamental forms from these symbols, and not from our 'normal' but distorted ones, if it is to achieve its own essential goodness."[15] As an exceptionally knowledgeable and sympathetic observer of the Catholic tradition, he suggests that the sacramental principle so central to Catholicism has been weakened by limiting the notion of "sacrament" to events affecting people only as members of the church and not simply as persons in the world at large. Thus, he notes, rebirth into the church is celebrated sacramentally but not birth into the human community.

> Baptism is not at all a sacrament of birth, of the divine gift of being, of life, of human existence, though our faith and our creed emphasize the centrality of the divine creation. On the contrary, baptism is solely a sacrament of the forgiveness of sins and of entrance not into the *human* but into the *religious* community! What a strange Marcionic vision within a Catholic system that names God "being," and then acts sacramentally as if the divine gift of being were secular and not worthy of sacramental notice![16]

Gilkey understands the Catholic sacramental tradition far too well to confuse it with any simple identification of the sacred and the secular. His point is not that birth is the real but disguised meaning of baptism; rather, he wants to be sure that the church remembers that baptism is the uncovery of the real meaning of birth.

The involvement of the churches in secular affairs may indeed be "frenzied," but it is not unjustified. And it is certainly not a confusion of the realms of the sacred and secular in any Catholic theology of grace. Indeed, any attempt to isolate the sacred and the secular from one another or simply to cast them in opposition to one another ends in the impoverishment of the secular and the trivialization of the sacred. But Leszek

Kolakowski is correct in his observation that conflict "can and often must exist" between the sacred and the secular[17] *if* "the sacred" is understood as the deep reality of the world and "the secular" as its self-distorting appearance. This is precisely why it is necessary for the believers in the Catholic tradition with its sacramental understanding of the relationship of grace and nature to enter into political conversation and action. For if it is the case—and we believe it is—that the world is grounded in the self-giving of God, and if it is also the case—and it surely is—that the world is not obviously seen to be so, then the church as "the sacrament of intimate union with God and the unity of all humanity"[18] must work to allow the world to be what it is. As Gilkey suggests that baptism both uncovers the real meaning of human birth and transforms any particular birth into what it is in fact, however hidden the fact may be, so believers must engage in transformative conversation and action so that human political, social and economic communities become what they are but so often obscure, the locus of the agape of God.

The reign of God is always *God's* reign, finally given not achieved. And yet believers in the Christian tradition have long understood themselves to be called and obligated to help bring about the reign. How is it that one must bring about what is gift? The answer lies in the claim that the world is rooted in grace but must be transformed so that it becomes what it truly is. Gerard Manley Hopkins wrote that "the just man justices; / Keeps grace: that keeps all his goings graces; / Acts in God's eye what in God's eye he is— / Christ."[19] As usual, Hopkins is precisely correct in his understanding of the sacramental principle. The just person is just by enacting justice; such a one becomes what he or she most truly is, Christ, by acting as Christ. If this is so, then the sacramental principle which provides the Catholic key to the correct understanding of the sacred and the secular can never be used to legitimate a gnostic claim that discipleship means possessing the key to the "real" meaning of the world or a purely aesthetic enjoyment of the play of grace beneath the surface of the secular. Christian discipleship is always a matter of action. We are in full agreement with Nicholas Lash when he writes that

> if it is in all the world's confusion, savagery, self-indulgence, and sheer "impossibility"; in a world in which most people go hungry and all people are threatened by the power and paranoia of a few; if it is in *this* world that, in pedagogy patterned according to the contours of the creed, Christians learn to respond to a word that sounds in silence and to celebrate a presence which (in view of our expectations in these matters) has all the hallmarks of apparent absence; if it is indeed in *this*

world that we bear precious knowledge of the saving mystery of God; then, however much still needs to be *said,* there is a great deal more that needs quite urgently to be *done.*[20]

The sacramental vision which is Catholicism's hallmark is not simply a matter for discussion but a pattern for action, politically, socially, economically.

A Sacramental Reality

Once one understands that all reality is sacred not profane then it is possible to appreciate the role of those events commonly referred to as "sacraments." Put simply, there are not seven sacraments, seven sacred rites, in a profane world but seven events which presume and seek to evoke awareness of the sacredness of all reality. Catholicism's sacramental vision, founded upon its theology of grace, teaches that God's gracious self-communication (grace) is always mediated. Where this vision is often misunderstood, even by Catholics themselves, is in believing that the mediation of God's grace is restricted to special rituals which are formally designated "sacraments." Such a notion of sacrament is an impoverished understanding of the Catholic theology of grace. It is a sacramental theology resting on a false division of sacred and secular, dividing life into realms of experience, one labeled "religious" and the other "everyday." But this is precisely what the Catholic theology of grace rejects, and thus any theology of sacrament which sets these rituals apart from the context of ordinary human experience must also be rejected.

The restricted vision of the sacramental principle can be corrected if we think in terms of three levels of sacramental mediation.[21] Mediation implies that God is experienced only through the world as created, sustained and fulfilled by the divine power. Further, as the Catholic theology of grace maintains, we cannot think of the world as profane, understood as untouched by grace. "Thus, the sea, a mountain, a people, a person—in fact, any creature—can and have so become 'symbols' of the divine being and activity. . . ." All reality is not only potentially a medium of God's self-gift but no element of the created order can be truly itself *unless* it is a symbolic expression of the divine. Creation is in the image of the creator, and the very integrity of the creature is to be itself, an entity brought forth, maintained and loved by God. The first level of mediation, therefore, refers to the conviction that the doctrines of creation and providence "mean that potentially every creature is a symbol, and even more that it is itself only *as* a symbol."[22]

Because the first level of mediation highlights the sacred within the secular, the graced character of nature, there is a worldly referent to religious symbols like creation, providence, sin, redemption and salvation. Appreciation for the first level of mediation transforms the way we think of the specific sacraments of Catholic liturgy.

> Worship, therefore, is primarily related to this presence of the divine throughout the human creature's existence. Its central purpose is to bring to awareness and to celebrate that universal presence, to shape that awareness into Christian form, and through that shaping of our natural existence by sacrament and word to elicit gratitude, contrition, recommitment, and transformation of that existence. It is the holy as it permeates our entire life as creatures, and at every level of that life, to which worship primarily responds: the holy that founds our being, inspires our creativity, that cements and deepens our relationships, elicits and demands our moral judgments, and directs our common efforts to recreate and liberate the world—and forgives and completes the waywardness in those efforts and grounds our hopes that they will be so completed. It is this ultimate dimension to our personal, social, and historical being that constitutes that divine presence in ordinary experience which provides the *real* basis of Christian worship.[23]

Without this first level of mediation religious symbols cannot be other than beyond human experience. But this is to return to the two realm approach to grace, a world of profane human experience and a separate world of "religious" experience which treats the sacred divorced from the secular. Inhabitants of a world which separates nature and grace cannot find the sacred in the secular, and in their worship they cannot relate religious symbols to their everyday life. By contrast, Catholic sacramental theology insists on the this-worldly referent to the experience of worship.

A second level of mediation addresses the fact that human beings are estranged from themselves. Due to sin, persons are unaware of their existence within the divine presence and so are out of touch with their graced nature and their role as symbols. Thus, apprehension of our true status must be awakened in us. This is where the second level of mediation comes into play, for there are special media "through which a particular revelation of the ultimate and sacred, universally present but universally obscured as well," can be "manifested in a particular form to a historical community, and so through which a group becomes newly aware of its own status as symbol (in the first sense), as existing in and through the power of the divine."[24] Within the Catholic tradition the foundational mediations of God's presence are the history of the Jewish community and the incarnation of Jesus. These symbols of special revelation are distinguished from the general revelation mediated by all of creation. It is by means of these second level mediations that the true nature of all existence is discovered. The revelation of God as concretized in particular and special events serves to underline or bring into relief what God is always already doing within all of the created order, communicating the divine gift of grace. Due to the alienation present within the created order, however, this second level of mediation is necessary so that human beings can grasp the essential truth of their nature and that of all creation. Awakening this sense of the sacred is a central task for any religion. Religion is but one symbol system within a culture, however. All cultures offer alternative, and often alienating, symbols to order and provide meaning for human existence. Because persons find themselves within cultures that distort the *humanum*, a second level of mediation, the originating symbols which mediate a particular religious revelation, is necessary to redeem us from the condition whereby we have forsaken our graced existence. The second level mediation of God's self-communication found in specific religious traditions reorients us to the foundational truth of all creaturely existence.

Over the course of history it is important for a community to pass on the truth communicated within the special revelation of an event like the person of Jesus. The effort to make this special revelation accessible to succeeding generations is accomplished through the emergence of a third level of mediation. Once more finite elements become the symbols which recall and reintroduce the holy as experienced in the particular moments of special revelation distinct to the community. The role of the seven sacraments in Catholic liturgy are one example of mediation at the third level. The power of these sacraments is found precisely in their ability to represent to participants the meaning, power and divine presence experienced in the originating symbols of the tradition. And these originating symbols speak to us insofar as they shed light on the experience we have of living within the created order, the world of everyday life. The mediation of levels two and three are for the purpose of revealing to us the dignity and role of our status as symbols (level one) who mediate the divine presence.

> Our argument is that, unless the symbols of our tradition in word and sacrament are brought into relation to the ultimacy that permeates our ordinary life, unless traditional symbols reawaken in us our role as symbols of the divine activity, there is

no experience of the holy. The Spirit must speak in and through us, and must reawaken us to *our* role as symbols, if the Father is to be known through the Son. In a secular age when ordinary life is separated in its self-understanding from its own transcendent ground, sacramental symbols unrelated to the transcendent dimension of our own existence in life become magical or merely traditional, and kerygmatic symbols change into empty theologisms or anachronistic signs of our moral and intellectual autonomy.[25]

The inclusion of kerygma in the third level of mediation points up the interdependence of word and sacrament. The centrality of preaching is due to the need for a word which is able to articulate the divine found within the finite medium, to assist in uncovering the sacred within the secular.

What this outlook suggests is that religious symbols are not demonstrated to be wrong or right, they either die or are enlivened by their ability to relate to the ordinary experience of participants. Properly understood the finite mediations of God's grace do not remove us to a sacred zone of human existence but provide the ability to thematize, inspire and guide human existence to its goal, life within the divine presence. Just as religious symbols are enlivened by reference to everyday existence, correlatively our everyday lives must be transformed by living our lives according to the symbols of religious belief. Without the mediations of levels two and three, humanity finds itself in a condition of estrangement from the truth of existence, the graced or sacred quality of life itself.

The Sacredness of Life

Because the graced quality of both everyday life and the divine presence within finite media is often "hidden," the sacred has to be proclaimed and interpreted. Unless there were prophets and apostles in Judaism and Christianity the divine presence in particular revelatory events might have been unnoticed. We require not only religious symbols but the witness of the word directing our attention to the sacred within the secular. Within the Jewish and Christian traditions one of the claims made by preachers and teachers is that human life is sacred, that our very existence is always graced existence. Just as the word is needed to interpret the meaning of the sacred in the symbol of the eucharist, so, too, the word is needed to interpret the meaning of the sacred in the symbolic mediation of human life. As part of that effort of proclaiming a revelatory word, Christian ethical reflection throughout the centuries has sought to articulate the moral implications of the claim that life is sacred.

First principles are notoriously difficult to justify. Typically they are argued *from*, not argued *to*, and a principle stating the sacredness or sanctity of life is no different. In our culture, by a variety of philosophical and theological formulations, the sanctity of life has attained wide acceptance.[26] But the appeal of this claim has less to do with the force of argument than with experience. Daniel Maguire has suggested that the touchstone of morality is "the experience of the value of persons and their environment."[27] Underlying all duties, rules, ideals or goals is an experience of the value of a person, in more religious language, the sanctity of human life. Unless an individual has experienced the value of human life no possible rationale can be provided which might justify any subsequent guidance for moral action. It is only by an appreciation of the sanctity of life that we are led to reflect upon what sorts of actions are befitting persons. Only because we value the person are we concerned that actions by ourselves and others are in accord with what is deemed to be of benefit to a human being.

The experience of the sanctity of life is, as Maguire suggests, characteristically both affective and a process.[28] Our initial moral awareness is located in the human affections. Affective experience is parent to reasoning. To engage the moral life seriously we must enter into a method of reflection, but that does not mean that reflection comes first. Initially we experience the value of the person and then we move to reasoning about what choices bespeak our valuing of the person.

The second characteristic of the experience of the sanctity of life is that it is a process. We grow in our ability to grasp the value of the other. That growth can take the form of greater depth, a more profound sensitivity to the sacredness of the other. We can become more attuned to the value of a person. Growth can also occur in the area of inclusivity, as a wider circle of humanity is drawn to include more whose life is held sacred. The process of developing a sensitivity to the value of life takes time, and some persons grow faster and deeper in this regard than others. Morally insensitive people are those incapable of genuinely interacting with another in a way that reflects the sacredness of each party. It is also possible that an individual can demonstrate sensitivity toward persons of one class, race, sex or nationality yet be slow to universalize the experience of value.

A difficulty for an ethic premised on the sanctity of life is the vagueness of the expression. In some camps the sanctity of life entails an absolute prohibition against killing, whereas other defenders of the sanctity of life develop an extensive casuistry which permits the deliberate taking of life under specified conditions. Most sanctity of life arguments do not value biological life as absolutely normative. "Certainly the majority of ethical systems that maintain a sanctity of life ethic hold that it is only generally or presumptively wrong . . . not to preserve and protect human life."[29] It is the vagueness of the sanctity of life principle which permits widespread support for the principle, but which also occasions the disputes that arise immediately after discussion begins about applications of the norm. So as not to exclude peremptorily any ethical theory which claims to be founded upon the sanctity of life we accept that a working definition of the sanctity of life norm is "a moral respect-for-life principle which states that it is wrong, whether absolutely or prima facie, to terminate or shorten or not to sustain a human life."[30]

A Consistent Ethic of Life

In recent years Cardinal Joseph Bernardin, archbishop of Chicago, has promoted what he calls a consistent ethic of life. His proposal is an example of a contemporary formulation of Catholic social teaching. Bernardin's intent is to weave together a number of positions on various issues in such a way that the thread of a commitment to the sanctity of life is seen in each topic. According to the cardinal, it is by developing consistency when addressing a spectrum of moral issues that the sanctity of life will be affirmed. In effect, the consistent ethic of life is meant to articulate the graced nature of all life and the value of human life too often obscured by various forces in modern society. It serves a kerygmatic as well as ethical purpose by pointing out the sacred dimension of human life.

A consistent ethic of life as espoused by Bernardin is marked by four qualities: it is analogical, comprehensive, dialogical and consistent.[31] By analogical is meant that such an ethic relates two things by noting the similarity amidst difference. The similarity is that each issue entails the promotion and protection of human life. Because all life is sacred, the loss of any human life is always to be regretted. There is no exception to this sentiment; all human life, be it of friend, stranger, or foe, is equal in the value it has. The difference within the consistent life ethic resides in the fact that not all life issues are similar in detail. Abortion is not war, poverty is not capital punishment. While each is a threat to the sacredness of human life, each threat is different and must be examined on its own terms. As Bernardin stated, "Each of these assaults on life has its own meaning and morality; they cannot be collapsed into one problem, but they must be confronted as pieces of a larger pattern."[32]

The consistent ethic of life is comprehensive in its concern for all significant threats to the sacredness of human life. Direct assaults on life's sacredness by wanton killing may be the most glaring but not the sole violation of life's sanctity. Not only the protection of human life but its promotion is addressed by the consistent ethic proposal. Thus, the denigration of life by crushing poverty, famine, pornography, and homelessness is an issue which any affirmation of life must confront.

A third quality, the dialogical nature of the consistent ethic of life, is found in the proposed posture of the church as it presses its moral position in the public forum.

> The style should be persuasive not preachy. . . . We should be convinced that we have much to learn from the world and much to teach it. . . . A confident church will speak its mind, seek as a community to live its convictions, but leave space for others to speak to us, help us to grow from their perspective, and to collaborate with them.[33]

Advocacy of the consistent ethic of life does not require an unbending conviction that the church alone has the truth about the value of human life or the solutions to practical dilemmas which touch upon the promotion of human life. Precisely because the sanctity of life is a moral experience available to all persons, the voices and insights of many contributors to public discussion must be heard. The Catholic community ought not to act as if its practical strategies for promoting human life are the only useful and valid ones available within society.

As the very wording of his proposal suggests, Bernardin believes that consistency is a necessary quality in a sound social ethic. The consistency striven for is not seen in the conclusions reached, for issues and their resolution will differ. But consistency in value is required. Adherents to a consistent ethic of life will, according to Bernardin, reject "an ad hoc approach" to the spectrum of issues which touch upon the sanctity of life. Instead there must be a persistent "attitude of respect for all life if public actions are to respect it in concrete cases."[34] The analogical, comprehensive, dialogical and consistent qualities of the ethic of life are important to the way Bernardin frames the question of how the sanctity of life is to be promoted.

Theology and Moral Vision

At the heart of the matter for Bernardin is the need to articulate a moral vision which will serve as a point of departure for assessing specific social issues. His proposed vision stems from an understanding of the graced condition of reality. Catholicism's understanding of grace highlights that life itself is a gift, physical existence is a graced event, and a person does not require a second religious "rebirth" to be ushered into the world of grace. By recalling to mind the graciousness of God present from the the outset of each life, Catholicism underlines the reality that God is the author and preserver of life. An understanding of God's purposes for human life has been manifested in the life and ministry of Jesus. In his teaching Jesus emphasized the value his Father placed on human life and the extent of God's concern which embraced all people irrespective of distinctions such as class, race, gender or nationality. Indeed, God's love is especially directed to the marginalized, those distinguished from the rest of society by some social stigma. It is evident that none of these statements resolve specific ethical dilemmas, however theologically correct they may be. Catholic theology's major contribution is not to be expected at the level of concrete moral choices. Instead, the understanding of grace found in the Catholic tradition provides an orientation, a perspective from which to analyze and address specific moral dilemmas. It highlights the sacredness of all human life and serves as a counterpoint to the biases of a culture such as the American tendency to adopt a functionalist mentality when assessing human life.[35]

A moral vision, the perspective by which one interprets reality, will raise certain issues to prominence and sustain specific dispositions. By speaking of the sanctity of life, the Bernardin proposal highlights the thread which runs through many present-day moral dilemmas. The consistent ethic of life reminds citizens that the way a given threat against human life is opposed "should be related to support for a systemic vision of life." This systemic vision of the sanctity of life helps prevent a person attentive to one issue among the many touching upon the value of human life from being "insensitive to or even opposed to other moral claims on the overall spectrum of life."[36] By promoting sensitivity to all dimensions of human experience the consistent ethic of life stands as a countervailing force to the fragmentation of moral life into discrete and random concern for social issues. Focus on the sanctity of life enables the moral imagination to grasp the interconnections among various threats to human well-being, so that underlying patterns in modern culture can be challenged. A moral vision can also help a person or community develop and maintain moral dispositions not supported by the wider culture. In a society like the United States there is a tendency to resort to a utilitarian calculus when assessing public policy proposals. Individual preferences are simply counted, and one chooses the policy which leads to the greatest good for the greatest number. A moral vision such as Bernardin's proposal encourages a more substantive style of ethical deliberation by its focus on values that are not easily quantifiable nor reduced to individual preferences.[37] An attitude of respect for the sanctity of the human person can serve as a corrective to the functionalist mentality of a culture that treats some with less respect than others because of intellectual achievement, financial success or physical appearance. The consistent ethic of life can preserve a moral disposition of respect for life that acknowledges the regret which ought to accompany any death-dealing action. Retaining a sense of the tragic nature of killing is an important safeguard from the callousness found in segments of a society. Taking the sanctity of life seriously is a stance in opposition to the social climate of the United States where citizens gather outside prison walls and celebrate the execution of prisoners.

In several speeches Bernardin has made explicit this element of vision in his promotion of a consistent ethic of life. "My purpose was to highlight the diverse issues touching upon the dignity and quality of life today. I also wanted to indicate the resources of the Catholic theological vision which are available to address the wide range of moral issues in a systematic, sustained fashion."[38] One of the chief benefits of articulating a moral vision is that it "pushes the moral, legal and political debate beyond an ad hoc or 'single issue' focus, setting our moral discussion in a broader context of concern for human life in diverse situations." The analogous nature of the consistent ethic must be maintained, however, since the purpose is not to "equate all issues or subsume the moral problem of protecting and promoting life into one proposition. Rather, its objective is to sharpen our moral sensitivity and to expand the intellectual framework for debate of the life issues." Situating a moral dilemma within a larger context—identifying the perspective brought to the discussion, naming the preferences and biases which shape the moral agent, making explicit the operative values—is the role of vision in ethical reflection. Bernardin's call for a consistent ethic is an effort to set discussion of an array of contemporary issues within a framework that heightens adherence to the sanctity of all human life and which points up the manifold ways that human life is threatened today.

The Need for Ethical Reflection

Moral vision orientates ethical reflection but does not replace such reflection. A consistent ethic of life roots itself in a moral vision, but moral principles must be developed which can guide decision-making and action. Principles are derived from the moral vision not so much by deductive logic as through discernment of those which "fit" with the overall vision. Thus, building consensus on a moral vision does not necessarily imply attaining complete agreement on ethical theory or moral choice. Yet, as we have suggested, the value of an interpretive and analytic context for moral reflection should not be underestimated. "A shared vision may not guarantee unity around ethical principles, but it may establish a kind of moral turf upon which we agree to work out enormously important public policy issues."[39]

One of the foundational tasks in any discussion of public policy is the determination of "which issues are public moral questions and which are best defined as private moral questions."[40] Within Catholic social teaching a topic was one of public morality if it involved the public order. Disputes may be contentious on which issues are counted as affecting public order, but it is a necessary part of societal organization to develop consensus on the matter. "A rationally persuasive case has to be made that an action violates the rights of others or that the consequences of actions on a given issue are so important to society that the authority of the state and civil law ought to be invoked to govern personal and group behavior."[41]

One of the striking things about American society is the movement toward privatizing issues which have customarily been thought of as public. Abortion has come to be thought of by many citizens as essentially a private decision by the pregnant woman. So strong is this current of thought that the father of the child and the parents of a pregnant minor have little or no legal recourse should they wish to have a say in the matter. More recently there has been an effort to cast the decision about terminating the life of medical patients in terms of privacy. As Bernardin notes, it is a "troubling attitude which seems to hold that killing—whether done in an official act or even from a humanitarian motive—only affects the victim."[42] A consistent ethic of life need not be understood as requiring an absolute prohibition of all abortion or a medical vitalism entailing heroic measures to extend the time of dying patients. But among the attitudes encouraged by a consistent ethic would be an appreciation that killing is a social act. Abortion and euthanasia affect the bonds of trust in society. Such acts can erode reverence for human life, and they assume consensus on who is to count as a member of the human community, as well as what is to count as a valued life.

A cult of privatization ignores the social dimensions of human actions, overlooking the societal requisite of ongoing public debate on matters which involve the taking of life and the need to attain a societal consensus on what acts of killing are legitimate. Even when the social dimensions are discussed, however, public discussion and consensus about the wisdom of taking a life can be undone if final decision-making is left in the hands of a lone individual. When public matters are shifted to the domain of the private, society does not establish procedures for who decides and how a decision is made. Thus, no social consensus is secure because no enforcement mechanism exists. Unless there are legal restrictions placed on a doctor's freedom to terminate a life, it does not really matter if society opposes death-dealing action by a physician. The same is true for the futility of discussing the morality of abortion if, after a consensus is achieved, the decision is still solely in the hands of the pregnant woman. Public morality requires the social institutionalization of procedures for adjudicating conflicting claims and measures to ensure compliance with society's norms. The centrality of life issues as part of public morality cannot be overstated. "It is hard to think of a more fundamental challenge to the moral vision and character of a society: deciding who fits in the circle of the legally protected human community."[43] Thus, when making determinations about the taking of life it is imperative that we as a people put in place decision-making procedures that are supported by a societal consensus. The difficulty with the Supreme Court's decision in the case of Roe v. Wade is that it reflected the American bias toward freedom of choice. But the substantive question of the sanctity of life was avoided by a focus on procedural matters. "The Roe rationale asks, 'Who decides?' but it does not focus on 'What is being decided?' By ignoring the second question, it evades and eviscerates the heart of the moral challenge posed by abortion. . . ."[44] A consistent ethic of life calls attention to the moral issue posed by abortion and insists that public discussion address this as a prerequisite for a just answer to the first question.

The Need for Public Debate

It is clear that attaining agreement as to what constitutes a question of public morality may be difficult. Yet our nation's history has found that such agreement is possible, and we have come to ascribe to some matters the designation "public" (e.g. civil rights, sexual harassment) while other matters are called "private" (e.g. liquor consumption, contraception). In our culture, debates about private and public morality take place in a climate heavily weighted toward privacy. Lacking an appreciation for the communal nature of our lives, individualism promotes the removal of more and more issues from the public arena. Guided by the impoverishing vision of individualism, a society finds less and less reason to see moral issues, especially intensely personal ones, as also having public significance. When community and society seem vague and unidentifiable, the only reality is the individual. A consistent ethic of life encourages a sensitivity to the public nature of life and death issues and opposes the privatizing tendencies of an individualistic culture. A consistent ethic calls for the rejuvenation of public life so that issues which affect the sanctity of life can be discussed and decided in a way that draws upon the moral wisdom of a people and not just an individual.

Bernardin has pointed out a second essential task for a social ethic founded on the consistent ethic of life. "How, in the face of an issue of public morality, should a public official relate personal conviction about religion and moral truths to the fulfillment of public duty?"[45] It is not possible for a person to set aside deeply held beliefs as if these will not form one's character and judgment in public life. The question then is the way moral conviction is translated into public policy choices. It is a complex process since it will be rare that a simple translation from moral norm to policy is possible. Thus, we can anticipate that subscribers to a consistent life ethic may adopt differing strategies for implementing public policy appropriate to their views.

Essentially, public policy proposals must pass through what has been called a "prism of feasibility." This entails consideration of four factors: the good of personal freedom which may be restricted, the factor of equity in the burdens created by the policy, consensus on the need for the policy in order to maintain public order, and the enforceability of any decision. Because of one or more of these factors some moral norms cannot be made into civil laws. Catholic social thought has long recognized that although law and morality are related they are not simply identical, for law is often a clumsy instrument to address moral values. There are many moral wrongs which are not best dealt with through public policy, and sometimes law can be but a partial expression of the morally right decision. As Bernardin states about his opposition to abortion and his openness to laws which may limit the number of fetal deaths without eradicating all abortion, "I am committed to teaching the moral law. But I am also committed to the search for what is possible and most effective in the civil arena."[46] His concern about law being "possible" and "effective" indicates awareness of the requirement for public policy to be assessed by the criterion of feasibility.

Personally Opposed But . . .

One of the most commonly stated positions on abortion by those in public life is that the individual is personally opposed to abortion but unwilling to support restrictive abortion laws. This view reflects the uneasiness that many have with simply considering abortion a good or morally neutral act. Such a position also demonstrates a sensitivity to the plurality of viewpoints on abortion in our nation and problems of trying to enforce a law when there is no consensus on the need or usefulness of a restrictive abortion law. It is a position which has been enunciated by many Catholic public officials, eager to be both faithful to their moral convictions and popular with the voters. In a variety of statements, press conferences and publications, the Catholic bishops of the country have attacked the "personally opposed but" stance of politicians. On August 9, 1984 the then head of the bishops' conference, James Malone, speaking on behalf of the U.S. Catholic Conference's executive committee, stated that such a stance was "not logically tenable."[47]

Several things must be clarified if this discussion between church and governmental figures is to go forward. First is the issue of why the "but" is added to the statement of opposition. If public officials are doubtful about the feasibility of a restrictive law, then their reluctance to press for such a law is understandable and defensible. A person can in good conscience believe abortion to be wrong yet still disagree with church leaders as to what should be done about abortion in the area of public policy. The relationship of morality and law admits of the distinction between these two realms. What can be asked of public officials is to state their opposition to present policies regarding abortion and to work toward conditions which would make abortion less necessary and a more restrictive public policy more feasible. Beyond that, church leaders cannot demand that officials endorse a specific law nor a specific timetable for passing such a law. If a public figure believes that a certain law, however valuable its intent, would be a bad law, then he or she can withhold support for such a measure. Being clear about this legitimate role for political judgment is necessary if politicians, especially Catholic politicians, are to avoid having a dark cloud over their heads created by bishops who demand that a civic leader must accept the policy recommendations of the episcopal conference. Supporters of a pro-life agenda must respect a public official's honestly held position that a given abortion law might not be feasible in the present situation.

It is possible, however, that some people who take the "personally opposed but" stance are against restrictive abortion laws not on the grounds of feasibility but because they are content to state their own view while not wishing to interfere in the exercise of another's decision to abort or not. Therefore they see no reason to work for a future law's becoming feasible and do not wish to see restrictive abortion laws passed even if feasible. According to this approach, abortion is a matter for each person to decide. This stance requires clarification of the expression "personally opposed."

Several years ago a prominent Catholic politician put it this way. "As a Catholic I accept the premise that a fertilized ovum is a baby. I have been blessed with the gift of faith; but others have not. I have no right to impose my beliefs on them. I firmly believe, given my current situation, that I could never have an abortion." At the outset it should be noted that the "gift of faith" may enable a person to perceive the value of fetal life, just as it may enable a person to see the horror of war or the equality of men and women, but such a judgment is not reducible to an issue of faith. Even a cursory glance at the Catholic teaching on abortion reveals that it is in no way similar to the teaching on the eucharist or the papacy. The church's view on abortion is like its views on racism, capital punishment or foreign aid: it may be motivated and informed by faith, but it relies upon moral reasoning, not appeals to faith.

The real difficulty with the position cited, however, entails the way it undermines the foundation of law. Those who wish to restrict access to abortion do so not on the grounds that abortion is a sin and all sin should be legally proscribed. Rather, abortion is opposed because it violates the "harm principle," namely, it causes harm to another person and laws should protect persons from significant harm caused by a second party. Normally, debates about law and the harm principle center on what constitutes *significant harm* to another; in the case of abortion there is no consensus on what constitutes harm to *another*. Those who accept abortion because they do not believe the fetus is a person with rights and thus cannot be harmed are logically consistent. Without a person to be harmed there is no substantive case to be made for restricting a moral agent's freedom. In the comment above, however, the public official admits that the fertilized ovum is a human person. So abortion, in this individual's eyes, must mean the destruction of human life. If so, then the only way that official can be indifferent to the taking of human life is to dismiss the harm principle. Choosing that option undercuts a large part of our legal system which has regularly employed the harm principle to justify laws which limit a person's freedom. In such circumstances, the sincerity of an agent's beliefs about whether he or she is causing harm is not a sufficient reason for others to ignore the harm they witness. Public order and law concerning harmful behavior may not be sacrificed to a person's claim that one should be free to do whatever one is sincere about.

Here, then, is the elemental failure of personal opposition but political acceptance of abortion. To acknowledge the fetus as a human person is necessarily a statement with legal and political consequences. According to both the 14th amendment to the Constitution and the United Nations' Declaration of Human Rights, to be a human person is to be entitled to the rights and equal protection of law accorded every other person. If we deny such legal status to a person we empty the word "person" of its meaning, which is public not just private. In effect, we declare some human beings to be non-persons in the public realm. Acknowledgement of another being as a fellow human person is inextricably a political statement.

To declare a fetus a human person is a political act in our nation, just as it would be to declare a black a human person in an age of slavery. To believe that the life in the womb is that of a human baby and yet to deny that child equal protection under the law is to choose one of two positions: 1) to ignore the political consequences of recognizing the humanity of another, or 2) to create a group of second-class human beings. To say that we believe someone is a person but we do not believe we need prevent others from treating that one as a non-person is to equivocate on the meaning of human personhood.

One way out of this indefensible position is to deny the human status of the fetus. But those who personally oppose abortion presumably do so because of their belief that the fetus is a person, as the statement of the Catholic politician indicates. Another way out of the dilemma is to oppose abortion and commit oneself to work against present policies permitting abortion even if at present one is unsure how to go about that; this is to employ the morality-law distinction. Yet the commitment to work against present policy is rarely made by those who take the "personally opposed but" position.

In truth, what we find in the case of many public leaders is confusion about belief and practice. If a person were to state, "I refuse to own slaves but I will not go around telling others what to do with their slaves," it would be correct to say that person does not practice slavery. However, can it be said that the person is really opposed to the institution of slavery? Many politicans do not practice abortion but they are mistaken to claim they are against it. To say that something is wrong for me (a practice) is not the same as saying that something is categorically wrong (belief). A minimal test of the sincerity of one's personal beliefs about abortion is whether one tries to persuade, not coerce, others to voluntarily renounce abortion. In many instances, those who "personally oppose abortion but" also oppose working for changes in abortion policy and so fail this test.

Single-Issue Politics and a Consistent Ethic of Life[48]

One of the persistent complaints about the Catholic Church's recent involvement in public policy debates surrounding abortion is that it has been prone to single-issue politics. Finding fault with single-issue political strategies is based on the belief that they undermine the work of building consensus in a democracy. Yet single-issue groups are not new and may not be any more powerful numerically than in the past. Even if their presence is more acutely felt, historical patterns clearly show that the intensity of commitment that one issue can evoke diminishes as the group's agenda widens. If the group is to survive as a viable political movement, then its agenda almost always widens. Thus, while single-issue politics may initially avoid the consensus-building process by working outside traditional party mechanisms, it cannot totally avoid the give-and-take that characterizes pluralistic democracies.

Yet a variety of observers still warn of the danger of factionalism—a narrow-minded pursuit of one's interest at the expense of the common good. Acting solely in one's self-interest, acting selfishly, is to be opposed. But a number of groups commonly labeled "single-issue" maintain that it is precisely a defense of the common good that motivates them. Certainly it is evident that a number of groups promote issues to which they are committed by reason of some social ideal rather than economic gain, e.g. conservationists.

Such movements do provide ways for people to participate in political life, making involvement manageable and comprehensible. People can feel overwhelmed by the complexity and number of issues facing them. A single issue can involve people who would normally stand bewildered on the sidelines of a political contest. Single-issue groups may also provide an important outlet for venting frustration over government unresponsiveness. Often they have stimulated debate on issues that might otherwise have been overlooked in political discussion. At times the quality of the debate is not high but the loud and shrill voices that eventually lose their strength perform the service of calling a nation's attention to an issue.

Single-issue politics can also encourage responsible voting. Voting in the 1950s for a candidate deeply committed to racial equality would have been quite justified if the opposition candidate were an advocate of Jim Crow—even if the civil rights advocate inspired some reservations in voters about other matters, like national security or fiscal policy.

Should the Catholic Church adopt such a style in its social teaching and action? To resolve the matter in an *a priori* manner would be unwise. Suppose the German bishops in the late 1930s had promoted opposition to fascism as the focal point of the church's social mission. Or perhaps the Catholic bishops of South Africa might have selected the dismantling of certain legal structures of apartheid as the predominant issue in recent years. Choices like these might not be indisputably wrong. At any time, the episcopacy might decide to promote exclusively some ideal or to oppose some evil. But such a position would be exceptional for two reasons. One has to do with the nature of the church, while the other has to do with the nature of politics.

Gaudium et Spes noted that the social mission of the church encompasses the defense of human dignity, the promotion of human rights, the cultivation of unity among humanity, and the provision of meaning to human activity in the world.[49] In such a wide perspective, it can be dangerously reductionistic to highlight one area of concern. For the church to reflect the whole spectrum of concerns that are entailed in the conciliar vision of social mission, a broad array of issues must merit attention from the people of God. Partly for this reason Bernardin proposed the consistent ethic of life. His aim of linking together various moral issues that entail the promotion of human life is meant to provide a unifying rationale for the church's stance on topics like capital punishment, abortion, care for the dying and warfare. This style of political engagement assures a public presence by the church which attests to the broad scope of its mission to the world.

Trying to isolate an issue when it has interconnections in public policy can be difficult. For instance, the abortion dilemma would be greatly eased if we, as a society, could eliminate the reasons why many women resort to abortion. Those reasons appear to be linked to significant social change. In our country, women still find themselves caught between the needs of child-rearing and economic solvency. Many mothers who work do so because they are single parents or because they supplement a spouse's modest income. Working women in America are not playing out a fantasy of "having it all"; they are trying to survive financially. Yet present economic and political realities penalize those who try to raise young children, especially single parents. If we are to create a social climate wherein abortion is not economic common sense, then we must promote a number of social changes including better prenatal care, greater maternity benefits, reasonable parental leave policies that protect job security, and good but affordable child care. As Bernardin notes, "the circumstances surrounding conception, and the resources needed to sustain a pregnancy and support children, are also part of the moral fabric of the abortion debate."[50] An intelligible strategy for decreasing the abortion rate is to get at the causes of abortion. Thus the so-called "liberal social agenda" may arguably be a pro-life program. A true anti-abortion position should advocate social reforms that strike at the conditions that incline women to choose abortion. Issues such as poverty, labor reform and social welfare would be included within a consistent ethic of life. Other issues, such as job-protected parental leave and abortion, are quite distinct—but they are related. This is what makes single-issue politics strategically problematic. Focusing too intently on an issue distorts a contextual understanding of the topic and obscures the array of policies needed to deal with the matter effectively.

John Coleman has written that a continual challenge for the church in its social mission is to avoid political irrelevance while also avoiding partisanship.[51] There is certainly political relevance to the church's involvement in issues like abortion. We must, however, distinguish between applying single-issue politics to political ends or principles and applying it to political strategies used to achieve those ends. Sometimes, when one major party or candidate endorses a basic principle but the other side does not, the church appears partisan if it supports a fundamental value. For example, advocacy of racial equality does not appear overly partisan in a culture when both major parties endorse the aim and differ only on strategy for its attainment. But if one candidate in an election had a record of opposing civil rights for African-Americans and defending white privilege, there would be a partisan edge in the church's defense of racial equality. The charge of partisanship in such an atmosphere should not deter church leaders if they are convinced that the basic goal is so central to the well-being of society that a single-issue approach is permissible. Single-issue activists sometimes have focused not on a political principle but on a strategy for bringing about their aim. Then the potential for polarization in the body politic greatly increases. Suppose in an election both parties endorse policies that, to correct past and present racial injustice, specifically address the special needs of the African-American community in the United States. One party's strategy includes a quota system for hiring by private firms that do business with the government, whereas the other party thinks this ill-advised. For the church to single-mindedly push for the quota strategy seems to entail a greater degree of partisanship than in the previous example.

Single-issue politics, even when justifiable at the level of principles, is questionable at the level of strategy. For the church to act on this level risks more than the accusation of partisanship, however. To advocate deciding an election solely on a judgment of strategy is political narrow-mindedness and theological trivialization: narrow-minded because it allows a disputed question to override all other matters; trivializing because it reduces the church's social message to one risky judgment on a matter several steps removed from the core elements of gospel faith.

Of late the U.S. bishops have become identified in the popular mind not only with opposition to abortion, but with specific means for reducing the number of abortions. During the last few elections, several of the bishops did not satisfactorily distinguish between those candidates who opposed the Catholic position on the value of fetal life and those who were sympathetic but disagreed as to the best means of developing societal support for protection of fetal life. The alarm felt by people over the abortion debate in this nation is due, in part, to the belief not only that some bishops have made abortion the overriding moral consideration in a consistent life ethic without persuasive reason but also that the issue has become one of strategy as well as goals.

When we move from generalities to specifics on moral questions, we of course do so with less certainty. That does not mean that church leaders cannot teach specifics, but they should do so with a becoming modesty in their claim to final wisdom on a topic. Claiming modesty is difficult if the most decisive issue in an election is whether candidates agree with our viewpoint. For that reason, single-issue politics should remain at the level of political ends or principles. It is outlandish for the church to practice single-issue politics at the level of strategy. When the specifics of public policy on abortion are held up as the single most important issue in a candidate's record, the risk of divisive partisanship and arrogant intolerance in the public forum is high. On balance, the consistent ethic of life is a more promising strategy than one that is single-issue. Not only may it prove to be more successful politically, but theologically it is a closer approximation to the breadth of the Catholic community's concern to witness to the depth of God's gracious presence in the lives of all people, to respect the sacredness of the lives of young and old, rich and poor, male and female.

5 | Creation and an Environmental Ethic

"In our day there is a growing awareness that world peace is threatened not only by the arms race, regional conflicts and continued injustice among people and nations, but also by a lack of due respect for nature, by the plundering of natural resources and by a progressive decline in the quality of life."[1] Without doubt the topic of the environment has become a more common concern among people. In John Paul II's message on the 1990 World Day of Peace we find evidence that ecological sensitivity has reached the higher echelons of church life. This concern among prominent persons has been matched in the political arena. The 1988 presidential campaign saw Messrs. Bush and Dukakis jousting over who should wear the mantle of the environmental candidate. And at the 1989 summit of the Group of Seven, the heads of state of the major industrial economies of the globe issued a communiqué giving further proof of just how "mainstream" environmentalism has become.

For many, of course, the environment has never not been an issue. Fetid garbage dumps, closed beaches, air that can be seen as well as breathed, the extinction of whole species—the causes for concern have long been with us. But the religious response to the ecological crisis has been more recent. Some have found the resources for such a theology and spirituality in eastern thought and practice. Others, like Joseph Sittler, Ian Barbour and Paul Santmire, seek out elements of the Christian tradition for the development of a more environmentally sound perspective.[2]

At the same time critics (e.g. Lynn White) have argued that the Christian tradition is suspect on the matter of the environment.[3] They argue that Judaism and Christianity have fed an anthropocentrism which, intentionally or not, demeans the rest of creation as it exalts those who are a "little less than the angels" (Ps 8:5). Certainly Hebraic monotheism declared that all others but Yahweh were "no-gods." Included among those thus denied divine status were the deities of Greek and Roman

104

mythology who protected streams, mountains, and forests. It is possible to see in this demythologizing a loss of reverence for nature. Christianity's contribution to the problem—its celebration of the incarnation—has promoted the centrality of humanity in the plan of creation and redemption and accorded secondary status to the rest of creation.

With a bit of poetic license and beyond-the-mainstream readings of the historical record, Matthew Fox has sought to re-present the tradition and demonstrate a different Christian attitude toward the created order.[4] Another approach, more dismissive of the tradition, is found in the work of Thomas Berry.[5] Geologian, rather than theologian, Berry has seemingly given up on the biblical tradition as a resource for a theology of the environment. Whatever else its merits, this work has borne fruit, in the sense that it has awakened among believers a degree of religious seriousness for addressing an issue that is more important and complex than the faddishness and trivialization which mass media politics inevitably encourages.

Despite these efforts, it is lamentable but true that the question still can fairly be asked, "What does Christianity have to say to the contemporary ecological movement?" That it has something to say is important to assert, but what it has to say is not primarily advice on public policy or clear moral judgments for settling disputes about economic growth versus ecological protection. In this regard, the Christian tradition is, in the words of Richard McCormick, "more a value-raiser than an answer-giver."[6]

The value that Christianity points to in the cluster of issues raised by the environmental crisis is humankind's essential relatedness to nature, an understanding of the created order, which is precisely what is at stake here. Too often the discussion over the ecosystem turns on arguments from self-interest, even if enlightened self-interest, a stance we believe is fundamentally flawed. Charles Murphy has written that "the environmental cause, from the beginning, was to an extent the special enthusiasm of a privileged and affluent minority who wished to preserve their particular lifestyle. . . ."[7] The same sentiment is captured in a cartoon which shows a snazzily dressed first-world tourist standing up through the sunroof of a large luxury car and yelling at an impoverished looking native about to chop down a tree, "Yo! Amigo!! We need that tree to protect us from the greenhouse effect!"[8] In the same vein, the economist Lester Thurow has commented on the "yuppie" image of the environmental movement. "We have simply reached the point where, for many Americans, the next item on their acquisitive agenda is a cleaner environment. If they can achieve it, it will make all the other goods and services (boats, summer homes, and so forth) more enjoyable."[9]

Of course, these criticisms do not capture the entirety of motives behind the environmental movement. Yet what they point out is that treating the environmental issue as primarily a calculation of long-term versus short-term self-interest maintains an attitude of instrumental rationality that is part of the problem.

The Proper Starting Point for Environmentalism

The Jewish and Christian understanding of creation, at least in one of its strands, is profoundly insightful and potentially transformative of modern ways of addressing the crisis of creation because it moves beyond instrumental rationality. Because "nature is never just 'nature' but retains a sacred quality as 'creation' " the Jewish and Christian approach calls for a sacramental consciousness which evokes a richer understanding of how we are to think about the created order.[10]

The needed transformation lies at the level of our deep convictions, our worldview. The relational dimension of the Jewish-Christian heritage must replace the atomized individualism of our current outlook. The mentality of consumerism, the myth of progress and our technological mind-set are all problematic in regard to the environment; they are also symptomatic. Each is the distortion of a human good, a distortion arising from the non-relational anthropology of our age. If our environmental sensitivity is to change, the transformation must take place at the root of the problem. But that transformation is more convoluted than might first appear.

The human abuse of non-human nature has spurred a harsh reaction by defenders of the environment, who exhibit a brand of ecological activism, an environmental romanticism, that borders on the anti-human. Nature is idealized. The achievements of human civilization are disparaged. The environmental romantic mirrors the fundamental outlook of the technocrats being criticized. Both see humanity at odds with nature. In one case, this leads to calls for more effective ways of manipulating, subduing, and dominating nature. In the other case, the result is opposition to technology, economic growth, and development efforts. In both cases humanity is set in opposition to the rest of creation. Either alternative is unacceptable from a relational worldview. To separate nature from human culture is environmental romanticism. To consider human culture apart from the non-human is to invite the impoverishment of the former and the devastation of the latter.

The Jewish and Christian traditions put before us a worldview in which humanity is not against nature but a part of it.[11] Neither element is rightly viewed in isolation. The exploration of this relational anthropology is the basic contribution theologians can make to the environmental movement. We can examine the religious tradition to see which developments have been distortions, which trajectories misguided, which insights forgotten. The constructive task is to illustrate how the resources of the Jewish and Christian heritage can be used in promoting ecological wisdom.

John Paul II has contributed to this constructive project in *Sollicitudo Rei Socialis*. The bishop of Rome identifies three points for reflection when considering the order of the cosmos: 1) respect for nature; 2) preservation of natural resources; 3) restriction of pollution.[12] The papal remarks are brief, however, and not fully developed. Drew Christiansen observes that only the first point is further commented upon by John Paul. Respect for nature entails "two strong ecological principles: 1) the independent moral status of other creatures and 2) the need to think and act in terms of whole 'environments' and ecological systems."[13] A renewed understanding of human dominion over nature that acknowledges God's sovereignty is the preferred metaphor in John Paul's writing.

While appreciative of the papal view, we do not feel that this continued reliance on the dominion theme in describing the relation of humanity to the rest of the created order strikes the proper note. However morally circumscribed, the emphasis on humanity's dominion over nature found in the first book of the Bible reinforces attitudes that lead to environmental abuse. A sharper break with the customary metaphors and rhetoric of the religious community when discussing the environment is needed if the desired change in fundamental attitude is to occur. In breaking with the customary categories we do not mean breaking with the tradition on issues of ecology; rather we advocate the retrieval of a neglected but important theme within the tradition for responding to the crisis of creation. Dominion is not the only creation theme found in Genesis.

Genesis

Like every myth of origin, the two Genesis stories of the beginning of all things (Gen 1:1–2:4a and 2:4b-25) have been used to explain and justify the ways human beings relate to one another and to the non-human world. As narratives of how things came to be and depictions of how things were and presumably ought to be, these creation stories have been elaborated into cosmologies and theories of the soul and twisted into ideological support for male dominance and industrial exploitation.

The first of the two stories has been the basis of both the overlordship and stewardship images for the role of humanity in the natural world.

> "Let us make the human being in our image and likeness. Let them have dominion over the fish of the sea and the birds of the air and the cattle and all the wild animals." . . . God blessed them, saying to them, "Be fertile and increase; fill the whole earth and subdue it; have dominion over the fish of the sea and the birds of the air and all the living things that move on the earth" (Gen 1:26.28).

Part of the human being's likeness to God is the exercise of dominion over the rest of creation. The twin images of being given dominion and being commanded to subdue the earth and all the creatures which fill it are closely connected with sovereignty. God's sovereignty is asserted often in the Hebrew scriptures; here the image and likeness of God, the human being, is entrusted with sovereignty. From the perspective of the first creation myth in Genesis, without such dominion and power over the rest of creation, the human being would not be "like God."

But there is a contrasting theme in this story of the beginning of all things. "And so God created the human being in God's image; in the divine image did God create the human being, male and female did he create them" (Gen 1:27). How is it that being created in the image of God results in the differentiation of male and female? Clearly the myth does not wish to attribute gender to God, much less dual sexuality. The point is not that God is male or female or male and female, but that God is relational. The only God that the Hebrew tradition knows is the God who is about the business of creating, i.e. the Hebrew scriptures contain nothing about God *in se*, God considered apart from the creating God. Even in one of its creation myths, the Hebrew tradition envisions God as the God of the covenant, God in relationship. To be the image of this God, the human being must be relational. Humanity is sexed in order that human beings may be driven into relationship one with another.

This is a central theme of the second of Genesis' creation myths (Gen 2:4b-25). The dominion motif is depicted in the first human being's naming all the animals that God has made and led before him "to see what he would call them" (Gen 2:19). All other creatures will be what the human being says they are—certainly an extraordinary statement of the power over creation given by God to humanity. But the context of this conferral is the human hunger for companionship. In the first of the creation myths, the first divine judgment on humanity is that it is "very good" (Gen 1:31). That judgment is made on humanity differentiated into male and female, relational being. The first judgment of God regarding human being in the second myth makes this even more explicit. Having fashioned the human being from the clods of the earth and breathed the divine breath into him, God announces that "it is not good for the human being to be alone" (Gen 2:18). Again there is the insistence that human beings are meant to be in relationship to one another. Thus, in this second creation story, companionship is the explicit ground given for the creation of the two sexes. But it is important to note that not only human beings are intended for relationship to one another. This is also the reason for the creation for "the various wild beasts and birds of the air" (Gen 2:19). The natural world is not merely intended for subjugation by human beings but for companionship.

Dominion over the earth and all that it contains, the command "to fill the whole earth and subdue it"—certainly this conveys power. Such a claim to power by human beings over all non-human creation contains the possibility, all too often realized, of domination and exploitation of the earth. Clearly the claim to power must be balanced by the call to responsibility, the traditional appeal to stewardship.[14] The relationship between humanity and the rest of creation has often been cast in the Jewish and Christian traditions as that of a caretaker, one charged by God with the maintenance of the earth. The non-human world has been given to human beings for our good, to be used responsibly for our self-development, to answer to our purposes and thus to fulfill God's purpose in creating it. To be sure, this stewardship metaphor prohibited wanton wastefulness, the mere exploitation of nature by humankind. The world is presented as a garden given into our care to be tended and nurtured. But undeniably the role of stewardship carries the implication that non-human creation is to be used.

Companionship

The theme of companionship, the relationship which exists not only between human persons but between human beings and non-human beings, has been largely submerged in the stewardship theme. We need to recover it. Companionship implies mutuality. It excludes the reduction of either side of the relationship to a tool of the other's purposes. Martin Buber, so deeply rooted in the biblical tradition, explored the meaning of companionship under the rubric "I-Thou."[15] The contrasting possibility is "I-It." The reduction of "thou" to "it" results from making the other into an extension of oneself. The other becomes *mine—my* husband, *my* wife, *my* child, *my* parent, *my* friend, *my* neighbor, *my* teacher, *my* student, *my* boss, *my* employee. "It" can be manipulated in order to fulfill the task which I set, for "it" belongs to me. "It" has no intrinsic value, only the instrumental value which I assign it. The other as "thou" cannot be possessed, can never become *my* "thou." When recognized and respected as "thou," the other is seen to be of inherent value, to be an end and not a means to an end.

As a human being can be reduced to an "it," so a non-human being can become "thou," in Buber's terms. "It" can be a possession but not a companion. "Thou" is always a companion. But in what sense, other than the mythology of the second creation story in Genesis, can one speak of the non-human world as companion to human beings? At a time of global ecological crisis, we certainly do not need a revival of the nineteenth century's romantic poets' personification of nature. Indeed, such personification is the very reverse of what Buber meant by treating the non-human world as "thou," for instead of allowing the other to be what the other is, personification insists that the other must be what I am if I am to enter into any relationship with it. Such personification is another more subtle way of reducing the non-human other to "it."

How then to present non-human creation as "thou," as companion to humanity? The Catholic tradition offers two important symbols that deserve to be explored as ways of reappropriating the biblical theme of companionship in creation: poverty and sacramentality.

Augustine of Hippo and Francis of Assisi

In Book 9 of his *Confessions*, Augustine recounts an incident that took place shortly before the death of his mother Monica as they stayed at Ostia on their way home to North Africa after his baptism in Milan.[16] Seated at a window overlooking the garden of their rented house, they speculated on the life of the saints in glory. As Augustine describes their experience, they entered into a rapturous ecstasy in which they had a foretaste of that life. Passing through all the spheres of the sun, moon, planets and stars of their Ptolemaic universe, they came to the outermost limit of their own minds and transcended even that. All the heavenly spheres ceased their music, Augustine writes. Everything that exists by passing away, i.e. all creatures, since the mark of creatureliness is temporality, fell silent after singing the song which they constantly sing: "We did not make ourselves, but were made by God who is forever."[17]

Eight centuries later, Francis of Assisi grasped the two central elements of this Augustinian song of all creation. As with so many charismatic men and women, the historic Francis has been lost in popular mythology. But two themes of the Franciscan legend seem rooted in Francis himself: poverty and the unity of all creatures. The singer of the Canticle of the Sun, who recognized the sun and moon, earth and air, fire and water, his own body, all animals and plants, and death itself as brothers and sisters, also entered into a mystical marriage with Lady Poverty. The Franciscan emphasis on poverty and the nature mysticism, which finds its legendary expression in Francis' preaching to the birds and the wolf of Gubbio, are grounded in one insight: all creatures are united in the depths of their being by the fact of being creatures. The discovery of one's finiteness is the recognition of one's poverty. When one grasps the "iffiness" of one's existence, the shocking fact that the source and foundation of one's being is not in oneself, then one knows oneself as truly poor. To be poor in this fundamental sense is a definition, not a description. True poverty, the poverty of the spirit, is the realization that there is no intrinsic reason for one's being at all.

This poverty unites all creatures. That Francis could address the sun and moon, the primal elements, birds and beasts and plants as his brothers and sisters rested on his perception that in his and their depths he and they were both absolutely dependent for existence. As Augustine knew, *all* can sing, "We did not make ourselves." In this fundamental poverty of creatureliness, there is equality. The human person has no more claim to intrinsic being than a plant or an animal, a star or a stone. The denigration of any creature as creature is therefore the implicit denigration of every creature.[18] If any creature is worthless, all creatures are worthless, because, precisely as creatures, all are equal. This is not in any way to deny the unique role which the human person plays in the divine economy. Indeed, in light of the Christian doctrine of the incarnation, that role is one of extraordinary dignity. But the role given to humanity is as sovereignly the gift of God as is the role of every other creature. The human person is the point in creation to which the fullness of the self-gift of God can be given. But the human person has been *created* as such.

The doctrine of *creatio ex nihilo* is not a claim about how the universe came into being, but *why*. It is the Christian response to the question that Martin Heidegger held was the beginning of all metaphysics: Why is there being rather than nothing?[19] If the question seeks a reason within being itself, it is doomed to remain unanswered. The doctrine of *creatio ex nihilo* insists on the fundamental poverty of the universe: the universe has no intrinsic ground for existence. When all else has been said, when the heavenly spheres fall silent, Augustine knew, the great truth that must be proclaimed is that we—all of us individually and together—did not make ourselves. And so Francis saw that it was neither an act of human self-denigration nor an effusion of poetic personification to address the sun and moon, the fire and the earth, and all animate and inanimate creatures as his brothers and sisters; it was the simple truth.

The only reason for anything to exist is the free agape of God. The universe exists because God loves it and wills to give God's self to it. Utterly poor in itself, creation is divinely gifted. Thus, to see creation as a whole or any creature in particular as what it is, namely, totally dependent on the gracious will of God, is to see revealed the grace which is its foundation in being.[20] Since everything that is exists because of the free act of God—the overflowing agape that is the source of being—then everything is a sacrament of the goodness and creative power of God.

Sacramental Vision

The themes of creation and poverty intersect in the Catholic vision of sacramentality. A sacrament is not a stand-in for something else, a visible sign for some other invisible reality. The essence of a sacrament is the capacity to reveal grace, the agapic self-gift of God, by being what it is. By being thoroughly itself, a sacrament bodies forth the absolute self-donative love of God that undergirds both it and the entirety of creation. The Catholic community has recognized seven particular events as being revelatory of grace. But every creature, human and non-human, animate and inanimate, can be a sacrament. The more richly developed our sacramental vision, the more sacraments crowd in upon us. Francis of Assisi's interweaving of poverty with the brotherhood and sisterhood of all creatures is profoundly Catholic because it is profoundly sacramental.

This Catholic sacramental vision is by no means limited to the Roman Catholic Church. When Jonathan Edwards described the marks of conversion in his great *Treatise on Religious Affections,* he gave as the first mark of such affections that they "do arise from those influences and operations on the heart which are *spiritual, supernatural,* and *divine.*"[21] In explanation of this first mark of the converted, Edwards wrote that

> in those gracious affections and exercises which are wrought in the minds of the saints, through the saving influences of the Spirit of God, there is a new inward perception or sensation of their minds, entirely different in its nature and kind, from anything that ever their minds were the subjects of before they were sanctified.[22]

The saints, to use Edwards' term, see reality differently from the unconverted. They do not see things that others do not see; rather they see what everyone else sees but in a different way. They see everything in its relation to God: they see it as creature. Edwards' "new inward perception or sensation" is the ability to hear the song of all creation that Augustine and Monica heard, to see the community of all creatures as creatures that Francis saw. At the risk of "catholicizing" the great eighteenth century Calvinist, one way of describing this "new inward perception" of the Edwardsean saint is to call it the capacity for sacramental vision.

The cultivation of sacramental vision is the richest way of recovering the companionship motif of the Genesis stories that the Christian tradition has to offer in the current global ecological crisis. The discovery that every creature, including oneself, is a sacrament of the love of God that causes all things to be provides the deepest foundation for reverencing creation. The recognition of the other as a creature and therefore that which exists because it is loved by God cannot occur where that other is regarded as "it." By its nature a sacrament requires that it be appreciated for what it is and not as a tool to an end; in Buber's terms, a sacrament is always "thou." Since every creature can and should be a sacrament, so every creature can and should be "thou," a companion. But this sacramental vision demands unflinching recognition of the poverty of one's own being—for many too terrible to be true—and joyful acceptance of the absolute agape that supports one's own being—for many too good to be true. This requires the expansion of the imagination.

Paul Ricoeur has written that "we too often and too quickly think of a will that submits and not enough of an imagination that opens itself."[23] Seeing the world sacramentally cannot simply be commanded. However necessary it may be for the survival of the planet in our time, sacramental vision cannot be made a moral imperative. It might better be understood as a Christian aesthetic which needs cultivation. The whole of Catholic praxis is training in sacramental vision. Liturgy and social action, marriage and parenthood, prayer and politics, music and dance and the visual arts, all educate us to appreciate the other as sacramental, worthy companions of our poverty and our engracedness. They teach us to see things as they are. In Gerard Manley Hopkins' words, "These things, these things were here, and but the beholder / Wanting."[24] At present, "beholders" are desperately wanted.

An Ethic Rooted in Sacramentality

If the ecological crisis is to be addressed effectively, the ethic of individualism must be replaced with an ethic of companionship. Such an ethic will move from the bold claim of human dignity inherent in our sacramentality to how human beings relate to the rest of the cosmos. The believer's conviction regarding human dignity is one of the legacies of the Jewish and Christian tradition, but this insight must be extended so that an ethic results which promotes a sound understanding of how persons are integrated within the rest of the created order.

Both creation myths in Genesis agree in their depiction of the hu-

man capacity for relationship as that which makes humanity "like God."
The exaltation of the individual at the expense of the community, which
in its crudest form becomes the "trickle-down" theory of social responsibility, stands in contradistinction to this foundational insight of the Jewish and Christian traditions. Not surprisingly, this individualist ethic has
debased the image of stewardship from participation in the creative activity of God into cost-benefit analysis. While it is important to attempt to
reassert the stewardship motif in its pristine form, it is also necessary to
strike at the heart of the problem, to confront impoverished and impoverishing individualism with the relational anthropology of the Jewish and
Christian traditions. The crisis of the environment is directly linked to
the problem of humanization. For unless non-human beings are treated as
"thou," human beings will be treated as "it." This is why the appeal to
self-interest cannot yield sufficient support in responding to the global
environmental crisis. Such an appeal merely reinforces the basic problem. Far more adequate and far more faithful to the Christian tradition is
the reappropriation of the companionship motif of the biblical creation
stories.

The religious discussion of human responsibility toward creation
must move beyond stewardship both for the sake of theology and for the
environment. Theologically, stewardship has been open to a deist interpretation whereby God is seen as having begun creation and then handed
over care of it to humanity. When the image of stewardship dominates
our imagination, God can be removed from the scene as human beings
are given oversight of the earth and move to center stage in the drama of
creation. Too easily the duty of caring for *God's* world becomes the task
of shaping *our* world. Just as stewards are not anxious for the master's
presence lurking over their shoulder, so humanity is often content to
keep God in a distant heaven.

Just as with theology, so, too, the environmental cause benefits by
retrieval of the companionship theme which evokes a different attitude
toward creation. This difference in attitude will be reflected in an environmental ethic grounded on a relational anthropology. Such an ethic
does not spring full-blown from the companionship theme. The movement from an over-arching frame of mind to an ethical method is more
complex. What the companionship motif provides is an orientation
which should guide us in devising an environmental ethic that does not
rest on instrumental rationality.

Constructing an Environmental Ethic

The first point of orientation the companionship motif provides is
the desirability of a transformed context within which to develop an

environmental ethic. Governed by images of stewardship and ruled by precepts based on self-interest, our moral imaginations are unable to envision an environmental ethic that is adequate to the Jewish and Christian heritage. In contrast, images of companionship encourage the moral imagination to consider that more than the good of the individual self is at stake. Once the intrinsic good of creation is seen, then approaches to the environmental crisis which treat creation only as an instrumental good for humanity become inadequate.

Basic to any ethic is, first, the recognition of the other, the "thou" who is not myself nor simply an extension of myself, to which I must respond. Then follows the determination of the moral standing of the "other" one encounters. The reduction of creation to "it" has promoted a loss of respect for nature and an attitude of instrumental rationality, whereby the purpose of nature becomes its use for human convenience. Doing justice to the environment becomes difficult when the context for decision-making is so one-sided. This is what John Paul wants to remedy by his call for a respect for nature that acknowledges the independent moral status of non-human creation.[25] Rediscovering the "thou" dimension of all creation provides a corrective to the tendency to relate to nature only as "it," moving beyond the technological vision of instrumental rationality to a reawakened sacramental vision of companionship. So fundamental a reorientation alters the context for assessing our responsibility toward the environment. The story of Noah in Genesis reminds us that all types of animals are to be saved, even those which might seem useless to humans. Furthermore, after the flood God announces to Noah that the covenant is established not only with Noah and his descendants but "with every living creature that was with you" and came out of the ark (Gen 9:10). In other words "the blessing which God gives to inaugurate the world after the flood is a single blessing for all his creatures, human and non-human." Yahweh also declares the rainbow to be a sign that never again shall earth be destroyed. "Inanimate nature thus joins the animals and humanity as joint recipients of the divine blessing and pledge."[26] For the author of the story, it is difficult to imagine humanity apart from the rest of creation which from the beginning was pronounced by the creator as good, and the inherent goodness of creation is reaffirmed by God after the flood.

The context of mutuality created by an awareness of both the poverty and the sacramentality of all the created order should yield an ethic less prone to denigrate the intrinsic worth of non-human creation. The poverty of the entire created order forces us to acknowledge our ties with the rest of creation in its dependence upon the creator. At the same time the sacramentality of all creation prevents any debasement of our common creaturely state. Our poverty as creatures and our dignity as sacramental mediations of divine grace must be held in tension as twin aspects of our organic connection with all creation.

Such a way of understanding the created order overcomes the anthropocentrism of much modern thought. In its place, however, the Catholic theologian proposes not a biocentric but a theocentric universe. As Drew Christiansen has observed, "Humanity needs to look more searchingly at itself as it is embedded in nature, not turn away to look at nature alone."[27] Coming to terms with one's creaturely state—both its poverty and sacramentality—and our relationship with the creator offers deeper resources for a transformed attitude toward the created order than biocentrism. Catholicism continues to affirm a distinction between God and nature which is lost in more exaggerated forms of biocentrism. Also a theocentric perspective provides a strong religio-moral motivation for humanity's reordering of its relationship with the rest of creation.

The second point of orientation for an environmental ethic is an expanded notion of the common good which includes non-human creation. The common good, in John XXIII's classic phrase in *Mater et Magistra*, embraces "the sum total of those conditions of social living whereby people are enabled to achieve their own integral perfection more fully and easily."[28] As a way of elaborating what those "conditions of social living" entail, John went on to list an extensive roster of human rights in *Pacem in Terris*.[29] Both Paul VI and John Paul II have continued to use the language of human rights when discussing the common good. John Paul has recently cited a "right to a safe environment" as a "right that must be included in an updated charter of human rights."[30] He maintains that the use of human rights in recent Catholic social teaching is a way of specifying the essential *needs*, basic *freedoms* and *relationships* with others that comprise the common good and serve human dignity.[31] In this chapter we have suggested a perspective which sees the created order as an "other" with whom we have a relationship and that this relationship is part of the common good. Protecting this relationship with *non-human creation* is properly one of the aims of *human* rights. John Paul's "right to a safe environment" is useful and correct, but there is more to the issue and there are other materials to draw upon within Catholic social thought.

Although not as widely studied as other papal teachings, the various addresses of Pius XII are important resources for social ethics. In a 1941 radio talk on the feast of Pentecost, Pius corrected the emphasis of Leo XIII on private property rights. In his desire to rebut socialism, Leo had stressed the church's support for the right of private property. While not denying this right, Pius XII made it clear that property rights are not primary but secondary. Private property is always subordinate to the more fundamental right of all people to the goods of the earth. In this Pius was faithful to the views of many of the church fathers and ironically was closer to Thomas Aquinas' position than was Leo, the pope responsible for the revival of Thomism.

Pius XII's reiteration of the priority to be given to the universal destiny of goods contains the germ of an important insight. Pius saw the relationship of humanity to the earth and the rest of its inhabitants as basic to the common good. We can also see in Pius' position a latent recognition of the fact that the resources of the earth are our ecological capital. When we consume our resources faster than they can be replaced or restored, and we are doing just that, we are depleting the capital which future generations will require. In effect several nations are on the brink of environmental bankruptcy in their management of the earth's goods, goods that were meant for more than the present generation.[32] There is no need to protect the environment by ascribing rights to nature or individual animal species.[33] It is humanity's fundamental right to relate to non-human creation and the right to share in the goods of creation that are the rights at stake in the ecological issue.

Of late, John Paul has developed the thought of his predecessor on this theme of the universal destiny of the goods of the earth. It is the original gift of creation by God that is the foundation for the universal destiny of earth's goods; no one has claim to any part of this gift in an absolute way. In the current bishop of Rome's mind, the destruction of the environment is traceable to "an anthropological error." That error is forgetting that any human labor "is always based on God's prior and original gift of the things that are." In this way the God-given purposes of creation are subordinated to human schemes which often tyrannize the rest of creation.[34] Resurrecting the patristic idea of the universal destiny of earthly goods as a fundamental human right is a needed part of an expanded theory of the common good. Setting this human right in the context of companionship is necessary, however, to prevent the human right to the universal destiny of the goods of creation from being interpreted according to a narrow mind-set of instrumental rationality.

The third point of orientation for an environmental ethic concerns the means whereby an expanded notion of the common good can be safeguarded and promoted. Here, too, the tradition of Catholic social thought has something to offer. In *Pacem in Terris*, John XXIII drew attention to the existence of the "universal common good."[35] The unity of the human family was the basis for John's espousal of a common good that transcended national boundaries. In the same encyclical John noted that the "whole reason for the existence of civil authorities is the realiza-tion of the common good."[36] The difficulty was that existing political institutions "no longer correspond to the objective requirements of the universal common good."[37] Subsequent popes have continued John's move from a national to an international to a trans-national plane when analyzing social questions.

Issues which touch upon the universal common good—and the con-dition of the environment is one of these—go beyond the competence of individual nation-states. It is necessary to develop structural vehicles which protect the well-being of the global environment. An international agreement like the Law of the Sea Treaty serves as an illustration of the kind of structure that the papacy advocates for the sake of the universal common good. In contrast, the tendency to define narrowly the self-interest of a nation remains a major obstacle to building effective vehicles for the universal common good.

The language of the common good challenges political arrange-ments not only at the level of trans-national issues. Ours is a nation that has prized individual liberty and has a strong attraction to free market economics. But we cannot avoid asking what social mechanisms on a national level must be devised so that the varied activities of citizens are directed to the common good, understood as including the good of cre-ation. Romantic calls for simpler lifestyles or ideological reliance on purely voluntary measures are simply insufficient. Debate on the specific nature of these necessary mechanisms requires political leadership nota-bly lacking at all levels of government.

William Ruckelshaus, former administrator of the Environmental Protection Agency, has written that transformed values are insufficient if the appropriate institutions are not in place to translate the values into public policies. Ensuring that market pricing includes the environmental costs of producing a good or providing a service, the implementation of market incentives to develop energy incentives, direct regulation of activ-ity through enactment of environmental standards—all these are exam-ples of the types of institutional arrangements which need to be put into place if government is to meet its responsibility toward the common good which includes the environment.[38]

Ecology, Justice and Economic Development

No proposed environmental ethic can avoid confronting the press-ing question of the relationship between ecology and economic develop-ment. A simple disavowal of economic growth may perpetuate injustice to humans in the name of non-humans. Ecology has to do with the relationship of organisms of the same or different species. Ecological balance has unquestionably been lost in the way that human beings have treated non-human nature. Righting the imbalance, however, cannot entail injustice to fellow human beings for the sake of other species. Poorer nations will not be willing to forego economic development at the behest of wealthier nations who have belatedly seen the results of their own assaults on nature in the quest for more and more expansion. To avoid a new imbalance, an environmental ethic must be informed by a careful analysis of the demands of economic justice.

Leonardo Boff makes the point that Francis of Assisi's sense of companionship, his extension of the ideal of fraternity to include non-human creation, was not born of romanticism. According to Boff, "romanticism is characterized by modern subjectivity; it is the projection onto the world of feelings themselves."[39] Romanticist attitudes toward nature point back to the human observer, to his or her feelings about nature. Francis, on the other hand, wished to rise above the ego to become engaged with brother wind and sister earth so as to sing a joint hymn of praise. What allowed Francis entry into this experience of the fraternity of all creation was the asceticism of poverty. Boff explains that such poverty "is a way of being by which the individual lets things be what they are; one refuses to dominate them, subjugate them, and make them the objects of the will to power."[40] Required for such an embrace of poverty is a "renunciation of the instinct to power, to the dominion over things," for it is the desire for possession that stands between true communication between persons with each other and with all creation.[41] As Francis became poorer, he became more fraternal; poverty was the way into the experience of universal fraternity. Francis, like the rest of creation, was a creature and thus was "not over things, but together with them, like brothers and sisters of the same family."[42] Before Francis could embrace nature he had first to embrace the poor of humanity who reminded him of his true nature, a dependent creature unable to be self-made, self-sufficient, and self-fulfilling.

Following Francis' insight means it would be folly to put environmental concerns at odds with the quest for global social justice. It would be an injustice to ignore our companionship with the poor of the world in the name of embracing non-human creation. Any environmental ethic that is suitable for believers must be an ethic that integrates strategies for economic development with those for ecological balance. What this means practically can be grouped under three headings: 1) determining the relative burden of restraint among nations, 2) the effect of international economics on development, 3) the link between poor populations and environmental destruction.[43]

With regard to the first heading, the nations with industrial and post-industrial economies have created most of the pollution. Reducing pollution ought not to be an excuse for keeping other nations in a pre-industrial state. Rather, the nations of the first world must acknowledge that they share the greater responsibility for reducing pollution since they are most responsible for the creation of the present situation.[44]

As to international economic activity, the second heading, there is a direct link between structures such as trade policies, foreign debt and the environment. One example is that many developing nations have resource-based economies.[45] What they have to trade in the global marketplace is their natural resources. Unless poorer nations are able to expand the range of tradeable goods as well as shift to more sustainable production for local consumption needs, there will be increasing pressure on the earth's resources. Trade relations that keep poorer nations in the position of being raw-materials suppliers for industrialized national economies leave the poor with little choice but to engage in greater deforestation and other unfortunate methods of securing income.[46]

Finally, it is becoming obvious that human poverty contributes to environmental denigration. The poor have higher birth rates which place greater strains on limited resources. The poor, because they are marginalized in a world economy requiring skills and knowledge, must eke out a living in ways that usually include inappropriate farming and pasturing techniques which, in turn, lead to desertification, soil depletion, and flooding.[47] Helping the poor with opportunities to move beyond a subsistence economy can, if done correctly, lead to ecological improvement.

The above comments make clear that no proposed environmental ethic can avoid confronting the pressing questions involved in the relationship between ecology and economic development. How are ecological concerns to be balanced with the creation of jobs for the poor? Is industrialization to be discouraged in nations with undeveloped economies for the sake of preserving certain animal and plant species? Because the common good cannot be a mere abstraction which prescinds from specific historical conditions, it is insufficient to speak about the global environment apart from the economic needs of the third world. At the same time, building a shared understanding on the matter of the common good and the place accorded to the environment among other goods is a crucial enterprise for any development strategy.

Catholic Thought on Sustainable Development

Since the time of John XXIII, Roman Catholicism has turned its attention toward the issue of development.[48] It was Paul VI who intensified this concern with his pleas for "integral development," a concept which required a broader set of criteria for development than simple appeals to GNP growth rates. In *Progressio Populorum* he spoke of the need for a development strategy that respected the culture and values of a people, thereby achieving a development which promoted a better way of life, not just more material goods.[49] Paul was proposing an approach which would reject the equation of development with the high consumption and material excess of first world nations. While his main concern was with the spiritual, moral and psychological costs of a narrow economic strategy, Paul's view was broad enough to include the environmental aspects of development plans. It is in that spirit that the bishops assembled at the 1971 Synod stated:

> Such is the demand for resources and energy by the richer nations, whether capitalist or socialist, and such are the effects of dumping by them in the atmosphere and the sea that irreparable damage would be done to the essential elements of life on earth, such as air and water, if their high rates of consumption and pollution, which are constantly on the increase, were extended to the whole of mankind.[50]

Donal Dorr has suggested that the episcopal view helps explain the use of the strong language about exploitation that is found in many third world pronouncements about the international economic system.[51] For too long the presumption was that the task was to "raise" poorer nations to the level of production and consumption found in richer countries. The 1971 Synod pointed out, however, that such a view, whatever other failings it has when compared to Paul's integral development, ignores the abuse of the environment that has accompanied development based on the first world model. Such development has come at the price of exploitation, directly the exploitation of the earth.

A consequent form of exploitation is the overuse of the universal goods of the earth for the benefit of a few, penalizing people in nations where economic development was slow in occurring. The earth cannot sustain everyone at the level of consumption found in the first world. The first nations to undergo modern industrialization have used more than their fair share of the earth's resources. Nations seeking economic development now must compensate for the abuses of those who benefited from earlier exploitation of the earth. According to third world leaders, the limits now proposed on development constitute an exploitation of poor nations. Current debates about Brazil's rain forests illustrate the point. No consensus yet exists on how to reconcile ecological concerns and development needs but some headway in resolving them is a *sine qua non* if the environmental movement is to make progress. It is certain that changes in first world nations will be necessary for a fair solution in the developing nations. In *Redemptor Hominis* John Paul II echoed this line of thought as he opposed a false development which is "dilapidating at an accelerated pace material and energy resources, and compromising the geophysical environment. . . ."[52] He followed this with remarks in a later encyclical about the "realization of the limits of available resources, and of the need to respect the integrity and the cycles of nature and to take them into account when planning for development. . . ." For John Paul, any "true concept of development cannot ignore the use of elements of nature, the renewability of resources and the consequences of haphazard industrialization. . . ."[53]

What we find in the recent record of Catholic social teaching is a growing sensitivity to the needs of nations with developing economies. Initially the popes expressed concern that strategies for development be just. This was followed by a desire that development also be "integral," respectful of the many dimensions which make for human well-being. More recently, church pronouncements have expressed an additional hope that economic development be ecologically responsible. In this the church is joining its voice to many others who have called for a world order that promotes just, sustainable development. Development which is sustainable means "paths of social, economic and political progress that meet 'the needs of the present without compromising the ability of future generations to meet their own needs.' "[54] Just development is concerned with equity among the nations of the globe; sustainable development is concerned with "equity between parents and their grandchildren."[55]

The Right Attitude

We have suggested that an attitudinal shift is foundational for dealing with the environmental crisis and that theology has a leading role to play in this endeavor. The main contribution of the church in the ecological crisis should be to foster a correct attitude toward all of God's creation. The motif of companionship is an important stage for establishing the imperative of a new way of relating to the created order. It is the opposite of that utilitarian approach which, in the words of John Paul, lacks "that disinterested, unselfish, and aesthetic attitude that is born of wonder in the presence of being. . . ."[56] The companionship motif is closer to the Hebraic vision of creation than it is to the prevailing western mentality. "[N]ature for the Greeks was 'dead,' only humanity was 'alive.' . . . The Newtonian conception of nature as a machine is not far from such a conception. In the biblical world-view, however, nature is not dead but alive. All the animals as well as humanity receive the divine 'breath.' "[57] Without that starting point of the Hebraic vision, the problems of fostering a politics and economics cognizant of the ecological common good will be multiplied.

We believe that humanity must rethink its place within creation so that human well-being is integrated within a wider setting, an ecological context. But this does not mean that the human is denigrated, nor does it mean the human does not have a special place in the plan of creation. A biocentric vision can lose sight of the fact that, while humanity is intimately related to the rest of creation, it has a unique role. Humanity alone is self-consciously aware of its creaturely status and dignity. It is vital to grasp the depth of the relationship that exists between humanity and all creation. It is as much a mistake to envision nature apart from humanity as it is to think of humanity apart from nature. The earth's environment is constantly evolving; non-human nature is not static. Other species than the human affect the global ecosystem.

> To maintain a preferred balance in nature (secure a flowing stream, preserve fish counts, rescue a mountain landscape, etc.), humans must intervene in natural processes. Likewise to arrest the depletion of the ozone layer, to check global warming, or to control acid rain, human beings must plan together and collaborate. . . . If the future of the earth itself is so entwined with conscious human decision, then one cannot avoid granting a special place to human beings in the cosmos.[58]

The theocentric vision of the Jewish and Christian traditions is able to correct the excesses of the anthropocentrism of modernity while avoiding the unrealistic biocentrism of those who relate humanity with non-human creation without distinguishing the unique role for the human species in the created order.

There is the danger that the language of companionship could be understood as simply fostering romantic anti-technologism. But a simplistic "back to nature" movement fomenting broad opposition to technology is a distortion of a proper theology of creation.[59] Technology is an outgrowth of our own human nature as creative beings. Unless we do violence to ourselves, technology will continue. What is needed is the wisdom to direct the process of technological change, not to stop it.

The question entails the relationship of technology, ethics and politics.[60] The primacy of ethics and politics over technology must be asserted. First, we must assess the goods which technology must serve. In order to guide change there must be a sense of the goods that are to be sought and an appreciation of the ranking of goods that may conflict.

Second, the political process is the locale where many of the moral choices will be worked through and implemented. Effective political action must follow careful ethical reflection. Only then can we know what policy choices are to be made, at what price, and what institutional arrangements are required for implementation. To fail in either of these realms is to permit technology to slip beyond human direction. From the outset, however, the scale of goods will be skewed unless humanity's relations with nature include an awareness of the "thou-ness" of creation.

A right attitude to creation is hampered by the predominant instrumental rationality of technologism.

> Western culture has a million ways of reinforcing the illusion that the world consists of inert stuff *out there* and that we are the active agents of change whose role is to get that stuff into shape. This is the assumption that has fueled the rapid development of technology. This is the assumption on which most modern education has been based, an education aimed at giving us the tools to exercise dominion over the earth.[61]

Theocentrism forces us to take another look at our assumptions. It helps us see that life is pure gift. If we can accept this, it is possible to admit that the world is not in our control. Within a theocentric vision the companionship motif of the biblical heritage encourages us to admit that "we do some shaping, to be sure, but we are also shaped by the relational reality of which we are a part. We are a part, and only a part, of the great community of creation."[62] Companionship strips us of the belief that the world is just *there*. We are in relation with a "thou" which is not of our making nor simply for us. Such an attitude serves to check the instrumental rationality which has fostered an abuse of the environment.

Although we believe that the retrieval of the companionship theme is required for the development of an environmental ethic, other elements are essential. A deepened commitment to the common good tradition and an expanded notion of the common good to include the good of ecological balance are necessary. Constructing new structures and institutions that can address the concerns which transcend existing territorial boundaries is also an essential aspect of an environmental program. Finally, development strategies which are both just and sustainable must constitute a significant part of an environmental ethic. But seeing the world rightly precedes our ability to act wisely and justly. The first task before us, that which theology can assist, is to revision all beings as united in their createdness, given to one another as companions, sacraments of the "love that moves the sun and other stars."[63]

6 | Incarnation and Patriotism

Christianity may seem to offer little assistance in responding to the problems posed by patriotism and nationalism. Indeed, it may appear to be a part of the problem. The Hebrew and Christian traditions have always lain open to the charge of scandalous particularism. On what possible ground can one justify the claim that God has singled out a particular people for a unique destiny? Has not the pretension to be a "chosen nation, a royal priesthood, a people set apart" led to exclusivism, chauvinism and sometimes expansionism thinly disguised as religious zeal?

By patriotism we mean a combination of affections for a nation-state. This can only arise if it is preceded by a set of feelings toward a place and a people. These two, place and people, go together, as Oliver O'Donovan has noted. " 'Place' differs from 'space' in that space is prior to culture or inhabitation. . . . A 'place' therefore is the fruit of civilization, an area of space that has been distinguished from other areas by the inhabitation of a community."[1] To develop a patriotic sense about a place is to form bonds of devotion and loyalty to a people who make that space their home. A country, a territorial area, becomes an object of patriotism when the people who civilize it establish claims of affection and faithfulness upon a person.

Patriotism must be distinguished from nationalism. The former is essentially defensive, but nationalism can be aggressive. Patriotism is concerned with a legitimate appreciation of the goods enacted by a given community of people and seeks to protect, promote and preserve those goods. Thus, an abiding loyalty and affection for particular communities of peoples is itself a good. Although nationalism may recognize restoring past injustices or advancing the national interest against other competing nation-states as valid rationales for war, the only justifying cause for war in Catholic social teaching is defense against aggression. Patriotism seeks the elements of the human good to be found in localism. Nationalism seeks the advancement of one group even at the expense of others and the greater common good.

The Scandal of Particularity

A theological rationale for a patriotism which is worthy of Christians and other people of good will must acknowledge, however, a seeming tension, even contradiction. It touches upon a fundamental issue in Christianity: How are we to think about "the scandal of particularity"? The problem of the value to be accorded being rooted in a given place and with a given people is both exemplified and immensely heightened by the claim of the incarnation. For the Christian tradition simultaneously proclaims the moral universalism of Jesus' message and maintains that God was incarnated in history at a particular moment as a member of a particular small but self-consciously chosen nation.

> When Yahweh your God has led you into the land you are to make your own, many nations will fall before you: Hittites, Girgashites, Amorites, Canaanites, Perizzites, Hivites and Jebusites, seven nations greater and stronger than yourselves. Yahweh your God will deliver them over to you and you will conquer them. You must lay them under ban. You must make no covenant with them: you must not give a daughter of yours to a son of theirs, nor take a daughter of theirs for a son of yours, for this would turn away your son from following me to serving other gods and the anger of Yahweh would blaze out against you and soon destroy you. Instead, deal with them like this: tear down their altars, smash their standing-stones, cut down their sacred poles and set fire to their idols. For you are a people consecrated to Yahweh your God; it is you that Yahweh your God has chosen to be his very own people out of all the peoples on the earth (Dt 7:1–6).

Even when Israel's understanding of God became sufficiently enlarged to include Yahweh's sovereignty over and interest in other nations, that sovereignty was seen as exercised for Israel's benefit, that interest was subordinate to God's predilection for the descendants of Abraham and Sarah. Thus God uses the rise of Cyrus for the return of Israel's remnant from captivity; Yahweh controls the destinies of the Babylonian and Persian empires for the sake of Israel (Ezr 1:1). When the later prophets celebrate the inclusion of other nations in the divine plan, they invariably depict those nations as coming to Israel; the Gentiles enter into Israel's felicity by recognizing the centrality of Israel (Is 60:1–16; Mic 4:1–4; Zech 14:16–19). In the constricted worldview of the ancient near east, amid nations each proclaiming its justification to dominance in accord with the will of its gods, Israel's claim to be a divinely chosen people may be understandable. But must not the pretension of any nation to a privileged position in history now seem both preposterous and dangerous?

The Perspective of the New Testament

Christianity seemed to have overcome the worst excesses of this claim to be a uniquely chosen people. Yet ambiguity pervades the gospels' depiction of Jesus himself. His attitude toward the centurion who seeks healing for a member of his household (Mt 8:5–13; Lk 7:1–10) and his parabolic response to the question of who one's neighbor is (Lk 10:29) seem to deemphasize the import of nationhood. The command to "make disciples of all the nations" (Mt 28:19a) sweeps aside the particularism of Palestinian life. But the dialogues with the Samaritan woman (Jn 4:7–29, esp. 22) and the Canaanite woman (Mt 15:21–28) show him as wedded to the particularism of nationhood, as able to advise his disciples not to visit pagan territory or enter a Samaritan town and to "go instead to the lost sheep of the house of Israel" (Mt 10:5b–6). The letters of Paul and the Acts of the Apostles demonstrate the struggle of the first generation of Christians to move beyond the confines of national religion to the perspective of a gospel without boundaries. The story of Peter's vision at Jaffa (Acts 10:9–16) culminates in his statement, "The truth I have now come to realize is that God does not have favorites, but that anybody of any nationality who fears God and does what is right is acceptable to him" (Acts 10:34–35). The unexpected success of the mission to Gentiles outside Palestine typified in the work of Paul and his companions led, however reluctantly, to the recognition by Jewish Christians that the salvation worked by God in Christ extended beyond their expectations and demanded the relativization of their own most dearly cherished assumptions. How difficult this expansion of the religious imagination was for even the most courageous of Jewish Christians can be seen in Paul. On the one hand, he insisted that, since all are "baptized in Christ, you have all clothed yourselves in Christ, and there are no more distinctions between Jew and Greek, slave and free, male and female, but all of you are one in Jesus Christ" (Gal 3:27–28). On the other hand, he could still worry over the status of Israel as a specially chosen people in the new dispensation and try to reconcile this privileged status with the universalism of the gospel on which his mission was predicated (Rom 9–11). The discovery that salvation in Christ knows no national bounds, that "God has no favorites" (Rom 2:11), is one of the greatest and most hard-won achievements of the first Christian generations.

But Christianity seems to harbor at its very heart a claim to particularism even more extraordinary than Israel's unique covenant relationship with God. "For of all the names in the world given to men, [Jesus Christ the Nazarene] is the only one by which we can be saved" (Acts 4:12). The central Christian claim is that the fullness of God's self-gift is given once for all and forever in the life, death, and destiny of Jesus. In him the full self-revelation of God is present in a unique and unsurpassable fashion. In him we have not simply words about God but the Word who is God. Consequently, there is no access to God save through him. "I am the way, the truth and the life. No one can come to the Father except through me. If you know me, you know my Father too. From this moment you know him and have seen him" (Jn 14:6–7). The self-communication of God, the mystery on which all that exists rests, is given absolutely once and once only, and then in the person of an itinerant Jewish prophet from a small town in a minor province of the Roman empire at the eastern end of the Mediterranean basin, who lived in the reigns of Augustus and Tiberius, who preached, apparently with little success, an apocalyptic proclamation of the imminent advent of God's eschatological kingdom, and who was betrayed by a close follower, denounced by his national and religious community, and executed by the governing Roman forces. Can the scandal of particularity be pushed to a greater extreme than this?

Christianity is not about timeless principles, eternal verities, unchanging moral norms. It is, first and foremost, an historical claim about the life, death, and destiny of a particular person, born of a particular ancestry in a particular nation, living in a particular place at a particular time under a particular government, speaking a particular language, praying in a particular religious tradition, who said and did particular things. "In the fifteenth year of Tiberius Caesar's reign, when Pontius Pilate was governor of Judaea, Herod tetrarch of Galilee, his brother Philip tetrarch of the lands of Ituraea and Trachonitis, Lysanias tetrarch of Abilene, during the pontificate of Annas and Caiaphas . . ." (Lk 3:1–2) is very different from "Once upon a time . . . ."

A now outmoded historical theology made great play of contrasting this insistence on the historical and particular with a subsequent "metaphysicalizing" of the gospel. This was often linked to a supposed "Hellenizing" of the original Palestinian "Hebraic" proclamation. The "christology from below" of the synoptic gospels was set out against the "christology from above" of the Pauline epistles and later New Testament literature. But this attempt to sort out two opposed lines of thought in the New Testament misses the point. The Christian proclamation is about the expression of the eternal in time and space. Even the earliest Christian documents, the letters of Paul, maintain that the salvation worked in Christ has been prepared from the beginning. Paul's argument in his letter to the Christians in Rome is that God's revelation has been made to all, through nature to the Gentiles, more explicitly through the law to Israel, and that all have been shown to be guilty. But this has all been in preparation for the great salvation now manifested in Christ: "Both Jew and pagan sinned and forfeited God's glory, and both are justified through the free gift of his grace by being redeemed in Christ Jesus who was appointed by God to sacrifice his life so as to win reconciliation through faith" (Rom 3:23–25). What has been revealed in Christ's life, death, and resurrection is a plan which begins with creation itself. Indeed, "the hidden wisdom which we teach in our mysteries is the wisdom that God predestined to be for our glory before the ages began" (1 Cor 2:7). This is the culmination which all creation has been groaning to bring to birth from its inception (Rom 8:22). The deutero-Pauline literature continues and develops these themes: "He has let us know the mystery of his purpose, the hidden plan he so kindly made in Christ from the beginning to act upon when the times had run their course to the end: that he would bring everything together under Christ, as head, everything in the heavens and everything on earth" (Eph 1:9–10). The itinerant prophet from Nazareth who suffered under Pontius Pilate is recognized as omnipresent in time and space:

> He is the image of the unseen God and the firstborn of all creation, for in him were created all things in heaven and on earth: everything visible and everything invisible, Thrones, Dominations, Sovereignties, Powers—all things were created through him and for him. Before anything was created, he existed, and he holds all things in unity. Now the church is his body, he is its head. As he is in the beginning, he was first to be born from the dead, so that he should be first in every way; because God wanted all perfection to be found in him and all things to be reconciled through him and for him, everything in heaven and everything on earth, when he made peace by his death on the cross (Col 1:15–20).

If these two themes, that of concrete and historical particularity and that of universality, are pitted against one another, the peculiar character of the Christian claim is missed. The heart of the Christian gospel is that the eternal plan of God is realized in a particular time and place, that the perfect self-expression of God has become flesh and dwelled among us (Jn 1:14). Any attempt to separate the particular and the universal distorts the mystery of the incarnation and necessarily misunderstands Catholicism. For the hallmark of Catholicism is its radical incarnationalism.

The Sacramental Principle and Concretized Love

Maintaining the incarnation in its fullness is the foundation of the sacramental principle: What is true always and everywhere must be expressed sometime somewhere. A sacrament is any person or thing, action or event, which occasions the realization and grateful acceptance of that which is always true but not always acknowledged. Thus the omnipresence of grace both allows and requires the manifestation of grace in particular acts and words. The notions of sacred time and sacred space are based on this principle. Because God is present everywhere, the divine presence must be attended to somewhere. The church or chapel is no more intrinsically holy than the parking lot or the supermarket. By consciously and deliberately noting the presence of God in the space consecrated as sacred, we may become aware of the divine presence in the unconsecrated secular spaces we more often inhabit. Likewise, because God is present always, the divine presence must be acknowledged sometime. We mark off certain times and days and seasons as holy. But surely all time is God's time, and Sunday is no more intrinsically the Lord's day than Tuesday or Thursday. But only by setting off some time as holy can we become sensitive to the sacredness of all time. The extraordinary becomes ordinary unless something ordinary is seen to be extraordinary.

A consequence of this sacramental principle is the crucial quality of the here and now. If the universal is experienced only in the particular, then the particular takes on great weight. The absolute can be found only in the concrete, the infinite in the finite, the divine in the creature. "Anyone who says, 'I love God,' and hates his brother, is a liar, since a man who does not love the brother that he can see cannot love God whom he has never seen" (1 Jn 4:20). Christianity is eminently practical and concrete. It does not exhort to love for the unseen. Rather, it maintains that the unseen can be loved only in the one who is seen. Agape, the prime metaphor for God in the Christian tradition (1 Jn 4:8, 16), is the effective willing of the good of the other, practical action in order to realize the best possible situation for the other. And the other cannot be dissolved into an abstraction, a faceless representative of an abstract humanity.[2] The other remains resolutely this particular person in this particular place at this particular time.

Of course, this insistence on concretized love for the particular person may appear parochial and narrow. After all, love for the people with whom we live and work and share our everyday lives can obscure our vision of a wider human community. It can cramp the heart and mind within a confined orbit of familiar, comfortable, like-minded persons. It reduces our capacity to build fellowship with those outside *our* circle, whether that circle be a neighborhood or town, a church or profession or social class, a language-group or nation. It may even seem that cosmopolitanism and localism are simply antagonistic, but a corollary of the sacramental principle is that one cannot exist without the other. The attempt to separate them is a denial of the principle.

Different Ways of Loving

Love, in English, names indiscriminately several distinct though related realities. Agape, self-gift, is the word which the Johannine strand of the New Testament uses as the least inadequate way in which to speak about God; it is the gift of the self to the other purely for the other's good. Eros is a movement of the self toward the other because of the other's capacity to satisfy the lover's desire. Sexual love is one obvious example, but the object of eros need not be personal; when one speaks of loving to play tennis or to hear a certain song or to eat some special food, the love in question is eros. Philia is a special form of eros. It is delight in the company of another; the satisfaction of the lover's desire is in the companionship of the one loved.

These three forms of what in English we name "love" are all good in themselves. But an over-spiritualized anti-humane exaltation of God's action at the expense of the creature's has in some versions of the Christian tradition not only distinguished agape from eros and philia but placed it in opposition to them. Then God alone is capable of agapic love, and agape alone is truly good. Eros and philia are always tinctured with some selfishness and are therefore, at least to some degree, evil. The love of God shed abroad in our hearts is agape, but it is always compounded with and adulterated by some admixture of human eros and philia. It follows that even our love for God is tainted by our erotic desire for the satisfaction of our restless hearts. Such a position rejects what has been called the Augustinian synthesis of divine agape and human eros in caritas. In this harsher non-Augustinian view, caritas is an alloy of natural inclination and the supernatural act of God which is agape. No human act of love has the purity of divine agape; it is always more or less debased by

the selfishness of eros or philia. To take pleasure in the beloved is the
sign that one's love is not agapic, and what is not agapic is not truly good.
The prejudice that virtue must always hurt is a popular form of this
antagonism between agape and eros.

The Thomistic strand within the Catholic tradition maintains that
nature is not the opponent of grace. Nature is that which is called into
existence by God precisely so that it can be the recipient of the divine
self-gift, the agape of God outside the Trinity which is grace. Nature
exists so that it can be engraced. Human love, necessarily expressed
erotically, i.e. as a desire of the heart seeking satisfaction, is not antagonistic to divine love, but complementary to it. Agape informs and finds
expression in human eros and philia. Taking pleasure in the one loved is
not a degradation of the love to which the gospel calls us. Love of those to
whom we are naturally attracted is no less fully Christian than love of
those whose company we do not spontaneously seek.

Thomas maintained the distinction but coordination of grace and
nature. "For there is no less order in the affection of charity, which is the
inclination of grace, than in the natural desire, which is the inclination of
nature; for both inclinations flow from the divine wisdom."[3] And it is
entirely natural *and good* that we find ourselves drawn more to some than
to others. Nor does this mean simply that proximity allows us to do more
for some than for others. Although we may not be able to extend *our*
"beneficence" to all, we are to be "benevolent" to all alike. Nevertheless,
"there is in fact another inequality in love from the simple fact that some
are loved more than others," and this is not necessarily wrong.[4] Thomas
admitted that one should love those who are good more than those who
are more immediately present to us but not as good, because love is
ultimately directed toward love itself, and the good are more loving. But
he added, "The intensity of love is measured with regard to the particular
person who loves. Accordingly, a person loves those who are closer to
him with a more intense affection for that good on account of which he
loves them than he loves those who are better for the greater good which
is theirs."[5] And this is perfectly correct, for those who are closer have
more relationships with us and can therefore be loved in more ways.

> For those who are not related to us we have no other friendship
> save that of charity. But for those who are related to us we have
> various other friendships according to the ways they are related
> to us. But since the good on which is based every possible kind
> of true friendship is directed as its end to the good on which
> charity is based, it follows as a consequence that charity re-
> quires the realization of every other kind of friendship, as the

art which concerns an end requires the art which concerns those things which are necessary for that end. And so loving someone because he is of the same blood or related to us or because he is a fellow-countryman or for any other reason whatever which is ordinarily in accord with the end of charity, can be required by charity. And thus, by both the prompting and the requirement of charity, we love in more ways those who are more closely related to us.[6]

As grace is expressed in and through nature, so agape is realized in and through our human eros and philia. Love for those closest to us—husband, wife, parent, child, brother, sister, friend, colleague, fellow citizen—is a sacrament of charity, universal love for all the creatures of God.

Moral Realism in Catholic Thought

A theology which pits nature against grace has an affinity with an individualist ethos. The separation of divine agape from human philia fits with an anthropology which sees relationship as more or less accidental to the human person. In such an anthropology, the fundamental constitution of the person is understood to be established quite apart from interaction with others. Indeed, entry into community with its obligations and responsibilities might be a hindrance to the freedom and thus the full development of the person. Having to assume roles with regard to others—parent, spouse, friend, neighbor, citizen, member of a profession, employee of a company—would then diminish one's individuality. One would be less oneself because of others. One would be fully oneself only in the privacy of the conscience "before God." In such a view, relationships of philia, companionship, partnership, friendship, cannot mediate the grace of God. They are too external to the "real person."

By the sharpest possible contrast, the Catholic vision of the human being is that one is by interacting with others. The actual, realized individual existence is achieved only in the interplay of countless relations, lifelong and transient, momentous and casual. Being this particular person means having these parents, those sisters and brothers, this spouse, these children, those teachers, speaking this language, living in that place at this time among those persons. Our relationships are who we are. If God graciously chooses to speak God's word to *us*, then God must speak through these relationships, for *we* are not to be found anywhere else. Our love for those to whom we are most intimately related is the way in which we experience divine love; we discover God's agape within our philia. This is the deep reason why the claim to love God whom we do not see apart from love for the brother or sister we do see can only be named a lie.

In a phenomenology of moral experience as seen through the Catholic perspective, the ethical demand is understood to arise not from an abstract natural law or from the positive revelation of the decalogue. Rather, the moral agent responds to the presence of the other, and in so doing responds to the Other. The human person finds himself or herself immersed in a sea of relationships which are simply *there*. The presence of the other may be welcome or not, desired or not, but the presence is not conjured up by the agent. The other stands before me as a presence to which I must respond.

Because we are born into the world with others, our moral development occurs as we move through various stages of growing sensitivity to the reality and worth of the others around us. These others may at times appear foreign or known, threatening or gracious. *How* we interpret and respond to the presence of the other is for us as moral agents to decide, but *that* we must respond is not open to our determination. Once the other's presence is part of our consciousness the only choice left is our decision whether to respond in a way that is appropriate or inappropriate. Non-responsiveness is impossible, but fitting or unfitting responses are possible.[7]

The sacramental principle of Catholic theology suggests that in each of these personal encounters there is always a depth dimension, whether acknowledged explicitly or not. The depth is evident to the person of faith who believes the response to the other is also a response to God. How one acts in relationship with other persons mediates how one relates with God. The Johannine axiom is true: We cannot claim to love God and not our neighbor.

The emphasis on the particularity of the other, which highlights the importance of personal relationships and local communities as the setting for encountering the universal, manifests itself in a variety of ways in Catholic social teaching. There is a long-standing bias toward the local and a disposition to favor natural communities in Catholic social thought. The principle of subsidiarity as articulated by Pius XI and subsequent popes reflects something of this sense.[8] So, too, does the social ideal of pluralism, the belief that a healthy society provides an array of intermediary communities between the individual and the larger institutions of societal life.[9] These formalized expressions of the tradition found in papal social teaching, however, do not create so much as reflect the Catholic imagination. Catholic social teaching articulates a view of social life as seen through the eyes of people already shaped by the sacramental principle.

Andrew Greeley has suggested that the vision of reality held by Catholics is the "low tradition" of Catholic social thought and it precedes the "high tradition" of such teaching as found in the modern papal encyclicals and conciliar teaching.[10] The hierarchy has tapped into the communal imagination of Catholic believers and expressed in precise if dry prose an interpretive grid or set of metaphors shared by many Catholics: an organic sense of societal organization, the central role of local communities, the importance of relationships for understanding personal identity, the unity of love of neighbor and love of God. By no means antipathetic to a universalist perspective, these are the way that people come to have concern for others beyond themselves.

As Paul Waddell suggests, the preferential love of friendship can school us in the virtues because "it demands getting outside ourself. . . ."[11] Because we cannot love in the abstract, we are trained in the art of love by loving concrete and particular persons. Waddell agrees with Thomas that, although we love those closest to us more intensely than those less immediate to us but who embody greater good, nevertheless we love those closest to us for the good we see in them. It is not just that we love *them*, but that we love the *good* in them.

A moral psychology that ascends above the particular in pursuit of the universal is thoroughly out of accord with the realism of Thomas and of the Catholic tradition at large which recognizes that the movement to the universal occurs only in the embrace of the particular. By the very fact that we are historically situated in company with some specific individuals we find ourselves able to love one group of human beings in more ways than we can love others. The exercise of charity takes place through a variety of forms, and those more closely related to us allow us to exercise that love in more ways, which, as Thomas noted, is by no means a hindrance to developing a true and universal charity. And so parenting, marriage, friendship and patriotism entail moral disciplines which develop the character of a person. "We think of ourselves not as human beings first, but as sons and daughters, fathers and mothers, tribesmen, and neighbors. It is this dense web of relations and the meanings which they give to life that satisifies the needs which really matter to us."[12] We love the good, but we can only love it as we experience it *in the concrete other*. Thus, because of its profoundly sacramental vision, Catholic social theory opposes the opposition of particular to universal.

The world is not on a pilgrimage from the particularist to the universalist; it is rather a combination of both. There may be rather more universalist norms and relationships available now than there were in the past, but that simply is because there are more relationships. The particularistic has survived and indeed probably provides the warmth and affection and support that makes universalistic behavior possible.[13]

The Quality of Loyalty

Patriotism, the love of one's community, nation and heritage, is a good to be fostered by the gospel precisely because it is a locus of our experience of love for others. As grace does not overcome the human but completes it, so patriotism is not an obstacle to Christian *caritas* which must be uprooted but a channel through which it can find expression. The core of Christianity is not an abstract expression of universal benevolence, the Christian tradition being far too tough-minded for such empty universals. The gospel of God become flesh is directed to flesh and blood human beings who live in a number of overlapping communities with multiple relationships.

The recent concern with narrative in moral philosophy and theology as a way of understanding the development of moral character also emphasizes the centrality of a person's relationships in any attempt to describe moral experience.

> Each one of us to some degree or other understands his or her life as an enacted narrative; and because of our relationships with others we have to understand ourselves as characters in the enacted narratives of other people's lives. Moreover the story of each of our lives is characteristically embedded in the story of one or more larger units.[14]

Among the candidates for such a larger unit is the country, and, as a result, the "contention of the morality of patriotism is that I will obliterate and lose a central dimension of the moral life if I do not understand the enacted narrative of my own individual life as embedded in the history of my country."[15] Then the value accorded not only the communal and particular but the quality of loyalty looms large.

Loyalty arises out of the experience of human life as incarnated. We are tied to a set of particulars—of place, time, ethos, relations. Coming to acknowledge, understand and act upon the responsibilities that emerge from such a thick web of connections is a major aspect of moral development. In Catholic social theory, loyalty is a basic assumption, for without it the creation of human relationships and communities is impossible.

But consideration of loyalty brings us to the ambivalence of the idea of patriotism. Patriotism is but "one of a class of loyalty-exhibiting virtues," e.g. marital fidelity, love of family, friendship, and devotion to institutions as diverse as schools and sports teams. All of these exhibit a "peculiar action-generating regard for particular persons, institutions or groups, a regard founded upon a particular historical relationship."[16] Of itself, loyalty appears to be a morally indifferent quality. The morally defining elements of loyalty are that to which one is loyal and why. In the case of patriotism, the object entails loyalty and devotion to a country. But the kind of claim which one's country makes on one's loyalty has been an emotionally laden question and never more so than in the last two centuries. Some answers to the question have been staggeringly destructive, for patriotism is easily confused with nationalism, and the latter has given the former a bad name.

Nationalism as Idolatry

However different in their presuppositions, Aristotle's *Nicomachean Ethics* and the first commandment of the decalogue (Ex 20:2-6; Dt 5:6-10) share a fundamental ethical wisdom. Aristotle built his treatment of the virtues on the principle that virtue stands as a mean between two opposed vices.[17] Or, put differently, vices are virtues taken to extremes. And similarly the prohibition of idolatry is placed at the head of the Mosaic code because all the subsequent evils condemned are rooted in the worship of false gods, the attribution of infinite value to what is of determinate finite value. Idolatry is the absolutizing of a relative good. It substitutes what is partial for the whole, the subordinate for the primary, the creature for the creator. Thus, sin, like vice for Aristotle, distorts reality by turning *a good* into *the good*.

Idolatry is always a temptation for Catholic Christianity, for it is a distortion of sacramentality. All too easily one moves from celebrating a sacrament, a creature in which the divine self-gift is communicated, to worshiping an idol, a creature which is identified with the divine self-gift. A sacrament uncovers the divine agape which grounds all reality in some particular person, place, thing, or event. An idol is a particular reality which claims exclusive presence of the divine within it. In the history of Christian thought the careful working out of christological formulae has been both intensely controversial and crucially important. For the claim of the incarnation stands perilously close to idolatry, and too frequently Christian devotional language runs to extremes which may claim the principle of the *communicatio idiomatum* as their justification but which in fact are monophysite or even docetic.

But often idolatry is not couched in explicitly religious terms. The idol is the meaning-giving, purposeful, empowering, and energizing element in life which claims an exclusive monopoly of meaning, purpose, power, and energy. Whatever it is of which one can say, "I live for that," or "because of that," is one's god. Such a god can be one's self or one's family, power or wealth, fame or pleasure, a job or profession, a system of ideas or a political program, the victory of science or the church or the party or "the revolution." An idol may be any good absolutized. The mark of all idolatry is that it is destructive, for the idolized good undercuts or swallows up all other goods. And for many, one of the most powerful and destructive idols of the last two hundred years has been nationalism.

The counter-enlightenment of the end of the eighteenth and the beginning of the nineteenth centuries was marked by a rejection of the claims for the all-sufficiency of either mathematics or the empirical method to resolve the questions of ethics and politics. The undeniable success of the method of observation and experimentation in yielding knowledge of the physical world had given rise to the optimistic expectation among many *philosophes* that the application of the same method to the human world would usher in an age of unprecedented social well-being. The achievement of happiness and freedom for all human beings in a conflict-free world of unimagined plenty was within sight, if not yet quite within reach. This dazzling vision justified the contempt with which many of the enlightened well-wishers of humanity regarded the ages prior to the burst of light which had broken on Europe in their own time. The remnants of those "dark ages"—feudal forms of government, monopolistic economies and, above all, the church—would now be swept away in order to usher in the new and glorious day of individual liberty and social progress. And the tool by which the walls of the decaying but still oppressive institutions of the past would be pulled down and the new enlightened world built was the inductive method of careful observance of data and uncovering of universally valid laws. The *philosophes* were confident that they knew what the goals of human life were —truth, happiness, justice, beauty. Knowledge of these universal goals was open to everyone, for they had been set, the deists and natural religionists said by God, the more religiously skeptical or straightforwardly atheistic said by nature. In either case, it was clear in what the good life consisted. The great question was how it was to be obtained. And the key to that question was now within the grasp of human beings—the correct application of the empirical method.

The counter-enlightenment questioned the possibility of transferring this method from the physical to the human world. Montesquieu firmly held that there were goals common to all persons in all ages, goods for which all should and do strive. But he emphasized that different cultures employ different means to those goals. A universal method seemed, in view of the facts of history and comparative cultural investigations, to be an unwarranted hope at best and a destructive imposition of one culture on another at worst. The most influential attempt to preserve the uniqueness of the specifically human realm, the domain of freedom and therefore of morality, from the mechanistic and deterministic laws yielded by the empirical method was that of Immanuel Kant. But there were those who went further and denied the fundamental presupposition of the *philosophes'* optimistic program, that the goals of human life were universal and recognizable by all rational persons.

Giambattista Vico insisted that even the goals of various cultures and of the same culture at various times in its history are incommensurable.[18] This he thought especially apparent in the study of poetry and literature. The kind of poetry written in one place and time is simply impossible for another place and time. The aristocratic heroic culture which produced the *Iliad* is entirely other in its vision of goodness, beauty and nobility in life from that of Horace or Dante or Shakespeare. The values which constitute the good life are simply different for one age and for another. Even if certain goals reemerge cyclically in human history, as Vico thought they did, universally valid and knowable goals are chimerical. Similarly, Herder and other German forerunners of romanticism, chafing under French hegemony in the arts and the intellectual world, embraced the uniqueness of particular languages and traditional cultures. Each cultural group is autonomous, striving for and in various ways realizing its own vision of truth, justice, beauty, true humanity, and this is mirrored especially in its linguistic history. Universal values are merely the abstractions of *philosophes* who would iron out the all-important differences between peoples and recast the world in their own "enlightened" image. Edmund Burke's vehement rejection of attempts to reform society in an accord with abstract universal principles, such as liberty, equality, and human fraternity, was rooted in the same recognition of historical particularity. Indeed, some insisted, the very notion of "humanity" was an unwarranted abstraction, a delusion of the *philosophes* which had addled their vision of reality and led to the bloody excesses of the French Revolution. Thus Joseph de Maistre complained,

The constitution of 1795, just like its predecessors, was made for *man*. But there is no such thing as man in the world. In the course of my life I have seen Frenchmen, Italians, Russians, etc.; I know, too, thanks to Montesquieu, *that one can be a Persian*. But as for *man*, I declare that I have never met him in my life.[19]

But if universal goals cannot be discerned, if, in fact, humanity is merely a theoretical term naming no concretely existing reality, then all values are localized and incommensurable. Truth, justice, beauty mean different things for different cultures and cannot be translated from one culture to another. Aristotle's sophist was correct: fire burns in Athens and in Persia, but the meaning of "justice" changes before our eyes. The locus of values can only be the cultural and ethnic group to which we belong and within which we share a common language and history. Thus an unintended result of the counter-enlightenment was the development of nationalism, understood as the claim that each nation has its own unique values, values which it does not and cannot share with foreigners, and which must be pursued if the nation is to be itself. This need not entail conflict. Herder, for example, stoutly maintained that each people ought to respect the integrity of other peoples' cultural values which are precisely the real values for those others. Being German was not a real or implied criticism of being French; it was simply different. That, Herder thought, was what the French *philosophes* did not appreciate. Technological means to ends were transportable across national boundaries, perhaps, but the ends remained distinct on either side. A German cultural hegemony would be as deplorable as the French cultural hegemony was.

But Herder's "Let-a-thousand-flowers-bloom" attitude was only one way to read the principle of national and cultural uniqueness. What if a nation's pursuit of its own historic goals brought it into conflict with other nations? Could Greece and Persia have simply lived side by side? Is "peaceful coexistence" always possible? What if a nation's natural and necessary historical development required *Lebensraum*? What if its "manifest destiny" ran athwart other peoples and cultures? The answer given by many was that a nation had to follow its genius ruthlessly, and the nineteenth century added that the law of the survival of the fittest demonstrated that a nation's success was the justification of its suppression or uprooting of others whose very inability to survive showed them to be inferior. The great rule of cultural history, and therefore of political and economic history as well, is, "To thine own self be true."

Thus each nation becomes the repository of its own unique goals. There is no good life for human beings, only the good life for Americans or for Germans, for Russians or for Chinese. The good of the nation is the only good its members can know. H. Richard Niebuhr described this reduction of universal goods to "our" goods as henotheism, a "social faith which makes a finite society, whether cultural or religious, the object of trust as well as of loyalty and which tends to subvert even officially monotheistic institutions, such as the churches."[20] Nationalism makes the nation's good the only knowable and available good; our good effectively, therefore, becomes the Good. In Niebuhr's terms,

> Nationalism shows its character as a faith whenever national welfare or survival is regarded as the supreme end of life; whenever right or wrong is made dependent on the sovereign will of the nation, however determined; whenever religion and science, education and art, are valued by the measure of their contribution to national existence.[21]

Nationalism subsumes all objects of loyalty under the nation. Like all idolatries, it is absolutist in its demands. To have but one object of loyalty is characteristic of the fanatic. But multiple loyalties both prevent extremism and produce moral quandaries, for sometimes our loyalties clash and one object of devotion must be given precedence over another.

The Nature of Loyalty

The problem of determining the proper object of loyalty is exemplified in an old philosophical conundrum. Two people are trapped inside a burning house. There is opportunity to save only one of the persons before the fire engulfs the entire house. One of those trapped in the building is a great social benefactor who has done much for society. The other person is one's mother. Which does one rescue?[22] Judged impartially, of course, a case can be made for the saving of the social benefactor. But few persons would have any hesitation in saving their mother because they do not make the judgment impartially but rather with a profound prejudice on her behalf. This comes from an instinctive sense of what is right. The particular relationship of parent and child gives rise to a set of affections which, in turn, are reflected in a sense of special responsibilities or duties toward one's mother.

Take another case, however. A man and woman apply for a job. Both possess the necessary credentials and qualities the job requires. It is clear that either one can fill the job vacancy adequately. But the employer is a man and decides to hire the male applicant because he is male. When challenged, the employer argues that he has a preference for workers of his gender and feels a special duty to promote their well-being. He makes this judgment based on his best instincts. Today such a position would be roundly condemned. This is obviously also true were "white" and

142 142   Fullness of Faith

"black" substituted for "male" and "female." Loyalty to one's gender or one's race does not receive the same approbation given to loyalty to one's mother. In the case of saving a parent's life we do not expect impartiality in treatment. In the case of hiring by gender or race, we have come to demand it.

Note that, in and of itself, the quality of loyalty is neither right nor wrong, neither wise nor foolish. Such judgments are appropriate only when we ascertain the object to which a person is loyal. Having affections of devotion and loyalty toward some particular objects, e.g. parents, is unexceptional. Having the same affections toward other particular objects, e.g. one's race or gender, is now deprecated. Whether one's country and its citizens are suitable as a particular object of loyalty is the question which must be asked about patriotism. This is not a question about loyalty or devotion per se. That there is a question about patriotism reflects the ambivalence people feel about whether a nation is a fit object of a person's loyalty. Is patriotism, like sexism or racism, an unjustifiable preference for a particular group which violates the norms of justice? Or is patriotism closer to love of one's parent, an understandable, indeed, admirable, partiality toward a group for which one rightly has special loyalty and devotion?[23]

Two issues must be distinguished. First, is one's country a proper object of loyalty? Second, since special duties flow from particular relations of loyalty and affection, how does one reconcile special particularist duties arising from patriotism, i.e. care for the well-being of fellow citizens, with the universal duty to love all people whether Jew or Greek, male or female, slave or free?

1. A Country as an Object of Loyalty

On what basis does a nation-state expect patriotism of its citizens? Why should a person exhibit loyalty and devotion to a country? Consistent with its anthropological premises, liberalism generally follows some sort of "mutual benefits" model of patriotic duty.[24] Society is essentially a contract entered into by individuals who come together for mutual benefit. Our obligations to our country derive from "our common participation in a practice from which all may expect to benefit."[25] This contractarian model of a nation-state emphasizes the social compact with others as being the result of a calculated judgment about personal benefit versus personal risk. In this view, it is permissible for the group to impose duties or even harms upon an individual, if some good comes of it, provided that the one suffering the harm is also a part of the society of mutual benefit. So we can ask things of the citizens of a nation which we would not require of those who are not part of the mutual benefit society, e.g. income taxes or military conscription.

Both the economic theory of liberalism and its political theory are grounded in this mutual benefits model. Public life, as experienced in political and economic society, is simply the coming together of those individuals who determine that the personal benefits of such association outweigh the risk. The nation-state provides us with security for person and property, organizes our transportation networks and educational system, and makes possible a number of other goods. We, in return, do our fair share to keep the enterprise going. Patriotism thus becomes an appreciative and willing holding up of one's end of the bargain.

There are a number of difficulties with looking at nation-states this way. First, it is not evident that "the scope of the mutual benefit practice coincides with existing social boundaries, rather than running within them or across them."[26] To justify nation-states as mutual benefit societies requires a more precise assessment of how benefits are produced and distributed than simply assuming that all within the territorial confines of a country share in anything resembling a fair distribution of benefits and burdens. There seems, on the face of it, reason to believe that the mutual benefits accrue on the basis of belonging to groups both smaller and larger than the nation-state.

Second, the mutual benefit model fails to describe the actual workings of societies. Were this model of society to provide the logic of our communal life, our duties only would be to those whose societal contribution benefited us. In accord with this logic, it is plausible to argue that persons with congenitally severe physical or mental handicaps should be excluded from the benefits of society.[27] Certainly it remains possible that those with some special compassion for the excluded group, e.g. their parents, might share some of the benefits they have earned with these handicapped persons, but nothing in the logic of the society requires such action. A mutual benefit model of social life leads to the exclusion of those persons or groups assessed to be non-contributors to the pool of benefits. "Yet," as Robert Goodin notes, "that does not happen, no matter how sure we are that handicapped persons will be net drains on the society for the duration of their lives."[28] This would seem to indicate that our social life operates on a standard other than the logic of the mutual benefit paradigm.

Another problem with the mutual benefit model, in addition to its inadequate description of the functioning of a national community, is its inadequate portrayal of the grounding of nationhood. The historical experience of being part of a nation is not that of a mutual benefit society so much as it is the warrant for establishing such a mutual benefit arrangement. "It is because we already share an attachment to our compatriots that we support the setting up of mutual benefit practices and the like."[29]

The recognition that we are already bound to a people encourages us to build political, economic and social institutions with them so that our commonalities might be enacted organizationally and thereby preserved and strengthened. Thus there are ties that precede the enactment of establishing mutual benefit structures.

Contrast the contractual way of seeing things with the communitarian model and its understanding of patriotism. In the communitarian view, the ties between persons are complex and spontaneous. Membership in a nation-state is not so much a reasoned judgment as an emergent reality beginning with experiences of kinship. Further, some goods, e.g. political self-determination, economic productivity in industrial society and enjoyment of a cultural heritage, positively require public life. Human beings are unable to live humanely save in society. Nationhood does not exist primarily as a legal reality but as a shared sense of being in union with others, of being in communion. A set of relations have been formed which form us. The organic nature of human society places us in a dense web of relationships that shape and bind us. Our ties to one another are more varied and less voluntary than the calculus of mutual benefit suggests. Patriotism in this context arises from the fact of association with a given people, place and way of life that provides elements of meaning and identity. There is a group to which one comes to feel loyalty and to which one wishes to contribute because membership in the group is integral to one's own sense of self. G.K. Chesterton suggested that patriotism is a common sense state of affairs.

> We all know a nation exists as we know a firm or a club exists; because we correspond with it, kick at it, hate it, owe money to it, or otherwise behave as if we were in communication with an agent and a personality. And the essence and necessity of a nation is nothing connected with its remote historic evolution; it is nothing even connected with its existing official scheme. A nation is a thing which recognizes a certain moral principle called patriotism, of which the opposite is treason.[30]

We find ourselves in a relationship with a country, a given place and people. Once relationships are established, expectations of faithfulness and affection develop. People come to see themselves as being part of the lives of others just as others become part of their lives. One's sense of self is bound up with the fact that one has this particular set of relations. The lesson of history confirms, and human nature seems to support, the claim that human beings identify with particular groupings of people.

But, as the recent history of central Europe and the Baltic republics indicates, the relationships associated with membership in a country must be actually experienced. A community must appear real before it can become an object of loyalty and devotion. We are not patriotic toward chimeras but only toward real countries. Here claims of loyalty can falter, for some nation-states do not constitute genuine objects of loyalty and devotion. Originally, social groupings began with family and extended kin, eventually expanding to ethnic ties. In some cases, as in the Baltics or much of central Africa, this is still the case. But in many countries a national character has been forged which transcends ethnic association without denying it. The English have developed a national character that would not have seemed possible to the Angles and Saxons and Normans. In a similar vein, Americans have from the outset of the United States as an independent country sought to create a unifying national character despite the multiplicity of ethnic groups making up the population.

National character must be forged over time, and there are elements of invention in creating such a distinctive identity among a people. Commonly found in the effort to build a country is an attempt to formulate a set of foundational myths about the origins of the country which ground certain values and folkways. Over time a distinctive, though not necessarily unique, communal narrative takes root in the collective imagination of a group. A way of life develops which reflects the shared values and aspirations of a people. Although at times hard to define, national character is what distinguishes one country from another. "Take away national character and all we are left with is *de facto* boundaries between states."[31]

Some countries are arbitrarily created territories, not truly reflective of a people. Some nations are not states, and some states are not nations. In such cases, the obstacles to patriotism are structural. Some communities of people do not live in a recognized territory with the freedom of self-determination, e.g. Tibetans. And there are territorial boundaries that encompass more than one people or divide a people who possess cultural integrity, e.g. Kurds in Turkey, Iraq and Iran.

But there is another kind of obstacle to patriotism, an obstacle found in countries such as the United States which do not have structural blocks to patriotism. The problem is cultural. In our country some people may not experience the nation as an object of loyalty because they do not experience social relations among fellow citizens capable of evoking affections of devotion and loyalty. Relations based on membership in a nation-state do not seem strong enough to influence us because of our growing inability to think about our relationships in ways other than the psychological. The lack of a vibrant public culture may lead some to doubt the existence of formative relationships which create a national character and shape personal identity. That a nation-state is a fitting object of loyalty and devotion, i.e. that patriotism is a natural affection, is only plausible once we acknowledge models of human relations that are not predicated on personal intimacy. One of the difficulties with understanding the communitarian vision is our woeful sense of public life impoverished by what Richard Sennett calls "the ideology of intimacy."[32] This "ideology" exalts intimacy and warmth and identifies impersonalism and coldness as the chief causes for human ills. It overemphasizes the psychological model of human relations and diminishes the political model. Human relations are deemed real and authentic only insofar as they approximate the familiarity achievable in one-on-one personal encounters, an arena which allows for intimate self-expression.

This imposition of the standards of private life on public life distorts the nature of public life. "We must learn to accept and appreciate the fact that public life is fundamentally impersonal. Relations in public are the relations of strangers who do not, and need not, know each other in depth."[33] The ideology of intimacy denies the worth of such public relations and makes the ties of social existence seem less real, less valuable and important than they are. In their quest for intimacy in public relationships and political life, people are inevitably disillusioned and may give up on social relations outside the circles of family and close friends. Only these latter seem real because they are intimate, and all other forms of social interaction are relegated to a shadowy backdrop.

Underestimating the value of public life as a result of measuring it by standards of private life leads to a dismissal of the nation as an object of allegiance. This bias of modern American society is based on a very restricted idea of human relationships. Other ages and peoples have understood that communities could be founded upon shared culture, mutually acknowledged obligations, a common history, even when the community was geographically dispersed and members not even personally acquainted.[34] To overcome the dominance attained by the categories of psychology when thinking about human relations, the communitarian model of society employs sociological and political renderings of human interaction. When social life is freed from the false expectations created by the ideology of intimacy, even essentially impersonal linkages among people may be recognized as creative of ties of affection and loyalty.

Nation-states *can* be seen as formative communities capable of inducing loyalty, if we understand that communities include groups of people who are socially interdependent, who share certain practices that define the group, and who participate in the decision-making of the group. National communities create a shared public culture. Communitarian theory attends to those aspects of social life which contribute to a person's sense of allegiance to and identity with a people. It understands particularistic bonds as inevitable and believes that they serve as necessary elements in the establishment of a person's identity.

2. *The Debate over Special Duties*

Granted that a relationship with a particular country is possible, the second question becomes important: Are there special duties of a patriot? It seems probable that there are since particular relationships almost always generate special duties, e.g. parenthood, marriage, friendship. But can an identity shaped by particular loyalties avoid standing in opposition to broader duties resulting from a universal regard for human well-being and a global awareness?

That some conflict does exist is obvious from the fact that particular relations do not justify any and all claims of preferential treatment. A daughter's duties toward her mother do not excuse favoritism in a court of law if the daughter is a judge and the parent the accused. Nor does a parent's special relationship with a child justify an elected official granting city contracts to a son who did not have to submit a bid in competition with others. In each of these cases, most people would readily agree that other more universal duties override the claims of any special duty. So, in any discussion of patriotism, careful attention must be paid to the way in which duties arising from the particular relationship with a country are reconciled with those universal duties which human beings have.

Moral universalism demands "that actions are to be governed by principles that give equal consideration to all people who might be affected by an action."[35] Particularism, on the other hand, suggests "one ought to give preferential consideration to the interests of some persons as against others, including not only oneself but also other persons with whom one has special relationships."[36]

The universalist approach diminishes the importance, the ethical significance, of national ties. In a century which has seen two world wars and hundreds of other small but bloody conflicts, it is appealing to offer a counter-weight to idolatrous nationalism. Have we not had enough of *Volk* and *Vaterland*? Have not enough died in the pursuit of ethnic rivalries? Must more die so that another group's "way of life" can be safeguarded or its "manifest destiny" achieved? Those who promote a universalist perspective can make a powerful appeal to recent history to support their belief that drawing the boundaries of moral duty too narrowly is a constant and dangerous temptation.

For the universalist, particularist loyalties stand in the way of establishment of a moral order that treats all justly. Instead of focusing on particularity, the universalist holds out a different approach to moral reflection, "namely, the view that the subject matter of ethics is persons

considered merely as such, independent of all local connections and relations."[37] This way of thinking entails a certain view of moral agency:
"The moral subject is seen as an abstract individual possessed of the
general powers and capacities of human beings—especially the power of
reason—but not fundamentally committed to any particular persons,
groups, practices, institutions, and so forth."[38] Such a description of
moral agency permits the full weight of our general duties to all humankind to stand out and override the various biases which we have due to
our personal histories. By focusing on universal duties we lessen the
risks of patriotic sentiment that permits one to favor some over others.
Certainly an ethic faithful to the gospel must be universal in scope. The
parable of the good Samaritan (Lk 10:25–37) clearly indicates the obligation to treat all people as neighbors; the particularist love for those near
to us is to be extended to embrace all people. Acknowledging special
duties seems, on the face of it, to undercut universal neighborly love.
Within modern Catholic social teaching the emphasis on human rights
reflects the universal duty of love of neighbor.[39]

In reply to the universalists' charge regarding the narrowness of
patriotism, particularists ask about the feasibility of a universalist position: Does such an abstract depiction of the human actor strip us of our
humanity by denying our incarnated nature? One defender of the particularist side in the debate believes that "[t]he attempt to depict a form of
human love which is without particularity, reciprocity or preference has
never yielded anything but a cold-blooded monstrosity."[40] The particularist school sees local loyalties and duties as central if human love is to be
anything more than an abstract wish. Only by rooting oneself in the
dense web of human relations and recognizing the weight and pull of
many personal bonds can one establish a self capable of responding to the
ideal of love. Thus for the particularist the acknowledgement of special
relations and the duties that arise from them is fundamental to human life.
Love, although the greatest of all, like the other virtues, must be prac-
ticed in actual historical settings.

To eradicate special duties, then, is neither possible nor desirable.
The particularity of our loving is one of the features of human life.
Special relations do not violate charity, for, as Thomas observed, we
express our love quite properly through the medium of particular relations with family, friends, co-workers, fellow-congregants, and
members of our nation-state. We acknowledge the good in them and so
love the good by loving them; the realism of Catholic theology reminds
us it is not only that we love the *good* in them but that we love the good in
them. In explaining our affection for a certain object we may "cite as
partially supporting reasons one's country's or one's spouse's merits,"

yet these are only partial reasons, "just because what is valued is valued precisely as the merits of *my* country or spouse. . . . The particularity of the relationship is essential and ineliminable."[41]

The particularist sees in the parable of the good Samaritan no denial of particular relations and special duties. Rather, the text serves to remind us that, perhaps like the priest and Levite who, preoccupied with their religious duties in Jerusalem, passed by the injured man on the road, we may espouse love of humanity but overlook actual persons. The Christian scriptures should not be interpreted as denying the urgency of special duties that arise from specific historical relationships. "Far from denying the significance of proximate relations, the parable [of the good Samaritan] discovers them where they are not looked for, nearer to us, not further away, under our very noses."[42]

Catholic social teaching reflects elements of both the particularist and universalist positions. It accepts both the inevitability and the value of particular relations as well as the special duties which flow from them. It also acknowledges and commits itself to the requirement that no person is excluded from the range of our moral concern. But this leaves unanswered the question how special duties can be reconciled within a view of morality that insists on the need for universal regard. Perhaps it is true, as Oliver O'Donovan argues, that "[t]he universal claim of every human being upon every other is, after all, more of a critical principle than a substantive one. To love everybody in the world equally is in fact to love nobody very much."[43] Yet we should not minimize what forms universal love can take.

Moral universalism can take many different forms, but the variant we find most attractive and which finds strong support in Catholic social teaching is that of human rights.[44] While love for the distant neighbor is quite unlike love for those with whom we have closer relations, it does not necessarily follow that love for all persons is a purely critical principle devoid of all substance. A commitment to human rights theory as articulated in modern Catholic social teaching is a useful way of expressing universal-regarding love. An interpretation of human rights theory illustrates how love of a particular nation can be reconciled with a global ethic that pushes us toward a universal love.

The growing centrality of human rights theory in Catholic social theory and pastoral strategy reflects the increased awareness on the part of the church of the need for a global ethic. According to Catholic teaching, human rights serve the aim of protecting and promoting those goods —personal, social, institutional—which secure human dignity and allow a person to enter into communal life. The necessary goods can be broadly divided into categories of freedom (political and civil rights) and well-being (social and economic rights). All persons have equal claim to these fundamental goods. The claims involved in human-rights theory generate corresponding duties upon others. Since all have the right, all have the corresponding duty. Thus, each person is called to active concern for the dignity of all people; since all are equal in dignity no one can be indifferent to the plight of another whose dignity is violated. No barrier of gender, creed, race, class, or nationality can be erected which places anyone beyond our moral concern. Because these rights are based on the foundational claim of human dignity, our support for them must be all-inclusive. No one can be excused from addressing rights-claims on the basis of territorial or national boundaries. We all have general claims against others by virtue of being human, and we all have general duties toward each other by virtue of being human.

At the same time, the Catholic tradition holds to the value of particularism. For in addition to general rights and duties, Catholic teaching admits of special rights and duties based on particular relations of family, friendship, occupation, citizenship, etc. These special duties can be thought of as "distributed general duties," i.e. special duties are the means "whereby the moral community's general duties get assigned to particular agents."[45] Special duties belong not only to individual persons but to social groups. Frequently it is efficient to set up social practices and institutions to secure rights. These group structures are then held to the standard of meeting the responsibilities generated by the special duties. Commitment to the human rights of all persons justifies the creation of social institutions which secure those rights and support their enactment. For practical reasons of administration, communication, and cost such institutions may be limited in scope to particular physical territories. As long as others not living in those areas are not denied the opportunity to develop their own structures, no harm is necessarily done by territorial limitation on membership. The loyalty and devotion proceeding from a person's experience of such social arrangements and personal interactions which provide for his or her freedom and well-being induces a commitment to protect and maintain those structural arrangements and human relations. Of course, it is hardly a matter of indifference how general duties get assigned. The assignment of general duties to particular agents ought not to be arbitrary. Certain personal and group relationships make some far better suited than others to be the primary agents responsible for addressing a rights claim. General duties designated to particular agents should reflect that human beings are incarnated beings, people with particular identities and histories.

This approach to countries, human rights claims, and the duties they generate fits well with the Catholic understanding of both moral psychology and the social principle of subsidiarity. We believe that it appreciates that personal relations can generate loyalties and that a bias toward the local and particular in social life is not necessarily wrong. Evidently patriotism is no more to be understood as hatred of all foreigners than friendship is to be interpreted as despising those with whom one is not acquainted. A preferential love of some should not be seen as antithetical to universal regard for all. Parents *do* have special duties toward their children, teachers to their students, public officials to their constituents, citizens to one another. As with family and friendship, so too with nation: by loving the particular we can love the universal. There is no inherent contradiction between patriotism and a deep attachment to the well-being of all people. Although our relationship with fellow nationals generates certain special duties, these duties are not the entirety of our moral duty. Patriotism can only be defended as part of a larger morality.

This latter point can be seen when those primarily responsible for meeting a duty fail, for then other agents can and ought to act, e.g. abusive parents can lose custody of their child to another who will care for it. When the social structures created to guarantee human rights fail, appeal is made to other agents to secure those rights which the agent ordinarily designated cannot or will not secure. In line with the principle of subsidiarity, there may be several levels of agents designated to secure a general duty. Thus, the government of a nation-state is not the only social institution responsible for human rights protection, even if ultimately it is often held responsible for this special duty. Persons rightly make claims which are to be met by fellow citizens acting through agencies such as the national government, but others beyond the territorial boundaries of the nation-state can also be responsible if the agents for the assigned general duty fail to act properly. Cases may arise when universal regard, often expressed in the language of human rights, requires something in addition to a love and respect for those living within the nation-state. In such cases, regard for human rights makes it necessary to acknowledge the moral duty one has to foreign neighbors whose human rights are not being protected by their own national government. Then, international non-governmental agencies—e.g. Catholic Relief Services, the Red Cross, the United Nations—may serve as the designated vehicles through which general duties correlative with human rights are met. A proper love of country can admit this, and the virtue of patriotism not only poses no obstacle to a commitment to universal human rights, it demands such commitment.

Catholic social teaching regards national sovereignty as a real but relative value. It recognizes the political structures, e.g. international law on sovereignty, which support the existence of particular national relationships. Human rights claims can, however, be of such urgency and significance that a relative good such as territorial sovereignty can be overridden. Particular duties and commitments are always contextualized by the requirement to serve the universal common good. But to assert the relative value assigned to love of country is not to deny the real value of the same. A value need not be absolute to be important, a duty need not be supreme to be significant, and love of country as expressed in a genuine patriotism can be a value and duty when ethically situated in the universal common good which relativizes it.

Patriotic Style

When the Spanish-American War was fought in 1898, many Americans patted themselves on the back and saw in their nation's victory a sign of the country's coming of age. This self-gratulation concerned William Graham Sumner. In assessing the outcome of the war, Sumner wrote:

> At present the whole periodical press of the country seems to be occupied in tickling the national vanity to the utmost by representations about the war which are extravagant and fantastic. . . . Patriotism is being prostituted into a nervous intoxication which is fatal to an apprehension of truth. It builds around us a fool's paradise, and it will lead us into errors about our position and relations. . . .[46]

Sumner found the patriotism of the "fool's paradise" dangerous because it celebrated policies which carried within them the seeds of destruction of that which a genuine American patriot should cherish, the institutions and culture of democracy. The great enemy of democracy, Sumner believed, was plutocracy. And in the struggle between these two styles of governance, "militarism, expansion and imperialism will all favor plutocracy. . . . They will take away the attention of the people from what the plutocrats are doing."[47] Sumner, the leading American spokesman for "social Darwinism," argued that the muscle and sinew of democratic life would be weakened by the misdirection of people's energy and attention to imperialistic adventures while the affairs of government fell into the hands of elites—political, bureaucratic, corporate and military. Focusing on the minor achievements of episodes like the war with Spain, Sumner held, blinded citizens to the true accomplishments associated with the creation of a democratic and pluralistic nation.

> There are people who are boasting of their patriotism, because they say that we have taken our place now amongst the nations

of the earth by virtue of this war. My patriotism is of the kind which is outraged by the notion that the United States never was a great nation until in a petty three months' campaign it knocked to pieces a poor, decrepit, bankrupt old state like Spain. To hold such an opinion as that is to abandon all American standards, to put shame and scorn on all that our ancestors tried to build up here. . . .[48]

Such was Sumner's harsh assessment of the state of American patriotism at the turn of the century.

After the 1960s, with the agony of Vietnam abroad, racial strife at home, and the accompanying social revolutions, and after the rise of the "Me Decade" in the 1970s, some Americans sensed that patriotism had died. No longer was Sumner's false patriotism a problem; rather, it was the lack of any loyalty to the nation that troubled people. In recent years we have seen what has been regarded as a revival of patriotism. The Olympic Games in Los Angeles in 1984 were the scene of boisterous protestations of love of country as the host fans constantly chanted that the U.S.A. was number one. In the 1988 presidential campaign much was made of the Pledge of Allegiance, while the Republican candidate's preferred backdrop for campaign speeches was a huge flag. Not long after that election, the Supreme Court ruling that burning the American flag is an act of protected free speech set off a chorus of voices calling for a constitutional amendment to reverse the Court's decision. Most dramatically (and tragically), the war in the Persian Gulf was accompanied by attention-grabbing calls for support for the troops. Yellow ribbons flourished, along with bumper stickers and flags. The long series of parades and celebrations following the war was interpreted as a new wave of patriotic pride sweeping the land. Common to all these elements was the demonstrative, we would suggest meretricious, manner in which patriotism was proclaimed. To a degree, it is a question of style: some like ticker tape, brass bands, and hoopla, while others prefer less grandiose expressions of love of country. But more than matters of style are at stake, since the risk is that the more showy approach to patriotism masks a lack of substance. There is the danger that love of country has been reduced to superficial exhibitionism, patriotism Las Vegas style—lots of glitter, neon, and noise, lacking any attribute of gravity, depth and inwardness.

Based on Sumner's complaint and our concern about the new patriotism, one might conclude that Americans are especially prone to this debasing of national loyalty. But it is evident in other nations, too. What is common to all such cases is misplaced affection, investing significance in what is marginal while at the same time losing sight of a nation's genuine achievements. G.K. Chesterton captured the essence of the problem in an essay which brought him much attention early in his career. In 1901, during the Boer War, he wrote a piece entitled "A Denunciation of Patriotism," in which he decried the "decay of patriotism" and protested that the true meaning of love of country had been lost. He opposed those who held the view, "My country, right or wrong":

> It is like saying, "My mother, drunk or sober." No doubt if a decent man's mother took to drink he would share her troubles to the last; but to talk as if he would be in a state of gay indifference as to whether his mother took to drink or not is certainly not the language of men who know the great mystery.[49]

Needed, Chesterton wrote, was a revival of sincere love of country, and this was not to be found in parades and ribbons. "For the first of all the marks of love is seriousness: love will not accept sham bulletins or the empty victory of words. . . . Love is drawn to truth. . . ."[50] For Chesterton, like Sumner, the sign of patriotism's degradation was that people had come to glory in the lesser things that marked the English nation. Why, he wondered, did the English beam over "trade, physical force, a skirmish at a remote frontier, a squabble in a remote continent"?[51] He observed the irony that those who thought themselves patriots did not really know the merits of the English people. Education was at fault in this, he concluded, for it did not teach the truly humane elements of the nation's heritage. Lack of historical knowledge led to a vulgar patriotism.

> [W]e have had our punishment in this strange and perverted fact that, while a unifying vision of patriotism can ennoble bands of brutal savages or dingy burghers, and be the best thing in their lives, we, who are—the world being judge—humane, honest, and serious individually, have a patriotism that is the worst thing in ours. What have we done, and where have we wandered, we that have produced sages who could have spoken with Socrates and poets who could walk with Dante . . . ? We are the children of light, and it is we that sit in darkness. If we are judged, it will not be for the merely intellectual transgression of failing to appreciate other nations, but for the supreme spiritual transgression of failing to appreciate ourselves.[52]

The agreement on the topic of patriotism between Sumner and Chesterton, who are so different in so many other ways, is striking. Both

saw the positive elements of love of country undermined by a championing of lesser qualities in a nation's experience. And both called for greater
appreciation for what they judged to be their country's true historical
achievements.

The cautionary words of both Sumner and Chesterton need to find a
hearing within American life at present. Such has been the decline in
education within our country that many even among those who graduate
from college have only a rudimentary knowledge and appreciation of
United States history, our political institutions, our social virtues, our
cultural strengths. In a society that has failed to pass on its historical
achievements we ought not to be surprised to find a citizenry which
glories in the trivialities of the moment. Our plight today is akin to that of
Chesterton's England in the Boer War: we do not know what we ought
to love about our nation, and so we express our misplaced love in a style
that is shallow and unserious. Because we do not understand what is good
about our nation, we have little grasp of what is good about other nations.
A healthy and wise love of the United States would attune us to appreciate other countries, just as genuine love of those who are family and
friends schools us in how to love beyond the circle of intimates. But
because our national pride is centered in lesser things and consequently
expressed in lesser ways—jingoism, triumphalism, chauvinism—what
passes for patriotism in this country easily becomes a threat to those in
other countries.

We need to reflect on what is truly of value in the American experience: self-government by the people, legislative and constitutional protection of the rights of minorities from majority abuse, non-violent
transfers of political power from one set of leaders to another, acceptance of pluralism not simply as a necessity for civic peace but as an
appreciative expression of the benefits of diversity, hospitality toward
new immigrants of different backgrounds, scientific and technological
creativity, works of literature, art, and music which feed the spirit. These
are the goods which this particular nation has embodied in history. Love
of these goods might lead to a more serious participation in the public life
of a nation through voluntary associations, public conversation, support
for public institutions, engagement with the political and electoral processes, and honest payment of taxes. Equating patriotism with flag-
waving and ticker-tape diverts our attention from the social practices of
genuine citizenship in a democratic nation. Replacement of the practices
of citizenship by highly demonstrative actions which require little self-
investment in public life is a symptom of a social illness, cheap patriotism
that knows little of sincere love of country. As Chesterton wrote: "People seem to mean by 'the love of country' not what a mystic might mean

by the love of God," but "something of what a child might mean by a love of jam."[53]

Idolatry is always present in human affairs when the universal is reduced to the particular. A peculiarly virulent form of this idolatrous tendency is the narrowness of nationalism which ignores the interdependence of persons and countries and the equality of all before God. This dark strand in the fabric of human history is not the whole story of particularist affections, however. Loyalty to country may in fact be a way of mediating our love of neighbor. And we propose that love of neighbor is, in truth, a mediation of what the mystic means by the love of God.

7 | The Communion of Saints and an Ethic of Solidarity

Americans seem to have a leaning toward proclaiming new world orders. George Bush's oft-repeated phrase for the international order which should follow the collapse of the bipolar world of the cold war is the latest echo of the revolutionary hopes of the generation of the nation's founders. Wordsworth's recollection of the boundless hope and promise inspired by the early stages of the French Revolution, "Bliss was it in that dawn to be alive, / But to be young was very Heaven!"[1] may seem to us more accurately to express the millenarian expectations of European romantics and revolutionary theorists than the sober classical figures of the signers of the Declaration of Independence. But the conviction that something totally new was happening, that the oppressive weight of the past had been sloughed off and humanity could stand upright again or perhaps for the first time, was not totally foreign to the gentlemen gathered in Philadelphia for the second continental congress. The French attempt to restart the calendar, beginning with September 22, 1792, the inauguration of the Republic, as the first day of the year I, was a more thorough attempt to enact the spirit of a claim made on the great seal of the United States.

America's Love of the New

Novus ordo seclorum reads the motto on the great seal and, lest we forget whence that new order of the ages begins, the numerals MDCCLXXVI are carved into the base of the pyramid depicted on the seal. History starts fresh with the founding of the new American nation, the motto about the bottom of the seal claims, and the motto above assures us that *annuit coeptis*, "He [presumably God] has favored our beginnings." The image on the seal is a proud claim, an assurance, and a prophecy. The pyramid, symbol of permanence amid the flood and decay of history, rises from the base marked with the date of American inde-

157

pendence to the pinnacle where an open eye surrounded by rays of light looks out upon us. The "new order" of time begins in the American revolution and culminates in a fully awakened humanity which sees clearly in the light. The new order of the ages culminates in the enlightenment of all.

Eight years after the date at the base of the pyramid, in 1784, Immanuel Kant published "An Answer to the Question, 'What is Enlightenment?' " which could well serve as a commentary on the great seal of the new nation across the Atlantic. "Enlightenment," he wrote,

> is man's release from his self-incurred tutelage. Tutelage is man's inability to make use of his understanding without direction from another. Self-incurred is this tutelage when its cause lies not in lack of reason but in lack of resolution and courage to use it without direction from another. *Sapere aude!* have the courage to use your own reason!—that is the motto of the enlightenment.[2]

The others from whose direction we must resolve to be free are not only the princes and powers of the present but also, perhaps even primarily, the dead. The past too easily and too often enchains the movement of the present toward the solution of that problem which is "the most difficult and the last to be solved by mankind,"[3] namely, "the realization of Nature's secret plan to bring forth a perfectly constituted state as the only condition in which the capacities of mankind can be fully developed, and also bring forth that external relation among states which is perfectly adequate to this end."[4] The founders in Philadelphia might not have agreed in every respect with the philosopher of Königsberg, but they thought that they had taken a long step toward the goal of history, true enlightenment based in real freedom, when they founded the new nation. They were laying the foundation of the pyramid from whose top one would truly see. But to do so, did they have to break with the past?

The claim that a "new order of the ages" had begun seems to say that they did. And certainly many who have celebrated them and the nation they founded have spoken as though they did. Almost immediately the hallmark of the new country's identity became newness and the concomitant rejection of the past. In 1782, Crèvecoeur tried to answer the question "What is an American?" in the third of his *Letters from an American Farmer*, and the answer turned out to be that the American is "new."

> He is an American, who, leaving behind him all his ancient prejudices and manners, receives new ones from the new mode

of life he has embraced, the new government he obeys, and the new rank he holds. He becomes an American by being received in the broad lap of our great *Alma Mater*. Here individuals of all nations are melted into a new race of men, whose labours and posterity will one day cause great changes in the world. . . . The American is a new man, who acts upon new principles; he must therefore entertain new ideas, and form new opinions.[5]

To be new meant to reject the old; if the future was to be embraced, the past had to be relinquished. "East were the / Dead kings and the remembered sepulchres: / Ahead of them was the grass," wrote Archibald MacLeish.[6] In the movement westward, across the Atlantic, across the mountains, across the Mississippi and the plains and the deserts, the great trek was from the east identified with the oppressive past ("dead kings") to space ("the grass") where time was overcome and a new order of the ages could begin.

The American Mind

Not only were dead kings to be abandoned, so too were dead thinkers and writers, dead poets and sages. They might provide inspiration, but the inspiration was to do something new, not repeat what they had done. They provided incentive, not models. "Meek young men grow up in libraries, believing it is their duty to accept the views which Cicero, which Locke, which Bacon, have given; forgetful that Cicero, Locke, and Bacon were only young men in libraries when they wrote these books," Emerson warned.[7] If to be an American was to be "new," as in Crèvecoeur's definition, with new ideas, new principles and new opinions, then an American could not learn from old books. Each generation had to think through the great questions afresh, learning something perhaps from the preceding generation but scarcely needing to go further back than that, save for inspiration. "Each age, it is found, must write its own books; or rather, each generation for the next succeeding. The books of an older period will not fit this."[8]

Newness was so constitutive of American-ness that America could be corrupted by the dead weight of its own past after it had existed a few years. It could maintain its purity only by an ongoing revolution. Reflecting on Shay's rebellion, Thomas Jefferson wrote to James Madison in 1787 that such public turbulence "prevents the degeneracy of government, and nourishes a general attention to the public affairs. I hold it that a little rebellion now and then is a good thing, and as necessary in the political world as storms in the physical."[9] Later that same year he returned to this theme in another letter to Madison: "The late rebellion in

Massachusetts has given more alarm than I think it should have done. Calculate that one rebellion in 13 states in the course of 11 years, is but one for each state in a century and a half. No country should be so long without one."[10] Throughout his long life, he argued for a peculiar plan to institutionalize periodic revolution whereby each generation would reform itself into a political community; by elaborate computation, he had arrived at nineteen years as the limit for all laws and public debts after which the slate should be wiped clean and new constitutions drafted.[11] Behind this odd scheme was the deeply rooted conviction that the present must be liberated from the past.

> On a similar ground it may be proved that no society can make a perpetual constitution, or even a perpetual law. The earth belongs always to the living generation. They may manage it then, and what proceeds from it, as they please, during their usufruct. They are masters too of their own persons, and consequently may govern them as they please. But persons and property make the sum of the objects of government. The constitution and the laws of their predecessors [are] extinguished then in their natural course with those who gave them being. This could preserve that being till it ceased to be itself, and no longer.[12]

> It is now forty years since the constitution of Virginia was formed. [European tables of mortality] inform us, that, within that period, two-thirds of the adults then living are now dead. Have then the remaining third, even if they had the wish, the right to hold in obedience to their will, and to laws heretofore made by them, the other two-thirds, who, with themselves, compose the present mass of adults? If they have not, who has? The dead? But the dead have no rights. They are nothing; and nothing cannot own something. Where there is no substance, there can be no accident. This corporeal globe, and everything upon it, belong to its present corporeal inhabitants, during their generation. They alone have the right to direct what is the concern of themselves alone, and to declare the law of that direction; and this declaration can only be made by their majority.[13]

> Can one generation bind another, and all others in succession forever? I think not. The Creator has made the earth for the living, not the dead. Rights and powers can only belong to

persons, not to things, not to mere matter, unendowed with will. The dead are not even things. The particles of matter which composed their bodies, make part now of the bodies of other animals, vegetables, or minerals, of a thousand forms. To what then are attached the rights and powers they held while in the form of men? A generation may bind itself as long as its majority continues in life; when that has disappeared, another majority is in its place, holds all the rights and powers their predecessors once held, and may change their laws and institutions to suit themselves.[14]

The dead have had their day and are silent; public conversation goes on among the living.

The "Mystic Chords of Memory"

And yet it should be noted that the motto on the great seal of the United States which proclaims the "new order of the ages" is drawn from Virgil.[15] One can scarcely invoke the words of a Roman poet to claim that the past is dead. Is liberation from the past possible? Is it desirable? Is it true that "the dead have no rights"? Are the dead "nothing"? Jefferson's insistence that the dead are indeed "nothing" and therefore can make no demands upon the living to which the latter need attend has been counterbalanced by Lincoln's invocation of "mystic chords of memory"[16] which unite us with preceding generations. In a statement which has become as hallowed a text in American life as Jefferson's Declaration, Lincoln insisted that "the living" must "be dedicated here to the unfinished work which they who fought here have thus far so nobly advanced." The dead do indeed make demands upon the living and rightly so. From them "we take increased devotion to that cause for which they gave the last full measure of devotion." The living are obliged to be "highly resolved that these dead shall not have died in vain." Only through fulfilling their obligations to "these honored dead" can the living effect something truly new, "that this nation, under God, shall have a new birth of freedom." And in fidelity to the future the living must determine "that government of the people, by the people, for the people, shall not perish from the earth."[17] For Lincoln, profound obligations and duties link the living with the dead and the unborn. The attempt to be free of the past is an unworthy illusion and to be free of the future a dangerous mistake. Far from society restarting itself every nineteen years, as Jefferson suggested, Lincoln reminded his contemporaries that they had an obligation to what had been done "four score and seven years" before.

On this issue, if not on others, Lincoln would have recognized Edmund Burke rather than Jefferson as a close companion in thought. Burke agreed with Jefferson that society is a contract but, he argued against the French revolutionaries' attempt to restart history, a very particular sort of contract.

> It is a partnership in all science; a partnership in all art; a partnership in every virtue, and in all perfection. As the ends of such a partnership cannot be obtained in many generations, it becomes a partnership not only among those who are living, but between those who are living, those who are dead, and those who are to be born.[18]

Burke's insistence was that society is far too complex in its aims, its methods and its institutions to be rechartered in every generation. He held that, at least in England, the rights of human beings, including presumably those with which Jefferson had declared they are endowed by their creator, are mediated to them by their history, i.e. from their ancestors, and are entrusted to them for their descendants. They are to be regarded "as an *entailed inheritance* derived to us by our forefathers, and to be transmitted to our posterity."[19] Community among human beings carries with it obligations which are not canceled by death. Any truly vital community transcends the lifetime of its currently living members and so involves the dead and the not yet living. The Jeffersonian maxim that "the earth belongs always to the living generation" requires careful conditioning if it is not to be a license for the destruction of future generations and a restriction of human life to the shallows. For once we forget our debt to the past, the future will receive scant notice. "People will not look forward to posterity, who never look backward to their ancestors."[20]

Tradition and Community

The Burkean view of society as trans-historical requires that responsible decision-making include "an extension of the franchise" to the dead, in G.K. Chesterton's term. This requires "giving votes to the most obscure of all classes, our ancestors. It is the democracy of the dead."[21] The present must care for the future by consulting with the past. Are Jefferson, Lincoln and Burke simply dead, become "nothing"? Or are they vital participants in the contemporary conversation about the rights and responsibilities of persons in society? As the founding generation of the country announced a new order of the ages through the words of a poet dead eighteen centuries, so we debate the condition of our communal life through the ideas of those long dead.

"The Catholic Church is the only thing that saves a man from the degrading slavery of being a child of his age," wrote Chesterton.[22] If we put aside the polemical bluster of "the only thing," his statement makes an important point. When Christian creeds describe the church as "one, holy, catholic and apostolic," what is claimed, among other things, is that there is a connection between unity, universality and trans-temporality and holiness. Describing the church as catholic means that it is spread throughout space, that it recognizes no intrinsic geographical barriers; describing it as apostolic means that it stretches through time, that it does not accept limits to its membership by mortality. If the church is one through space and *time*, then the dead are members in good standing. If the franchise has been extended to them, then living members cannot be merely children of their own place or time. The church is a communion of the dead and the living and the not yet born, a communion of saints.

The Communion of Saints

Communion among believers is grounded in the person and work of Christ in and through whom we participate in the life of God. Christ has established commonality of life with us by sharing humanity (Heb 2:14), and therefore we share in the life of God. Our communion with one another is our experience of that communion with God in Christ. According to the first letter of John 1:3, we have communion with the Father and the Son, which means that we live no longer in darkness but in the light; living in the light means that we have communion with one another. This common life with one another is how we share in the blood of Jesus which cleanses us (1 Jn 1:7). For living in light means loving our brothers and sisters; anyone who fails to do so is still in darkness (1 Jn 3:11). Anyone who claims to live in communion with God must live as Jesus did, i.e. must live in accord with God's command (1 Jn 2:5–6). That command is nothing new; we have heard it "from the beginning" (1 Jn 2:7). The message heard from the very beginning is that we are to love one another (1 Jn 3:11). Thus the immediate experience of communion with God is living in loving communion with one another. Anyone who claims the former without the latter is a liar (1 Jn 4:20). Because God is love, to live in communion with God is to live in loving communion with one another (1 Jn 4:16).

This communion with one another, this shared life, is our union with God and therefore the source of holiness. Oneness with God is given through unity with one another, and so unity and holiness are intimately connected in the Christian life. One of the most often quoted statements from the Second Vatican Council is that found in its Dogmatic Constitution on the Church, *Lumen Gentium* (1,1): "By its relationship to Christ, the church is a kind of sign or sacrament of intimate union with God and the unity of all humankind." The church is here described as the effective sign of *both* "intimate union with God," i.e. the sanctifying mission of the church, *and* "the unity of all humankind," i.e. the social mission of the church. This is a restatement of the teaching of the synoptic gospels that the two great commandments are not only interrelated but substantially identical (Mt 22:34–40; Mk 12:28–34; Lk 10:25–37). To recognize that the love of God with one's whole mind and heart is inextricably connected to the love of one's neighbor as oneself is to be "very close to the kingdom of God" (Mk 12:34). Indeed, the quality of one's gift of self to the least of one's brothers and sisters is so determinative of one's relationship to Christ that what one does to the former is done to the latter (Mt 25:31–46). This synoptic identification of the commandments to love God and one's neighbor is radicalized in the fourth gospel's reduction of the two to one new commandment: love one another (Jn 13:34; 15:17). Not only is obedience to this commandment the hallmark by which true disciples can be recognized (Jn 13:35), it is the entry into true communion with God, for the Father and the Son will come and dwell in the one who fulfills this commandment (Jn 14:23; 15:9–10).

But if communion of life with others is our communion of life with God, who are the others with whom we have communion? On one level, this question must call to mind the defensive response of the scribe in Luke 10:29 who asks, in response to Jesus' identification of the two great commandments, "And who is my neighbor?" The parable of the good Samaritan which follows expands the notion of neighbor, of the ones with whom we have commonality of life, to include not only strangers, but enemies, those of different races and religions. As Paul insisted, in the Spirit in whom we all participate through baptism, there is "neither Jew nor Greek, neither slave nor free, neither male nor female" (Gal 3:28); in Christian communion, national, social, and gender differences become insignificant. Thus, the oneness of Christian life, which is the source of holiness, is catholic, universal, unbounded.

The Mystical Body and Social Thought

The doctrine of the communion of saints means that race, nationality, class, gender, even space and time pose no limitations within the shared life of people. It is an expression of the metaphor used in Roman Catholic ecclesiology that the church is the mystical body of Christ, that is, membership in the church entails a dynamic relationship with Christ and other believers. For the American Benedictine Virgil Michel, who popularized this ecclesiological metaphor in the United States during the 1930s, the mystical body underscored the organic union that existed among persons, and the import of contributing to the development of that union. This graced union of believers was not foreign to the person, Michel maintained, but was the supernatural form of our human condition since community and participation were vital for human development. Michel often used the doctrine of the communion of saints to illustrate the lesson of the mystical body. In terms reflecting the theology of his time he described the communion of saints as the contribution of believers to a common treasury of merit from which each could draw upon as needed. All should participate as givers since all have received from the storehouse of grace derived from the work of Christ. The mutual generosity and need which marks the communion of saints' treasury of merit was indicative of the attitude that members of the mystical body should have in all things. In Michel's opinion this supernatural sharing of the communion of saints offered a telling analogy for the way that earthly society should be structured.

Separation from the communion of saints hinders the sharing of supernatural life. In a similar way, to be cut off from the society of persons is a most serious deprivation in human life. And just as there is a responsibility on the part of all believers to promote the spiritual well-being of others by contributing to the common treasury of merit, so too there is a serious responsibility to promote the material well-being of others by serving the common good. The theme of the mystical body in the spiritual life was a reminder that individuals, due to the work of the group, have benefited disproportionately from any personal achievement. In the course of earthly life, "the achievements of every individual are in part also the result of the entire heritage of the ages of material and intellectual contributions on the part of past men, and are therefore due to a common treasury of human possessions." Awareness of this should lead people with even "the slightest instinct of fairness" to avoid "drawing on this heritage constantly without in turn contributing their share to the common good. . . ."[23]

In line with this understanding of the centrality of participatory community, Michel opposed any barriers within the social order that prevented persons from entering into communion with others. "Just as each member of the mystical body has access to the common spiritual treasury according to his good will, efforts, zeal, charity, etc., so must it be in things material."[24] For Michel this meant that there could be no artificial barriers to the participation of individuals in the social life of the nation. Again his conclusion was based upon the ideal society of the mystical body and its expression in the communion of saints. In such a communion "no member is *per se* restrained from attaining the fullest share of spiritual goods. The getting of them is open to all without exception; and the maximum of opportunity is equally within reach of all. Neither birth, nor race, nor education can interfere there."[25]

The Practices of Communion

Within the experience of pre-Vatican II Catholic life the communion of saints was no abstraction but was regularly reinforced in a variety of ways. Philip Murnion notes that his naming at baptism gave him a sense of being in a special relationship both with his father's favorite uncle and a New Testament disciple. In later years his family's daily prayer regularly invoked the intercession of his dead father to continue to watch over them all. The picture of the pope prominently displayed in the home, the statue of Mary on a mantle, Mission Sunday celebrations in the parish—all these brought home the truth that as a young man he was in relationship with many persons, close and distant, present and past. As he looks back on his youth, Murnion writes,

> that period was filled with suggestions and expressions of familial ties to the wider families of church and society, which furnished a basis for our obligations to them. Evidence of, celebrations of, symbols of both our separate identity and the communities of church and society with whom we were in solidarity were a critical part of that era.[26]

It was an era where parish activities were supported by all members even if, as with the parochial school, not all members directly benefited. "The school was a project (today we'd say ministry) of the entire parish, not a service for those who wished to pay for it."[27] People gave, Murnion continues, out of a sense of obligation to the community, not because of what they got out of it. There were symbols, rites and social practices which taught people they were part of a network of relationships that transcended personal acquaintance.

Our self-understanding is informed by an imaginative view of ourselves as being in relation to others. Experience of being in communion with others beyond a narrow circle of intimacy provides a view of the self that differs from the ideology of individualism. Fred Kammer offers a suggestive way of appreciating the impact of a relational notion of the self. He asks: What does it mean to be a parent, to understand oneself as a father or mother? The answer is that the identity of the parent is "to-the-child-ness." To be a parent is to see oneself strongly oriented to the child.[28] One's values, priorities, activities are chosen with an eye toward their impact on the child. So, too, to be a child is to be oriented to the parent. That relationship shapes one's whole way of being, for it promotes the orientation of our thoughts, affections, and behavior. We are different because we understand ourselves to be in relation to someone else. The process of maturation entails the expansion of those with whom we are in relationship and the sorting out of our values and priorities in the face of the many persons to whom we are related, the different way that being a child, a friend, a lover, a spouse, a parent, a neighbor, a citizen, an employee, orients us.

Being attuned to the communion of saints promotes attention to the identity of being a fellow believer with others past, present, future. Admittedly, as with other identities, being part of the communion of saints can have large or small impact on the orientation of our lives. Yet one of the potential benefits of such an identity is that it fosters a sense of solidarity with those whom we do not know personally; it suggests that solidarity should not be limited to the immediate group near at hand. The various means, some recalled by Murnion, that the church has used to create awareness of the communion of saints were, in effect, disciplines of solidarity which is the moral expression of the communion of saints. Schooling people in the reality of the communion of saints was training for a virtue essential to Catholic social teaching.

Like all other virtues, solidarity requires formative training. People must be encouraged to develop the quality of moral character which we call solidarity. Perhaps the best way of doing so is to provide people with experiences of solidarity, "the actual sharing of life with a group of persons." Out of such experiences bonds of affection grow which link people to one another. "The lived experience of solidarity and the feelings that go with it are the normal way in which commitment grows."[29] Finding communal practices that engage people in sharing is a vital element in developing solidarity among people. It is likely that many of the activities of the past that formed a sense of the communion of saints are unavailable to us now, e.g. May crownings. But parishes can create new strategies which teach solidarity. Liturgical celebrations which highlight the multi-cultural nature of the church, parish partnerships between suburban and urban churches, the adoption of sister parishes in foreign lands, ecumenical projects which bring various religious traditions together, promoting fund-raising for, and awareness of, Catholic Relief Services and the Campaign for Human Development—these are some possible opportunities to encourage solidarity. Another important dimension is for parishes to resist what Murnion calls the "fee for service

mentality" which allows people to be donors rather than genuine contributors to a community. Solidarity arises out of participation in the life of
others, not simply contributing money for the direct benefits and services one receives from the work of others.[30]

The Backdrop for Catholic Social Thought

When the Catholic community adopts practices to foster solidarity
it is giving expression to deeply rooted beliefs about the nature of human
life, the nature of the church, and the role of the church in society. These
theological convictions are reflected in the Pastoral Constitution on the
Church in the Modern World, *Gaudium et Spes*, of Vatican II. In that
document the social mission of the church was given extended treatment,
building on what *Lumen Gentium* hinted at in its statement that the
church is the sacrament of the unity of humankind. In *Gaudium et Spes*
the council fathers aver that the church has no political mission, properly
speaking, but serves a religious mission. However, they then proceed to
affirm that this religious mission has implications for action in the world
since out of this religious mission comes "a function, a light, and an
energy which can serve to structure and consolidate the human community according to divine law." In the same paragraph the bishops continue by quoting *Lumen Gentium* in *Gaudium et Spes*, 42: "For the promotion of unity belongs to the innermost nature of the church, since she
is, 'by her relationship with Christ, both a sacramental sign and an instrument of intimate union with God and of the unity of all humankind.' "
They saw in this text an affirmation that the church's task of fostering
unity includes admonishing not only believers but all persons "to overcome all strife between nations and races in this family spirit of God's
children, and in the same way, to give internal strength to human associations which are just."

Earlier in *Gaudium et Spes*, in chapter two (23–29), there is a medita-
tion on the foundation of the church's teaching about society. Several
theological themes are recalled which serve to ground the conciliar vision of how humanity is to live together. On the basis of our creation in
the image of the creator it is stated that the plan of God is that humanity
"should constitute one family and treat one another in a spirit of brotherhood." This social nature demonstrates that "social life is not something
added on" to human life but is essential to our development. As a result
the promotion of the common good is a vital concern for all persons
since it is through participation in the shared life of a community which
respects the good of all that each person fulfills his or her worldly responsibilities. The inclusion of all persons and groups in any project to advance the common good is a moral imperative.

> In our times a special obligation binds us to make ourselves the
> neighbor of absolutely every person, and of actively helping
> him when he comes across our path, whether he be an old
> person abandoned by all, a foreign laborer unjustly looked
> down upon, a refugee, a child born of an unlawful union and
> wrongly suffering for a sin he did not commit, or a hungry
> person who disturbs our conscience . . . (27).

This imperative includes not only the stranger but also "those who think
or act differently than we do in social, political, and religious matters,
too" (28). Reverence for the dignity of the person accounts for this moral
concern that is all-embracing. The sacredness of the person, in turn, is
founded upon a cluster of theological claims: creation (our common
origin), redemption (our common gift), discipleship (our common vocation), and eschatology (our common destiny). All these elements contribute to the communitarian vision of the Catholic tradition.

This theological vision of humanity as one family and the church as
a sacrament of that unity serves as a backdrop to the ethic espoused in
Catholic social thought. The communion of saints as a theological statement has its counterpart in an ethical principle of solidarity. As we shall
see, this principle generates moral norms regulating the political and
economic framework found in Catholic teaching. For now, the point to
make is that solidarity serves as the "deep theory" of recent Catholic
social teaching.[31] By this expression we refer to the taken-for-granted
understanding of justice in an ethical theory. It is the "tacit intuition or
vision that undergirds a conception of justice."[32] When the Catholic
imagination envisions a just society, it depicts a situation in which humans exist in right relationship to one another. This entails more than the
regulation of personal rights. Within the Catholic imagination the human good is related to the experience of communities which practice
forgiveness, mutual respect and honor, and love. As a result the Catholic
understanding of justice demands the creation of genuine community,
and while rights must be met in any true community, there is more that is
necessary. For we are more than bearers of rights. Our rights may be
respected and yet our true dignity denied. Belonging, respect, friendship,
forgiveness, love are essential to human well-being, but they are not
easily addressed by the language and concept of rights. What is central to
the Catholic theory of justice is the recognition that, as the U.S. bishops assert, "human dignity can be realized and protected only in
community."[33]

Defense and promotion of human life requires more than a strict
observance of each other's rights. When the American bishops devel-

oped the idea of community in their pastoral letter they employed the theme of participation as a component of just community; persons must be able to participate in the life of a community. John Paul II does not use this exact language, but his thought runs along the same lines: he speaks not of participatory community but the need for an "authentic human ecology," that is, a societal environment which reflects the conditions for human well-being: solidarity and participation.[34]

A communitarian vision is the "deep theory" of Catholic social thought. When debates about justice arise, the background or stance which informs the formulation of norms in Catholic teaching is a commitment to a society where the experience of community is made real through the ordering of societal institutions and made available to all through the practice of solidarity. A recent study of Catholic social teaching concludes that "encyclical social teaching coheres around a theologically inspired communitarian ethic." As a result Catholic social teachings regularly "decry the classical liberal model where society is understood as an artificial contract between autonomous individuals 'undertaken for self-interest rather than fraternal reasons.' "[35]

Solidarity and Interdependence

A common claim made today is that we live in an interdependent world. In this context solidarity is seen as the moral correlative to the fact of interdependence. Such a view, while fundamentally correct, may overstate the reality of interdependence in our society and world and thus be misleading about the challenge that solidarity poses to our society. Today, as in the past, wealth and power can provide significant opportunities for people to isolate themselves from one another. One observer of American society has cited the disturbing trend of people losing interest in public goods while using private means to avoid the harm stemming from the decay of public life.[36] This "secession of the successful" suggests a variation of John Kenneth Galbraith's claim that private wealth requires public expenditure.[37] He sensibly argued that private automobiles relied upon publicly financed roads and private jets required a whole network of publicly financed air traffic control and airports. Thus, it is not just the poor or working class who have a vested interest in maintaining public goods, according to Galbraith.

While it is true that many wealthy still rely on public monies in a variety of ways, it is also true that today there is a growing disengagement with public life on a broad scale and a narrowing of concern to one's immediate locale. The language of community is spoken but the difficulty is that "most Americans no longer live in traditional communities." Instead we live in "suburban subdivisions bordered by highways and sprinkled with shopping malls, or in tony condominiums and residential clusters." Those who do not live this way are often in "ramshackle apartment buildings and housing projects." People do not work at home but commute and socialize with others "on some basis other than geographic proximity." The one thing neighbors generally have in common is similar incomes. And this is what constitutes the new and false notion of community for Americans.

> The renewed emphasis on "community" in American life has justified and legitimized these economic enclaves. If generosity and solidarity end at the border of similarly valued properties, then the most fortunate can be virtuous citizens at little cost. Since most people in one neighborhood or town are equally well off, there is no cause for a guilty conscience. If inhabitants of another area are poorer, let them look to one another. Why should we pay for their schools? So the argument goes, without acknowledging that the critical assumption has already been made: "we" and "they" belong to fundamentally different communities.[38]

The process of the secession of the top one-fifth of high earners from the rest of American society is a gradual one and takes a variety of forms. Many wealthy people now live in residential enclaves which employ private companies for security, trash collection, even road maintenance, while nearby municipalities are too financially strapped to provide such services adequately. Privileged children attend private schools, summer camps and other activities available only to those who can pay for the entrance fees. "As public parks and playgrounds deteriorate, there is a proliferation of private health clubs, golf clubs, tennis clubs, skating clubs and every other type of recreational association in which costs are shared among members."[39] It is not hard to detect in the "taxpayers' revolt" of the present time or the political pandering behind pledges of "no new taxes" a lost sense of solidarity whereby citizens contributed to public services and goods which were not directly beneficial to them. Resentment over taxation may spring from a variety of sources but the fragmentation of society and loss of solidarity which undergirds citizenship is evident in much of the public rhetoric concerning taxation.

Patterns of public benevolence also illustrate the tendency of the successful to secede from the larger society. Reich notes that studies demonstrate the charity of the affluent does not go mainly to social welfare for the poor. "Instead, most voluntary contributions of wealthy

Americans go to the places and institutions that entertain, inspire, cure or educate wealthy Americans—art museums, opera houses, theaters, orchestras, ballet companies, private hospitals and elite universities."[40] As a percentage of income, the wealthy (those making more than 100,000 dollars a year) give considerably less to charity than those making below 10,000 dollars a year. And, Reich adds, corporate philanthropy follows the same generally self-serving pattern. Business-giving during the 1980s to primary and secondary education was less than the amount granted corporations in the form of tax breaks and subsidies by host communities who need tax revenue for education.[41] If one looks at the annual debate over foreign aid in the U.S. Congress, and if the amount of military aid is subtracted from the total figure, the general paucity of American support given to the poorer nations of the world reflects something of the same pattern as domestic contributions to public welfare. Indeed, a recent article written from the perspective of the third world suggests that, with the demise of communism, there is less strategic importance given to third world nations. If the nations in this category are no longer valuable politically in the superpower competition, it remains to be seen whether they will now be valued economically. There are some indications that the situation is not promising as the cheap labor found in the third world is less necessary.

> Today, unlike a century ago, most of the third world's population is superfluous from the perspective of the first world's economic needs. The third world's seas, air and natural environment are still in demand, even if only as a toxic waste dump; and its raw materials continue to be needed. Even though certain raw materials have become less important, the third world continues to be key for the ongoing development of the first world. What is no longer necessary is the majority of its population.[42]

Interdependence may be an increasingly important dimension of human life within our nation and among nations, but it remains true that some isolate themselves successfully from much of the experience of their interdependence with the poor and marginalized. Catholic social teaching on solidarity recognizes that the appeal of interdependence may not be heard by all. The claim of solidarity is not presented simply as a prescient recognition of interdependence but as a moral imperative that is generated by a belief in the fundamental unity of the human family. Like other moral imperatives, it calls for conversion in the lives of people: it asks for change in the ways that we have structured our societal and global order. Among the rich the acknowledgement of interdependence remains sufficiently weak that people, classes and whole nations still run the risk of being written off as beyond the bounds of concern. For this reason solidarity, as used within the Catholic tradition, must be distinguished from interdependence. An argument for moral concern based on interdependence might suggest that solidarity is nothing more than enlightened self-interest, that commitment on the part of the "haves" for the "have-nots" is good social planning and will benefit all. Within Catholic social teaching, however, solidarity is a virtue; it requires conversion of mind, heart and will. It is not inevitable that the articulated interests of people can be harmonized. There is no presumption in Catholic teaching of an "invisible hand" guiding self-interested people to act in ways that benefit all. Solidarity must be a conscious choice of people who seek ways of improving the good of all, if a commitment to the common good demands that some place limits on their own desires or stated interests that should be done. Catholic social teaching argues not from enlightened self-interest but from a theological claim about the unity of the human family and the moral obligations which arise from a vision of the community of persons.[43]

Solidarity and Justice

Catholicism's vision of the unity of humankind and its theological representation in the communion of saints have heightened appreciation for the moral importance of solidarity. The lesson of the communion of saints that neither time nor space can destroy the essential unity of the human family has found expression in the claim that solidarity is global and trans-generational. Catholic social teaching refuses to allow parochial or national loyalties to stand in the way of moral claims made by persons who are not our near neighbors or citizens. The championing of human rights is an important dimension to solidarity if the tendency to exclusivity rather than inclusivity is to be avoided. Marginalization, however, not particular loyalties, is the real enemy of a solidaristic stance. Solidarity as a vision of the universality of our duties to one another means that there ought to be a constant vigilance on the part of the center toward the periphery. Those already participating in vibrant and sound communal relations need to reach out to those who are left without the means or opportunities to participate in community. Just as human rights have grown in prominence as a vehicle for defending a genuine solidarity in Catholic social thought, so, too, has the option for the poor emerged as a central component of Catholic teaching on justice informed by solidarity. People must be welcomed into community, and those who are on the margins provide a stimulant to the rest to focus energy and resources to remove barriers toward full participation. Solidarity serves the common good. But, as Gregory Baum argues, if we recognize that society is organized in such a way that injustice is perpetuated, then it becomes an act of solidarity to take the side of social reform leading to greater justice.[44] Siding with segments of the community, even when it entails defiance toward other segments, is not a breach of solidarity but an intimation of a truly participatory community.[45] Solidarity, therefore, does not require an absence of partisanship in Catholic social teaching. The preferential option for the poor within the context of solidarity requires a strong prejudice in favor of actions which promote a lessening of marginalization.

Solidarity has given new emphasis to the connection between justice and participatory community. Because of its solidaristic vision, Catholic social teaching places weight on the ability of persons to be in relationships if they are to achieve their integral development. As our reflection on the Trinity in chapter three made clear, relationship is key for understanding personhood. Persons are called to be self-giving, to transcend self-interest through altruistic action. Participation is crucial for developing opportunities to be self-donative. If people are left outside the circle, not seated at the table, then they are encouraged to act irresponsibly, not altruistically. Thus the opportunity to enter into the life of a community, to give oneself away to others in mutually supportive ways, is a marker for assessing whether society is rightly ordered. "Basic justice demands the establishment of minimum levels of participation in the life of the human community for all persons. The ultimate injustice is for a person or group to be actively treated or passively abandoned as if they were nonmembers of the human race."[46] More and more one finds in Catholic social thought a stress on the element of participation as a key feature for understanding the meaning of justice in modern society.

In addition to the three facets already mentioned—the universal nature of some moral duties, the importance of the option for the poor and the accent on participation in community—there is yet another lesson for Catholic teaching on justice which can be drawn from an ethic shaped by solidarity. A commitment to the unity of the human family, the "deep theory" of the Catholic social tradition, coupled with the stark reality of growing inequality within and between societies, has given rise to a moral norm of relative equality. This norm entails "that wealth and resources ought to be regularly redistributed to redress the differences between groups, sectors, and even nations."[47] Relative equality is the normative expression of the theological vision of solidarity.

Drew Christiansen describes Catholic social teaching as favoring a "strong" form of egalitarianism. Strong forms of egalitarianism are characterized by two things: 1) a discounting of the weight accorded other principles of justice while not entirely dismissing these other principles, e.g. inherited rights, contract, utility, so as to advocate "economic and social institutions which attempt to approximate equal allocation of resources as a norm"; 2) as a consequence of the first characteristic, support for "substantial redistribution of material goods, establishing guaranteed welfare floors, socio-economic rights" and other strategies.[48]

A further comment on the norm of relative equality is that the word "relative" means that the equality aimed at is not absolute, a level "in which everyone gets the same benefits and shares the same burdens." The idea behind relative equality is that "inequalities are held within a defined range set by moral limits." A variety of factors such as need, contribution and the common good may justify differences but there are limits set on differences to be permitted.[49] Not only floors below which one should not fall but ceilings above which one should rise are set for the sake of limiting inequality. The limits and the differences serve the same aim of promoting solidarity among people so that the unity of humankind can be enhanced. There is in this latter aim the intimation of a conclusion reached by recent popes that the grow of significant inequalities in social existence has led to the further dissolution of communal life.[50] It is the divisiveness caused by inequality which makes it such a concern for the church because the resultant breakdown of community stands in contrast to the theologically informed communitarian vision of Roman Catholicism.

The judgment about inequality frustrating solidarity has come to clearer expression as Catholic social teaching has employed the method of reading the signs of the times—that is, an attempt to study how the events, ideas and trends of history stand in relation to the values of the reign of God. Since a significant aspect of the experience of God's reign is the achievement of unity among God's creatures, the reading of the signs of the times has focused attention on the obstacles to community, including a growing gap in the possession of the material conditions for human well-being.[51]

The New Social Question for Catholic Social Thought

When Leo XIII wrote *Rerum Novarum* he considered the condition of the worker to be the social question of his time. Later Pius XII wrote from the perspective of a new social question, the task of establishing a political order after World War II. With the advent of John XXIII, and in subsequent writings of Vatican Council II and the papacies of Paul VI and John Paul II, we find another description of the social question of the age. Today it is inequality which has become the dominant social concern of the church. It is the huge division of societies and the globe into "the haves and have-nots" that is the sign of the times which Catholic social thought must address.

Confirmation of this reality comes from many sources. Raymond Flynn, the mayor of Boston, writing a few weeks after the termination of the Persian Gulf War, called upon the nation to turn its attention to the "other gulf crises—the widening gulf in wealth between the rich and the poor, and the growing gulf in competitiveness between the U.S. and other industrial nations." Flynn went on to delineate some of the sobering statistics about the state of our nation.

> More than 33 million Americans—one out of seven—live below the poverty line. The figure for children is yet more alarming: one out of every four lives in poverty (among blacks one of every two). Compared with a decade ago, today's poor are poorer, and likely to be poor for longer periods. More people today are likely to earn their poverty on the job—the "working poor." More and more poor people are concentrated in our cities, while more of the jobs are located in the suburbs, inaccessible by public transportation.
>
> During this decade of increased destitution, a small number of wealthy Americans became even richer. The richest 1 percent of all Americans (those with average incomes of $549,000) now receive nearly as much income, after taxes, as the bottom 40 percent combined. The average income of those at the very top rose $236,000 during the decade—an increase of 75 percent—while the poorest one-fifth of the population saw its income drop by 3.8 percent. . . . [T]he share of national income going to those in the middle is now lower than at any time since World War II.[52]

Other statistics, reported by Flynn, are equally troubling. Infant mortality in the nation ranks nineteenth in the world, and among black Americans the rate is comparable to that of third world nations. Housing is in a state of crisis. Apart from the homeless population, there are large numbers living in overcrowded apartments. A huge share, eighty-five percent, of low-income renters pay too much of their meager incomes for housing. Two-thirds of this group pay half or more of their income for rent. "As a result, millions of Americans are just one rent increase, layoff, illness, or other emergency away from becoming homeless."[53]

Among the most vulnerable in our society are children, and as the American bishops have stated clearly, "our nation is failing many of our children."[54] The episcopal reading of the signs of the times underscores this judgment. Children are the poorest segment of the population, "nearly twice as likely to be poor as any other group. Among children, the younger you are, the more likely you are to be poor in America."[55] Child poverty means that young people start out in life missing the basic goods—food, shelter, health care—which are needed for development. This deprivation at the outset stays with children throughout life. Forty thousand children die before their first birthday. Teen suicide has tripled in occurrence over the last thirty years. Our nation has the highest rate of teen pregnancy in the western world. One-fourth of all teenagers drop out of the educational system before graduating high school.[56] Children are having children, as more than one out of four children are born outside marriage; thirty years ago the figure was one in twenty. One of every three children now comes to maturity dependent on welfare.[57]

> Too many of today's children and adolescents will reach adult-hood unhealthy, illiterate, unemployable, lacking moral direction and a vision of a secure future. . . . Many young people believe they have little to lose by dropping out of school, having a baby as an unmarried teenager, using and selling dangerous drugs, and committing crimes. When they lack a sense of hope and the opportunity to get a good job, support a family and become a part of the mainstream adult society, teenagers are frequently not motivated to avoid dangerous or self-destructive behaviors.[58]

This assessment of the state of children, as tragic as it is, takes on an even more challenging tone when seen in the context of Reich's charge about the "secession of the successful" and the privileged experience of one segment of our society. There has been a retreat from public support for programs with proven track records that might begin to remedy some of the ills besetting poor children, e.g. Head Start, the WIC program (Women, Infant, Children), Child Health Services. The plight of these government sponsored programs during the decade of the 1980s was but one sign that public concern about the poor was on the wane. Withdrawal of support for government programs assisting the needy is a product of the secessionist mentality of an elite who no longer feel committed to programs that are aimed at improving general welfare.

The decline in interest about children in poverty is abetted by a new trend. In the nineteenth century only about twenty percent of U.S.

households were without children under eighteen whereas now the percentage has risen to approximately sixty-five percent. Daniel Moynihan cautions, "Raising children is now carried out with the incomes of a minority of adults. Child welfare becomes a minority interest."[59] This demographic trend, coupled with the legacy of racial and ethnic discrimination in this nation, leads to the possibility that poor children have become marginalized. Our government spends $11,000 on every American over sixty-five years of age but less than half that, $4,200, on each American under eighteen years of age.[60] A recent study of social indicators in the U.S. reports that during the last two decades "while children were growing poorer relative to the rest of the population, state and federal governments were cutting the principal income support program for poor children—Aid to Families with Dependent Children—by 43 percent in inflation-adjusted dollars."[61] Neglect of children by the wider society portends an ominous future according to the National Commission on Children. We are creating a society in which future generations will have significant numbers of people who are not just unemployed but unemployable, not just poorly educated but illiterate in an information-based society, not just angry but asocial and without moral direction.

If one turns to the wider global picture, the spectre of inequality grows even larger. The statistics about global poverty are so overwhelming that it is helpful to bring the picture into a scale that is more understandable. Imagine the world as a village of one hundred families. Seven families would own sixty percent of the land, consume eighty percent of the available energy and possess all the consumer luxuries. Sixty families would have to live on ten percent of the land. Sixty-five families would be illiterate. Seventy families would have no drinking water in their homes. Only one family would have a member with university education.[62]

As with domestic inequality, so, too, at the global level it is often children who are most vulnerable and marginalized. Millions of children die each year from poverty, hunger, and disease. The United Nations estimates that forty thousand children die each day of the year from diseases related to malnutrition. Worldwide more than seven million children live in refugee camps and a larger number have been forced to leave their home countries as a result of war and natural disasters. Child labor in many countries, totaling over eighty million persons, entails harsh conditions, scandalous wages and physical danger. Thirty million children throughout the world live in conditions that UNICEF describes as "especially difficult," driven to crime, begging and prostitution simply to survive. In their letter on children and family life the American bishops note that "poverty around the world falls most heavily and directly on women and children. . . . Their future is mortgaged to flawed 'development,' which increases a nation's gross national product but worsens its distribution, helping the rich at the expense of the poor." The bishops remind their readers that statistics can be emotionally numbing, but "behind each of these numbers is a sister or brother, a child of God."[63]

When the U.S. bishops discuss economic justice they are concerned that just being born into the human race does not guarantee that one will be treated as a person, as a participating member in the life of a society. David Hollenbach, an advisor to the bishops in the writing of their 1986 pastoral letter, put the moral challenge presented by poor children and others in need this way: "The problem is that many would prefer not to reflect on what it means to say that these marginalized people are members of the human community and we have a duty to treat them as such."[64] It is a breakdown of solidarity which allows entire classes of people and whole nations to be put on the periphery of our field of vision. Building a truly inclusive social and global order is the hope held by those who believe in the communion of saints, who have a vision of life which sees community as central to human existence. What, then, is needed if a people is to remove the blinders of marginalization and acknowledge that those on the fringe of community life are also brothers and sisters to us? What might be the agenda for a society that desires to practice solidarity and a church called to witness to the reality of the communion of saints?

The Politics of Generativity

Erik Erikson, the prominent psychologist who studied the process of maturation as persons pass through various stages of life, has referred to the importance of generativity in the later years of adult life. For Erikson, generativity refers to the care that one generation gives the next as the life cycle continues within the human community. The authors of *The Good Society* have borrowed this theme of Erikson in their call for a politics of generativity. They ask, "With what kind of society will we endow our children and our children's children, what kind of world, what kind of natural environment?" They observe that many of the problems we face as a national society and as a global community call for precisely the generativity which Erikson saw as a virtue of the mature. And the "most obvious problem is the perilous neglect of our own children. . . ."[65] Poverty and despair fester as a result of the inequality found both at home and abroad. Future adults are now living in conditions so marked by inequality that we are virtually guaranteed both a society and a planet where the gulf between rich and poor will not only continue but widen. Environmental damage is another example of how we seem indifferent to the future, as is the massive indebtedness of present generations that will be left to later generations of citizens. In our country the lack of resources committed to building necessary infrastructure and improving education is a further example of a lack of generativity in our political sensibilities. We are living in a society and a world which lives off the generosity of past generations and the postponed payment of present debts that will be the inheritance left to the future. This is in striking contrast to an ethic which is derived from a sense of solidarity across generations. Paul VI reminded us that obligations fall upon those who have been "heirs to generations gone by" and therefore have "no right to put aside all concern for those through whom the human family will be enlarged after we have filled the span of our own life." For Paul the "mutual bond" of all humanity "is a reality" which "not only confers benefits upon us but also imposes obligations."[66]

Robert Bellah and his colleagues see in a politics of generativity the ideals of "social inclusion and participation as a key theme. . . ."[67] In this the politics of generativity sounds several of the same notes struck by Catholic social teaching. Indeed, the authors explicitly note that the social teaching of the Catholic tradition is an example of the fresh thinking that a politics of generativity requires, an approach that is not identified with existing political options. Such a politics can develop within a given political party, or it may begin as a social movement that comes to be aligned with a political party. But generativity as a societal ideal is not easily captured by existing political ideologies. One of the elements of the Catholic tradition attractive to Bellah and his fellow authors is the understanding of justice as both a personal and a social virtue, having elements of solidarity and participation.

> A just social system is impossible without people being just. Justice is first and foremost a virtue, and it inheres in individuals and institutions that carry out God's commandment to care for one another—to feed the hungry, heal the sick, and enable the able-bodied to work and contribute to the commonweal.[68]

Describing the duties of a politics of generativity one might draw upon those duties outlined in Catholic social teaching as the duties of justice, charity and solidarity. These were first outlined in Catholic social teaching by Paul VI in his encyclical on development, *Progressio Populorum*. The duties of social justice entail the structure of international economics especially trade policies and the need for a new international economic order. Duties of charity touch upon the attitudes which a person ought to have in acting as a member of the human family. There ought to be a spirit which sees the other as a brother or sister. Proper treatment of the immigrant, refugee, and guest worker, and an openness to cross-cultural dialogue, are signs of the right attitude which charity requires. Charity asks us to build genuinely human ties among people. Solidarity creates duties that fall upon those well-off to close the gap between themselves and the least advantaged. It entails a willingness to sacrifice for the sake of creating greater equity, capital transfers through aid programs, and both personal and national actions which narrow the gap between rich and poor. If the Catholic tradition's understanding of original sin is correct, then the call to practice agape and justice is not beyond the capacity of sinful persons. Self-interest is real but can be overcome, as we suggested in chapter two. Charity establishes an internal commitment to relate to others in a humane manner, justice demands the restructuring of institutions to promote participation in economic life, and solidarity requires an effort on the part of the privileged to work on behalf of the less advantaged.[69]

What Paul and later John Paul II are proposing in their writing is a heuristic understanding of development that moves attention beyond simply the economic to include other concerns, for example, moral and political values. Development must not be reduced to economic factors alone. This view of development does not offer detailed plans but suggests a vision of how people ought to live within nations and between nations. It is what Paul called "integral development." What is offered in Catholic social teaching on development is a set of criteria which permits one to assess any proposal for advancing the human prospect. There is no Catholic development plan, but there are standards by which any plan can be evaluated according to the duties generated by charity, justice and solidarity.[70] The politics of generativity seeks to create a society which meets the duties outlined under the headings of charity, justice and solidarity. People are called upon to act not out of self-interest but concern for the other. There is a strong moral component to true development, for human beings can only attain development by creation of communities wherein each and every person is able to give of himself or herself for the sake of the well-being of all. Self-development is not opposed to the common good of all, for development is not a zero-sum game. It can be construed as such only if we reduce development to material wealth and someone's gain becomes another's loss. Development understood along the lines of a politics of generativity sees that mutual benefit is vital to development. Economic success within an unjust social order cannot be equated with human development.

The Communion of Saints and a Solidaristic Vision

It is a commonplace to note that a person's moral vision affects his or her decisions. We all see the world through different eyes, and there are a variety of ways in which the human reality can be described. It is impossible to decide reasonably about issues which we overlook or see only in a distorted manner. Thus, seeing the human situation rightly precedes our ability to think ethically about it properly. In any number of ways our moral vision will affect the decisions our country must make concerning domestic and international life. Attitudes toward the poor, toward government's role in society, about America's place in the world —there are fundamental convictions at work when such topics arise which preemptively determine much of political argument and debate. Seeing the other through the lens of a doctrine like the communion of saints secures a different vantage than viewing the same person through a vision of society as a social contract.

Throughout this volume we have proposed that the Catholic theological tradition and its consequent social teaching offer a distinctive vision of human life, human community, the goals of a just society. The communitarian vision of Catholicism promotes a social ethic of solidarity. Seeing the world in this way leads to a set of emphases which differ from much present-day public discussion. The isolationism of some public officials' pronouncements on foreign policy stands in sharp contrast to a belief in the unity of the human family. The operative isolationism of many within our society contradicts the Catholic belief in the communal nature of human life. The apathy of the secure ignores the call to a common good which embraces all. Despoliation of our earth denies the sacramentality of the created order. Our public officials are often shallow, pandering to our darkest instincts. Our public discourse is so narrow that we struggle to find language that can speak to something besides the crassness of self-interest.[71]

Before we resolve the specifics of public policy we need to train our eyes to see reality more clearly and our minds to articulate more accurately what it is we find when we look beyond ourselves. Until this is done, there will be strong resistance to many of the public policies we would like to see implemented. The inclusion of theology in public discourse is an important step toward moving our society in a better direction. But theology must be made public by theologians who strive to make the central symbols of the tradition accessible to society. The wisdom latent within the tradition of a religious community must be explicated so that those who are not members of that body can ascertain the foundational elements of a believer's vision of the good society. Then discussion and debate can occur and, finally, decision and action. In much of what we have written we acknowledge there is room for debate; indeed, we hope that debate will result precisely in the theological terms whose public significance we have tried to explore. As was said at the outset of our volume our aim is primarily to help people see the linkage between a profession of faith and ideas about how we are to live in society. The public significance of theology cannot be denied by believers and ought to be acknowledged by all. This book is an attempt to explain and demonstrate why that is so.

Epilogue

At the close of the first chapter of this book, we referred to John Milbank's contrast between Augustine and Nietzsche. Milbank evokes Nietzsche's contrast between the viewpoints of eagles and sheep in *On the Genealogy of Morals*.[1] Nietzsche's parable pits the "morality" of the strong against that of the weak:

> That lambs dislike great birds of prey does not seem strange: only it gives no ground for reproaching these birds of prey for bearing off little lambs. And if the lambs say among themselves: "these birds of prey are evil; and whoever is least like a bird of prey, but rather its opposite, a lamb—would he not be good?" there is no reason to find fault with this institution of an ideal, except perhaps that the birds of prey might view it a little ironically and say: "we don't dislike them at all, these good little lambs; we even love them: nothing is more tasty than a tender lamb."[2]

Nietzsche seeks to derive the morality of the strong from a fundamental way of being, viz. strength. The lambs, on the other hand, invert the morality of the strong, imagining weakness to be the paradigm of goodness. In both cases, morality is a justification of one's own fundamental character and situation. The difference is that the eagles are content to be eagles and to let the lambs be what they are, i.e. their prey; but the lambs want the eagles to turn into lambs. Indeed, they construct a model of perfect goodness, and it turns out to be a lamb—or, as Nietzsche undoubtedly intended us to recognize, the Lamb. But eagles will go on being eagles, unless the terrible inversion occurs, and the lambs impose their "slave morality" on the great birds of prey.

What best counters a parable is another parable, and so Milbank wisely observes, "Given the dedication of the strong to a narrative which invents their strength, it is possible for the weak to refuse the necessity of this strength by telling a different story, posing different roles for human beings to inhabit."[3] So, he suggests, what is required is a story "which simply changed the metaphors: which, for example, proposed a humanity becoming sheeplike, pastoral." Such a story has been narrated in Augustine's *City of God*. Indeed Milbank brilliantly describes Nietzsche's *Genealogy* as a "kind of jeu d'esprit, a writing of the *City of God* back-to-front from a neo-pagan point of view."[4]

We differ with Milbank, however, on the final outcome of the Christian story in which humanity becomes "sheeplike, pastoral." For he sees "the absolute Christian vision of ontological peace" as now providing "the only alternative to a nihilistic outlook" and points to its consequences as "the emanation of harmonious difference, the exodus of new generations, the path of peaceful flight. . . ."[5] But the peaceful flight which he prescribes is also an abandonment of politics as a realm given over to Nietzsche's birds of prey. We offer another contrast of images, this between Nietzsche and the gospel of Matthew.

At the beginning of *Thus Spoke Zarathustra*, Nietzsche's hero/spokesman comes down from the mountain where he has dwelt in solitude for ten years in order to proclaim the "Overman" to humanity because he is moved with pity for human beings. Failing to find a hearing because he has come too soon (like the Madman who announces the death of God in *The Gay Science*[6] and Nietzsche himself who entitled his earlier essays *Untimely Meditations*[7]), he gathers a group of disciples about him. But realizing that he cannot come to his "stillest hour"[8] and greatest joy in the company of any others, including his disciples, he returns along to his mountain where eventually he is transfigured before his three animal companions, the serpent, the lion and the eagle. And there, at the end of the book in its original form, he remained in splendid aloneness.[9]

In Matthew 5:1, Jesus proclaims his message from a mountain. But instead of proclaiming the "Overman," he announces that the truly happy are the poor in spirit, the single-hearted, those in mourning, the peacemakers, the humble, those thirsting for justice and all who are persecuted in his name. Twelve chapters later, he returns to a mountain in order to have a "stillest hour" with three disciples and is transfigured before them (Mt 17:1–8). The suggestion is made that remaining on the mountain is good and that Jesus should abide there (17:4). But the story ends with Jesus leading his disciples back down the mountain to continue a mission which will lead to his death (17:9). And so he rejoins the crowd who cannot fathom his message (17:17), for it is "untimely"—"until the Son of Man is raised from the dead" (17:9).

The possibility of remaining apart on the mountain, husbanding one's strength, enjoying one's capacities, fulfilling one's desires without

interruption and without care for the others may seem attractive sometimes to everyone and at all times to some. Much of American life has
celebrated the individual, the pioneer, the "mountain man" who relies on
himself alone and neither needs nor wants a companion, the entrepre-
neur, the self-made person. Zarathustra on the mountain has been popularized as Shane riding off into the sunset, alone but free of the family and
responsibilities which would trammel him. A peculiarly individualist variant of this is a temptation for Christian believers: to retreat to the mountain and pitch tents there, to leave the cares of the valleys and markets and
towns, to take "the path of peaceful flight." But the fullness of faith
requires that we return down the mountain to struggle with the seemingly intractable problems of living together.

Nicholas Lash has wisely observed that there are various ways of
viewing the desert or, in the image of Matthew and Nietzsche, the
mountaintop.

> In some accounts, the desert experience (whether construed
> literally or metaphorically) is an ideal goal, even if only attain-
> able by a few; in others, its role is that of representative protest;
> in yet others, it is to be a staging post from which return is
> necessary. Perhaps we could say that, according to the first,
> God is most truly and purely to be found only in solitude, in the
> desert; for the second, he is sought in the desert because his
> presence has been obscured by the circumstances that obtain in
> the city; for the third, he is to be sought in the desert in order
> that his presence may be better discerned, and his purposes
> more purely obeyed, on return to the city.[10]

The Catholic Christian tradition has always appreciated the vocation of
those who go to the desert or the mountaintop, so long as their motive is
love of the city. But the one who retreats from the cares and concerns of
his or her brothers and sisters because those concerns seem a distraction
from God simply does not know what the word "God" means in Christian discourse. And so we cannot abandon politics, in its classical meaning, the attempt to construct a society which makes the good life (however we may understand that) possible for human beings. We cannot
attempt to become that strangely American oxymoron, a "private citizen." And we may not be simply sheep in the midst of wolves—or eagles.
"Peaceful flight" is an inadequate description of Christian mission. Eagles or lambs are false alternatives. For the Christian who would live the
fullness of faith, a more accurate image is to be found in the charge given
by Jesus that we be both "wise as serpents and innocent as doves"
(Mt 10:16b).

Notes

1. The Public Church and Public Theology

[1] Martin Marty, *The Public Church* (New York: Crossroad Publishing, 1981).

[2] Marty, *The Public Church*, p. 37.

[3] Marty, *The Public Church*, p. 1.

[4] Marty, *The Public Church*, p. 14.

[5] Marty, *The Public Church*, p. 1.

[6] Marty, *The Public Church*, p. 6.

[7] Among the many books on this question two commonly cited ones are Andrew Greeley, *Unsecular Man* (New York: Schocken Books, 1972) and Peter Berger, *The Sacred Canopy* (Garden City: Doubleday and Company, 1967).

[8] That this effort is something which is present throughout Catholicism is demonstrated by an interesting and candid comment of Jacques Gaillot, bishop of Evreux in France. "The church must look for a new way of relating to civil society. We must definitively renounce any attempt to dominate this society or to claim that we are still the only group able to speak the truth to that society or to propose the best way of acting for society. We have to learn how to take part in debates on all the questions that this society brings forth. . . ." "The French Church in Crisis," *America* 160 (1989): 576–578, 595–596 at 577.

[9] David Hollenbach, "Editor's Conclusion" in David Hollenbach, Robin Lovin, John Coleman, J. Bryan Hehir, "Theology and Philosophy in Public: A Symposium on John Courtney Murray's Unfinished Agenda," *Theological Studies* 40 (1979): 700–715 at 714.

[10] Due to the overly narrow popular understanding of the word "political" in our country we find the better expression to be public theology. We seek to avoid any connotation that theology is, therefore, a rationalization for power blocs made up of Christian believers seeking to impose their will upon others. Nor do we wish to be associated with any view of society which would reduce all of public life to the political

realm, or, even more narrowly, to the realm of government. Finally, we wish to avoid any implication that the best way for the church to be a public presence is for its clergy to take publicized partisan stands on the important issues of the day. It is our hope that the reader will find the term public theology less laden with the baggage that might accompany a project labeled political theology.

A commonly cited charter document in the movement of political theology is Johann Baptist Metz, "Religion and Society in the Light of a Political Theology," *Harvard Theological Review* 61 (1968): 507–523. While it can be argued that the various liberation theologies which have emerged are also responses to the divorce of religion from public life, we prefer to follow the thinking of many liberationists themselves that their theology is more a response to the experience of oppression than privatization, while liberationists would, of course, oppose separating religion from public life that was not the social context which gave rise to their movements. The "magna charta" of Latin American liberation theology is the well-known work by Gustavo Gutierrez, *Theology of Liberation* (Maryknoll: Orbis Books, 1973).

[11] William James, *Pragmatism* (Cambridge: Harvard University Press, 1975), p. 30.

[12] Martin Marty, "Foreword," in *Religion and American Public Life*, ed. Robin Lovin (New York: Paulist Press, 1986), pp. 1–4 at 1.

[13] Richard Bernstein, "The Meaning of Public Life," in *Religion and American Public Life*, pp. 29–52 at 32–33.

[14] Bernstein, "The Meaning of Public Life," p. 33.

[15] Robert Bellah, Richard Madsen, William M. Sullivan, Ann Swidler, and Steven M. Tipton, *Habits of the Heart: Individualism and Commitment in American Life* (Berkeley: University of California Press, 1985).

[16] Bellah, et al., *Habits of the Heart*, pp. 20–21.

[17] William M. Sullivan, *Reconstructing Public Philosophy* (Berkeley: University of California Press, 1986), pp. 157f: "The contemporary starting point for understanding the classical conception of the citizen must be the recovery of a sense of civic life as a form of personal self-development. The kind of self-development with which the theorists of civic life have been concerned is in many ways the antithesis of contemporary connotations of the notion of self-development in a 'culture of narcissism.' Citizenship has been traditionally conceived of as a way of life that changes the person entering it. This process is essentially a collective experience. Indeed, the notion of *citizen* is unintelligible apart from that of *commonwealth*, and both terms derive their sense from the idea that we are by nature political beings. Self-fulfillment and even the

working out of personal identity and a sense of orientation in the world depend upon a communal enterprise. This shared process is the civic life, and its root is involvement with others: other generations, other sorts of persons whose differences are significant because they contribute to the whole upon which our particular sense of self depends. Thus mutual interdependency is the foundational notion of citizenship. The basic psychological dynamic of the participants in this interdependent way of life is an imperative to respond and to care." Sullivan offers an exceptionally insightful attempt to recover civic republicanism as a basis for American public life.

[18] Bellah, et al., *Habits of the Heart*, p. 20.

[19] Bellah, et al., *Habits of the Heart*, pp. 102–110.

[20] Bellah, et al., *Habits of the Heart*, p. 25.

[21] Bellah, et al., *Habits of the Heart*, p. 24.

[22] Bellah, et al., *Habits of the Heart*, pp. 152–155.

[23] Bellah, et al., *Habits of the Heart*, p. 153.

[24] Bernstein, "The Meaning of Public Life," p. 44.

[25] Bernstein, "The Meaning of Public Life," p. 47.

[26] Bernstein, "The Meaning of Public Life," p. 46.

[27] John Courtney Murray, *We Hold These Truths* (New York: Sheed and Ward, 1960), p. 18.

[28] Murray, *We Hold These Truths*, p. 19.

[29] Murray, *We Hold These Truths*, p. 20.

[30] Murray, *We Hold These Truths*, p. 21.

[31] Murray, *We Hold These Truths*, p. 22.

[32] Murray, *We Hold These Truths*, p. 23.

[33] Murray, *We Hold These Truths*, p. 24.

[34] Murray, *We Hold These Truths*, p. 28.

[35] Murray, *We Hold These Truths*, pp. 33–34.

[36] In this way Murray made the case that there was compatibility between Catholicism and American life since the natural law heritage was the bridge between the founders of the republic and the Catholic tradition. His exposition of the affinity between Catholicism and American experience was for the benefit of his fellow Americans. It was the flip side of his work on religious liberty and U.S. church-state relations which was directed toward answering criticism of the U.S. arrangement by his fellow believers. Murray's genius at explaining Roman Catholicism to America is sometimes overlooked due to his notable effort at explaining America to Rome.

[37] Murray, *We Hold These Truths*, pp. 90–91.

[38] Murray, *We Hold These Truths*, p. 81.

[39] Murray, *We Hold These Truths*, pp. 79–89.

[40] Murray, *We Hold These Truths*, p. 80.

[41] "Murray, in short, envisioned a public theology in which biblical theology and religious imagery would be used sparingly at best." Dennis McCann, "Natural Law, Public Theology and the Legacy of John Courtney Murray," *The Christian Century* 107 (1990): 801–803 at 802. Also note the comment of David Hollenbach that one of Murray's "central methodological convictions" was the belief that the church's contribution to public discourse was best "formulated in the categories of philosophical reason rather than expressed in the symbols of religious belief." Hollenbach, ed., "Theology and Philosophy in Public," p. 700.

[42] For a commentary on Murray's debt to a theological position in the presentation of his natural law philosophy see David Hollenbach, "Public Theology in America: Some Questions for Catholicism after John Courtney Murray," *Theological Studies* 37 (1976): 290–303.

[43] Hollenbach, "Theology and Philosophy in Public," pp. 700–701.

[44] John Coleman, "A Possible Role for Biblical Religion in Public Life," in "Theology and Philosophy in Public," *Theological Studies* 40 (1979), p. 705.

[45] Coleman, "A Possible Role for Religion in Public Life," p. 702.

[46] Coleman, "A Possible Role for Religion in Public Life," pp. 705–706.

[47] Coleman, "A Possible Role for Religion in Public Life," p. 706.

[48] Coleman, "A Possible Role for Religion in Public Life," p. 706.

[49] Robin Lovin, "Resources for a Public Theology," in "Theology and Philosophy in Public," *Theological Studies* 40 (1979), p. 707.

[50] Lovin, "Resources for a Public Theology," p. 708.

[51] Lovin, "Resources for a Public Theology," p. 709.

[52] Hollenbach, "Public Theology in America," p. 299.

[53] Hollenbach, "Public Theology in America," p. 302.

[54] David Tracy, "Particular Classics, Public Religion, and the American Tradition," in *Religion and American Public Life*, pp. 115–131 at 115.

[55] "To be human means to live in a world—that is, to live in a reality that is ordered and that gives sense to the business of living. It is this fundamental characteristic of human existence that the term 'life-world' is intended to convey. This life-world is social both in its origins and in its ongoing maintenance: the meaningful order it provides for human lives has been established collectively and is kept going by collective consent." Peter Berger, Brigitte Berger, and Hansfried Kellner, *The Homeless Mind: Modernization and Consciousness* (New York: Random House, Vintage Books, 1973), p. 63.

For narrative theology, see Stanley Hauerwas and L. Gregory Jones, eds., *Why Narrative? Readings in Narrative Theology* (Grand Rapids: Eerdmans, 1989). The emergence of narrative-based theology has been due in large part to the increased appreciation of "sociology of knowledge," especially as that field has been developed by Peter L. Berger and Thomas Luckmann; see their *The Social Construction of Reality: A Treatise in the Sociology of Knowledge* (Garden City: Doubleday and Company, 1966). "It can be said without too much simplification that the sociology of knowledge is an enormous elaboration of Pascal's insight into the social relativity of human notions of truth. Put differently, the sociology of knowledge understands and studies the constructed character of what human beings mean by 'reality.' " Peter L. Berger and Hansfried Kellner, *Sociology Reinterpreted: An Essay on Method and Vocation* (Garden City: Anchor Press/Doubleday, Anchor Books, 1981), p. 59.

[56] One more than usually thoughtful version of this position is that advocated by George A. Lindbeck, *The Nature of Doctrine: Religion and Theology in a Postliberal Age* (Philadelphia: Westminster Press, 1984), the thesis of which is "that intersubjective communicative systems are the source rather than the product of distinctively human experience, whether religious or nonreligious" (p. 44, n. 18).

[57] Tracy, "Particular Classics, Public Religion, and the American Tradition," pp. 118–119.

[58] Tracy, "Particular Classics, Public Religion, and the American Tradition," p. 118.

[59] Tracy, "Particular Classics, Public Religion, and the American Tradition," p. 119.

[60] David Tracy, *The Analogical Imagination* (New York: Crossroad Publishing, 1981), pp. 99–154.

[61] Tracy, "Particular Classics, Public Religion, and the American Tradition," p. 123. See his description in *The Analogical Imagination*, p. 108: "My thesis is that what we mean in naming certain texts, events, images, rituals, symbols and persons 'classics' is that we here recognize nothing less than the disclosure of a reality we cannot but name truth. With Whitehead, here we find something valuable, something 'important'; some disclosure of reality in a moment that must be called one of 'recognition' which surprises, provokes, challenges, shocks and eventually transforms us; an experience that upsets conventional opinions and expands the sense of the possible; indeed a realized experience of that which is essential, that which endures."

[62] Tracy, *The Analogical Imagination*, p. 163: "Like all classics, religious classics will involve a claim to meaning and truth as one event of disclosure and concealment of the reality of lived existence. Unlike the classics of art, morality, science and politics, explicitly religious classic

expressions will involve a claim to truth as the event of a disclosure—concealment of the whole of reality *by the power of the whole*—as, in some sense, a radical and finally a gracious mystery."

[63] Tracy, "Particular Classics, Public Religion, and the American Tradition," p. 120.

[64] Tracy, *The Analogical Imagination*, pp. 6–28.

[65] Tracy, *The Analogical Imagination*, p. 31.

[66] Tracy, *The Analogical Imagination*, p. 29.

[67] Tracy, "Particular Classics, Public Religion, and the American Tradition," p. 125.

[68] Tracy, "Particular Classics, Public Religion, and the American Tradition," p. 126.

[69] In his essay "Social Contract or a Public Covenant" Robin Lovin has sought to show how the use of the biblical symbol of covenant can offer a way of thinking that is helpful in developing a more communal notion of social life. His interpretation of the symbol continues the Niebuhrian tradition and reflects the proposal of Tracy that the public test of an idea is in its effects not its origin. See *Religion and American Public Life*, pp. 132–145.

[70] Robert Bellah, Richard Madsen, William Sullivan, Ann Swidler, Steven Tipton, *The Good Society* (New York: Alfred Knopf, 1991), p. 179.

[71] Bellah, et al., *The Good Society*, p. 180.

[72] Bellah, et al., *The Good Society*, p. 180.

[73] Richard P. McBrien, *Caesar's Coin: Religion and Politics in America* (New York: Macmillan Publishing, 1987), p. 11.

[74] McBrien, *Caesar's Coin*, p. 25.

[75] In a frequently cited footnote in his commentary on the Declaration on Religious Freedom John Courtney Murray explains the public order as having a "threefold content": an order of justice (protection of basic rights and processes of adjudication), an order of peace (domestic tranquility), and a moral order (minimal standards of public morality). Thus, the public order entails juridical, political and moral values, all of which are part of the common good. But the common good also includes values beyond the powers of the limited constitutional state to enforce. See Walter Abbott, ed., Joseph Gallagher, trans. ed., *The Documents of Vatican II* (New York: New Century Publishers, 1966), p. 686, n. 20.

[76] Robert Bellah, "Civil Religion in America," *Daedalus* 96 (1967): 1–21.

[77] Bellah, "Civil Religion in America," p. 186. Bellah is very aware of the possibility that America can fail by the standards of its civil religion. He has examined the question whether that is precisely what has

happened in Robert N. Bellah, *The Broken Covenant: American Civil Religion in Time of Trial* (New York: The Seabury Press, 1975).

[78] On this point we differ with Marty's use of the term public theology. See p. 16 of *The Public Church* where he clarifies his use of the expression. For Marty it is closer to civil religion than our usage.

[79] It can also be said here that throughout the book the reader will notice that our commitment is to the Christian tradition with a preference for the Roman Catholic interpretation of that tradition. Because a genuinely Catholic reading of the tradition is ecumenical, we hope that a good deal of what we write will appeal to Christians of other communions. Furthermore, insofar as we achieve the aim of doing a public theology, we believe that what we write will be understandable to people of all or no religious persuasion.

[80] As quoted in Douglas Sturm, "Religious Sensibility and the Reconstruction of Public Life: Prospectus for a New America," in *Religion and American Public Life*, pp. 53–87 at 54.

[81] Robert Reich, "Introduction," pp. 1–12 at 1 in Robert Reich, ed., *The Power of Public Ideas* (Cambridge: Ballinger Publishing, 1988).

[82] Reich, "Introduction," p. 4.

[83] Bernstein, "The Meaning of Public Life," p. 37.

[84] See Reich, "Introduction," pp. 4–5.

[85] Paul Ramsey, *Who Speaks for the Church?* (Nashville: Abingdon Press, 1967).

[86] Bellah, et al., *The Good Society*, pp. 192–193.

[87] John Milbank, *Theology and Social Theory* (Oxford: Basil Blackwell, 1990).

2. Original Sin and the Myth of Self-Interest

[1] Gary Orren, "Beyond Self-Interest," and Steven Kelman, "Why Public Ideas Matter," both in Robert Reich, ed., *The Power of Public Ideas* (Cambridge: Ballinger Publishing, 1987), pp. 13–29 and 31–53.

[2] Kelman, "Why Public Ideas Matter," p. 43.

[3] John Rawls, *A Theory of Justice* (Cambridge: Belknap Press, 1971), and Robert Nozick, *Anarchy, State, and Utopia* (New York: Basic Books, 1974).

[4] Epitome, A.1, aff.3.

[5] III–IV C. a.1.

[6] C. VI, 2.

[7] C. VI, 4.

[8] David Carlin, "This, Too, Shall Pass," *Commonweal* 115 (1988): 8–9 at 9.

[9] Thomas Hobbes, *Leviathan, or the Matter, Forme, and Power of a*

Common-wealth Ecclesiasticall and Civill, ed. C.B. Macpherson (New York: Viking Penguin, 1968), p. 186.

¹⁰ Hobbes, *Leviathan,* p. 87.

¹¹ Hobbes, *Leviathan,* p. 185.

¹² Thomas Hobbes, *De Cive,* ed. S.P. Lamprecht (New York: Appleton-Century-Crofts, 1949), p. 24.

¹³ Richard Cumberland, *A Treatise of the Laws of Nature,* trans. John Maxwell (London: 1727).

¹⁴ Anthony Ashley Cooper, Earl of Shaftesbury, *Characteristics of Men, Manners, Opinions, Times,* ed. John Robertson (Indianapolis: Bobbs-Merrill, 1964).

¹⁵ Pierre Nicole, *Essais de Morale,* 4 vols. ("Luxembourg": 1671–1678).

¹⁶ Adam Smith, *An Inquiry into the Nature and Causes of the Wealth of Nations,* ed. Edwin Cannan (New York: Random House, Modern Library, 1937), p. 14.

¹⁷ Adam Smith, *The Theory of Moral Sentiments* (New York: Augustus M. Kelly, 1966), p. 120.

¹⁸ Smith, *Wealth of Nations,* p. 13.

¹⁹ Smith, *Wealth of Nations,* p. 421.

²⁰ Council of Trent, session 5 canon 1.

²¹ Council of Trent, session 6 cap. 1.

²² Council of Trent, session 6 canon 7.

²³ National Conference of Catholic Bishops, "Economic Justice for All: Catholic Social Teaching and the U.S. Economy," 28.

²⁴ Andrew Greeley, *No Bigger Than Necessary* (New York: Meridian Books, 1977), p. 92.

²⁵ Philip Gleason, "American Catholics and the Mythic Middle Ages," in *Keeping the Faith: American Catholicism Past and Present* (South Bend: University of Notre Dame Press, 1987), pp. 11–34.

²⁶ In this paragraph we have drawn on Christopher Lasch's essay "The Communitarian Critique of Liberalism," in Charles Reynolds and Ralph Norman, eds., *Community in America* (Berkeley: University of California Press, 1988), pp. 173–184 at 176–177.

²⁷ Hannah Arendt, *Men in Dark Times* (New York: Harcourt Brace Jovanovich, 1968), p. 24.

²⁸ Lasch, "The Communitarian Critique," p. 178.

²⁹ Our list is gleaned from various points mentioned in Allen Buchanan, "Assessing the Communitarian Critique of Liberalism," *Ethics* 99 (1989): 852–882, and Chantal Mouffe, "American Liberalism and Its Critics: Rawls, Taylor, Sandel and Walzer," *Praxis International* 8 (1988): 193–206.

[30] Greeley, *No Bigger Than Necessary,* p. 108. Greeley notes it is unfortunate that "very few American Catholics have bothered to reflect on the interpenetration of Catholic social theory and American political practice, which has been at the core of the American Catholic experience."

[31] J. Messner, *Social Ethics; Natural Law in the Modern World,* trans. J.J. Doherty (St. Louis: B. Herder Book Co., 1949), pp. 114–115.

[32] Greeley, *No Bigger Than Necessary.* This quote and the subsequent citations describing the three principles are all found on page 10.

[33] For a reflection on the role of the local church congregation as a mediating structure see, Kenneth R. Himes, "The Local Church as a Mediating Structure," *Social Thought* (1986): 23–30.

[34] See for example the use of scripture as found in the American bishops' pastoral letter "Economic Justice for All."

[35] Dennis McCann, "The Good to be Pursued in Common," in Oliver Williams and John Houck, eds., *The Common Good and U.S. Capitalism* (Lanham: University Press, 1987), pp. 158–178 at 164.

[36] Charles Curran, "The Changing Anthropological Bases of Catholic Social Ethics," in Charles Curran and Richard McCormick, eds. *Readings in Moral Theology, No. 5: Official Catholic Social Teaching* (New York: Paulist Press, 1986): 188–218. In our view, this essay will be considered among Curran's best in a long and distinguished career. We rely heavily on it in this section of the chapter.

[37] Curran, "Changing Anthropological Bases," p. 191.

[38] "For its part, authentic freedom is an exceptional sign of the divine image in man." *Gaudium et Spes,* 17.

[39] A closely argued analysis of this evolution is Drew Christiansen, "On Relative Equality: Catholic Egalitarianism After Vatican II," *Theological Studies* 45 (1984): 651–675.

[40] The various drafts of the pastoral letter are available through the National Catholic Documentary Service's periodical *Origins.* The first draft, which was entitled "Catholic Social Teaching and the U.S. Economy," may be found in volume 14 (1984): 336ff. The two questions are located in the opening paragraph of the letter. By the second draft of the letter, found in volume 15 (1985): 258ff, the additional question about participation was added. It remained in all subsequent drafts and the final version of the letter.

[41] For a more detailed argument supporting this conclusion including an explanation of the Augustinian and Thomistic basis for a nontotalitarian view of the state in communitarian thought, see David Hollenbach, "The Common Good Revisited," *Theological Studies* 50 (1989): 70–94.

[42] Christiansen, "On Relative Equality," p. 660.

[43] Christiansen, "On Relative Equality." This paragraph summarizes points made on pp. 657–658.

[44] Christiansen, "On Relative Equality," p. 674.

[45] Christiansen, "On Relative Equality," p. 675.

[46] Dennis McCann, "The Good to be Pursued in Common," p. 166.

[47] John Courtney Murray, *We Hold These Truths*, p. 33.

[48] Another point of difference between Murray and McCann is that the latter does not believe it is necessary to exclude overtly theological discourse from public discourse provided it meets the standards for public communication. On this topic, see chapter one. Among the similarities between Murray and McCann is that both authors have noted that the practice of public conversation by the church in society will eventually redound to the good of the internal life and structures of the church, moving it toward increasingly open, free and honest communication.

[49] Dennis McCann, "The Good to be Pursued in Common."

[50] Hollenbach, "The Common Good Revisited," p. 88.

[51] An illuminating essay explaining this development within Catholic social teaching is "Global Human Rights: An Interpretation of the Contemporary Catholic Understanding," in David Hollenbach, *Justice, Peace, and Human Rights* (New York: Crossroad Publishing, 1988), pp. 87–100.

[52] Buchanan, "Assessing the Communitarian Critique of Liberalism," p. 855.

[53] The notion that the common good includes the well-being of social groups as well as individuals is reflected in the teaching of Vatican Council II. There the common good is described as "the sum of those conditions of social life which allow social groups and their individual members relatively thorough and ready access to their own fulfillment. . . ." *Gaudium et Spes*, 26. This topic will be taken up at greater length in chapter 6.

[54] Maryanne Glendon, *Abortion and Divorce in Western Law* (Cambridge: Harvard University Press, 1990).

[55] Charles Wilber, "Economic Theory and the Common Good," in *The Common Good and U.S. Capitalism*, pp. 244–254.

[56] Garrett Hardin, "The Tragedy of the Commons," *Science* 162 (1968): 1243–1248.

[57] Wilber, "Economic Theory and the Common Good," p. 248.

[58] A recent book which advocates proposals that are in accord with our view on community-based organizations is David Osborne and Ted

Gaebler, *Reinventing Government* (Reading: Addison-Wesley Publishing, 1992), especially chapters 1, 2 and Appendix A.

[59] Many of the ideas listed under the heading of policy implications were taken from Greeley, *No Bigger Than Necessary*, pp. 127–151.

[60] A fine collection of studies that argues against liberalism's emphasis on self-interest is Jane Mansbridge, ed., *Beyond Self-Interest* (Chicago: University of Chicago Press, 1990). The volume contains essays representing an array of disciplines in addition to political science and economics.

[61] See Douglas Sturm, "Religious Sensibility and the Reconstruction of Public Life," in *Religion and American Public Life*, pp. 53–87, esp. 61–68.

3. The Trinity and Human Rights

[1] John XXIII, *Pacem in Terris*, 11–27 in William Gibbons, ed., *Seven Great Encyclicals* (New York: Paulist Press, 1963).

[2] Hollenbach, *Justice, Peace, and Human Rights*, p. 87.

[3] National Conference of Catholic Bishops, "Economic Justice for All: Catholic Social Teaching and U.S. Economy" (Washington, D.C.: United States Catholic Conference, 1987).

[4] Augustine, *De trinitate* 8, 10, 14.

[5] Augustine, *De trinitate* 7, 6, 11.

[6] Thomas Aquinas, *Summa theologiae* I, q. 29, a. 3; the general principle is found in I, q. 13, a. 2.

[7] Aquinas, *Summa theologiae* I, q. 29, a. 4.

[8] Rowan Williams, "Trinity and Revelation" *Modern Theology* 2 (1986): 197–212 at 199.

[9] Norman Gottwald, *The Tribes of Yahweh: A Sociology of the Religion of Liberated Israel 1250–1050 B.C.E.* (London: S. C. M., 1979).

[10] Williams, "Trinity and Revelation," p. 200; the reference is to Paul Ricoeur, "Toward a Hermeneutic of the Idea of Revelation," and "The Hermeneutics of Testimony," in Lewis Mudge, ed., *Essays on Biblical Interpretation* (Philadelphia: Fortress Press, 1980), pp. 73–118 and 119–154 respectively.

[11] Williams, "Trinity and Revelation," p. 200.

[12] Walter Kasper, *The God of Jesus Christ*, trans. by Matthew O'Connell (New York: Crossroad, 1984), p. 311.

[13] Aristotle, *Politics*, 1253 a.3.

[14] *Gaudium et Spes*, 12, 40–42.

[15] *Gaudium et Spes*, 24.

[16] John Paul II, *Centesimus Annus*, 41.

[17] S.I. Benn and R.S. Peters, *The Principles of Political Thought* (New York: The Free Press, 1959), p. 108.

[18] Here we accept David Hollenbach's suggestion of the pluralistic nature of a world church as a backdrop for understanding why the papacy has come to embrace so closely human rights theory. See *Justice, Peace and Human Rights*, pp. 87–100. The rest of this section will draw upon Hollenbach.

[19] More than any particular passage in the document *Dignitatis Humanae*, it is the very document itself, acknowledging the diversity of cultures, beliefs, persons and patterns of social organization, which indicates the church's awareness of the reality of a pluralistic world.

[20] Karl Rahner, "Towards a Fundamental Theological Interpretation of Vatican II," *Theological Studies* 40 (1979): 716–727.

[21] Paul VI, *Octogesima Adveniens*, 4.

[22] 1971 Synod of Bishops, "Justice in the World."

[23] National Conference of Catholic Bishops, "Economic Justice For All," 79.

[24] For a reflection on the fact that humans are "more than rights-bearing creatures," see Michael Ignatieff, *The Needs of Strangers, An essay on privacy, solidarity and the politics of being human* (New York: Penguin Books, 1984), pp. 13–14.

[25] John Paul II, *Redemptor Hominis*, 16.

[26] Barrington Moore, *Reflections on the Causes of Human Misery* (Boston: Beacon Press, 1973).

[27] David Price, "The Quest for Community and Public Policy" (Bloomington: Poynter Center, 1977), p. 3.

[28] Maurice Cranston, "Human Rights, Real and Supposed," in D.D. Raphael, ed., *Political Theory and the Rights of Man* (Bloomington: Indiana University Press, 1967), pp. 43–53. See also an earlier article by Cranston for his criticism of Catholic social thought in this area, "Pope John XXIII On Peace and The Rights of Man," *Political Quarterly* 34 (1963): 380–390.

[29] Cranston, "Human Rights, Real and Supposed," p. 53.

[30] David Watson, "Welfare Rights and Human Rights," *Journal of Social Policy* 6 (1977): 31–46 at 35.

[31] D.D. Raphael, "Human Rights Old and New," in *Political Theory and the Rights of Man*, 54–67 at 64.

[32] Joel Feinberg, "Rights: Systematic Analysis," in Warren Reich, ed., *Encyclopedia of Bioethics* (New York: Macmillan Company, n.d.).

[33] Cranston, "Human Rights, Real and Supposed," p. 52.

[34] It must be admitted that not everything proposed as a right should actually count as one. Even the United Nations Declaration may go too far in stating that paid vacations are human rights. Nevertheless, abuse of a sound principle should not obscure sound use.

[35] Watson, "Welfare Rights," p. 40.

[36] Thomas Paine, *Rights of Man*, ed. Henry Collins (Middlesex, England: Pelican Books, 1969), esp. chapter 5. See also D.D. Raphael, "The Liberal Western Tradition of Human Rights," *International Social Science Journal* 18 (1966): 22–30 for additional historical examples.

[37] Carl Friedrich, "Rights, Liberties, Freedom," *The American Political Science Review* 57 (1963): 841–854 at 846.

[38] It is even more difficult to explain a duty corresponding to the right of self-giving. However that duty is to be delineated, it presumes a degree of human relatedness. For this reason, Catholic social thought maintains there is a communal context for human rights, for without such a context it is hard to fulfill the duty which is the correlative of the fundamental right to give oneself away. Perhaps one might postulate there is an *in rem* duty to build and maintain community implicit in Catholic social teaching.

4. Grace and a Consistent Ethic of Life

[1] Leszek Kolakowski, "The Revenge of the Sacred in Secular Culture," in *Modernity on Endless Trial* (Chicago: The University of Chicago Press, 1990), pp. 68–69.

[2] Kolakowski notes in another essay the familiar story in the synoptic gospels and correctly rejects the interpretation of it which would justify two independent sources of power or authority, church and state. In line with his insistence on inevitable conflict between the sacred and the secular, he interprets it as a religious devaluation of the secular in an extreme eschatological context: "To read into [Jesus' statement] a general theory of two independent, or partially independent, legitimate sources of power was an extremely inflated and distorting exegesis. Still, Jesus' saying is quite in keeping with his teaching if it means, 'Give to Caesar the earthly goods he desires, his power is short-lived anyway in the face of the imminent descent of God's kingdom. Caesar is not important; all his glory will soon evaporate without a trace.' The oncoming Apocalypse is the never-fading framework of Jesus' preaching." "Politics and the Devil," in *Modernity on Endless Trial*, p. 183.

[3] *Faust*, Part I, ll. 1335–1336.

[4] Ll. 1337–1344.

[5] *Inter multa alia, Summa theologiae* I, q. 4, ad. 3.

[6] Ignatius of Loyola, *Spiritual Exercises,* trans. Anthony Mottola (New York: Doubleday and Company, 1964), p. 75 and passim.

[7] David Tracy, *The Analogical Imagination,* p. 212.

[8] *Summa contra gentiles,* III, 70.

[9] Nicholas Lash, *Easter in Ordinary: Reflections on Human Experience and the Knowledge of God* (Charlottesville: University Press of Virginia, 1988), p. 249.

[10] E.g. see Emile Durkheim, *The Elementary Forms of the Religious Life,* trans. by Joseph Ward Swain (London: George Allen and Unwin, 1915; New York: Free Press, 1965), pp. 235–272.

[11] Langdon Gilkey, *Reaping the Whirlwind: A Christian Interpretation of History* (New York: Seabury Press, 1976), p. 68. Gilkey acknowledges that his analysis of the ultimacy of politics draws heavily on the work of Paul Tillich; see Gilkey's fine discussion of Tillich's early political writings in relation to his later theological work, in *Gilkey on Tillich* (New York: Crossroad Publishing Company, 1981), pp. 3–22.

[12] Langdon Gilkey, "The Political Dimensions of Theology," in *Society and the Sacred: Toward a Theology of Culture in Decline* (New York: Crossroad Publishing Company, 1981), pp. 42–56 at 45.

[13] Gilkey's statement of the need for political "demythologizing" has strong echoes of the classical Protestant view of the human person as *simul justus et peccator*; see *Reaping the Whirlwind,* p. 68: "Because the call to us is fragmentary and the called partly unclean, the condemnation is on us and on the immediate future we will help to create as well as on the world and on the world's past and present."

[14] Karl Rahner, "The Experience of God Today," in *Theological Investigations* 11 (New York: Seabury Press, 1974), pp. 149–165 at 154. We are expanding Rahner's point from individual experience to communal experience, an expansion justified by Rahner's own recognition that the person is radically communal in construction.

[15] Langdon Gilkey, "Symbols, Meaning, and Divine Presence," *Theological Studies* 35 (1974): 249–267 at 261.

[16] Gilkey, "Symbols, Meaning, and Divine Presence," p. 266.

[17] Kolakowski, "The Revenge of the Sacred in Secular Culture," p. 69.

[18] *Lumen Gentium,* 1,1.

[19] Gerard Manley Hopkins, *The Poems of Gerard Manley Hopkins,* 4th ed., rev. and enl., ed. by W.H. Gardner and N.H. MacKenzie (London: Oxford University Press, 1967), p. 90.

[20] Lash, *Easter in Ordinary,* pp. 284f.

²¹ In the remainder of this section we summarize ideas of Gilkey found in "Symbols, Meaning, and the Divine Presence," pp. 255–262.

²² Gilkey, "Symbols, Meaning, and Divine Presence," p. 256.

²³ Gilkey, "Symbols, Meaning, and Divine Presence," p. 257.

²⁴ Gilkey, "Symbols, Meaning, and Divine Presence," p. 258.

²⁵ Gilkey, "Symbols, Meaning, and Divine Presence," pp. 260–261.

²⁶ For a sampling of the variety of rationales for the sanctity of life as a moral principle see, David Thomasma, *Human Life in the Balance* (Louisville: Westminster/John Knox Press, 1990), esp. chs. 5–7.

²⁷ Daniel Maguire, *The Moral Choice* (New York: Winston Press, 1979), p. 72.

²⁸ Daniel Maguire, *The Moral Choice*, pp. 84ff.

²⁹ Warren Reich, "Quality of Life," *Encyclopedia of Bioethics*, v. 2 , pp. 829–840 at 832.

³⁰ Reich, "Quality of Life," p. 831.

³¹ We are indebted to James Walter for pointing out the analogical, comprehensive and dialogical qualities of Bernardin's proposal. See Walter's essay which was originally part of a symposium held at Loyola University in Chicago, "Response to John C. Finnis: A Theological Critique," in Thomas Fuechtmann, ed., *Consistent Ethic of Life* (Kansas City: Sheed and Ward, 1988), pp. 182–195.

³² Joseph Bernardin, "Enlarging the Dialogue on a Consistent Ethic of Life," *Origins* 13 (1984): 705–709 at 707.

³³ Joseph Bernardin, "The Consistent Ethic After 'Webster,'" *Commonweal* 117 (1990): 242–248 at 248.

³⁴ Bernardin, "Enlarging the Dialogue," p. 709.

³⁵ A helpful essay discussing the role of theology in moral reflection is Richard McCormick, "Theology and Bioethics," *Hastings Center Report* 19 (1991): 5–10.

³⁶ Bernardin, "Enlarging the Dialogue," p. 708.

³⁷ A critical commentary on the American predilection for utilitarian methods of public policy calculus, such as cost-benefit analysis, can be found in Robert Bellah, et al., *The Good Society* (New York: Alfred Knopf, 1991), ch. 4.

³⁸ Joseph Bernardin, "Religion and Politics: The Future Agenda," *Origins* 14 (1984): 321–328 at 325. The subsequent quotes in the paragraph are also taken from this source.

³⁹ Thomasma, *Human Life in the Balance*, p. 64.

⁴⁰ Bernardin, "Religion and Politics," p. 326.

⁴¹ Bernardin, "Religion and Politics," p. 326.

⁴² Bernardin, "The Consistent Ethic After 'Webster,'" p. 242.

⁴³ Bernardin, "The Consistent Ethic After 'Webster,'" p. 243.

⁴⁴ Bernardin, "The Consistent Ethic After Webster,'" p. 244.

⁴⁵ Bernardin, "Religion and Politics," p. 326.

⁴⁶ Bernardin, "Religion and Politics," p. 327.

⁴⁷ James Malone, "Religion and the '84 Campaign," *Origins* 14 (1984): 161–163 at 163.

⁴⁸ This section is largely an excerpt from Kenneth R. Himes, "Single Issue Politics and the Church," *America* 156 (1987): 377–381.

⁴⁹ *Gaudium et Spes*, 42–44.

⁵⁰ Bernardin, "The Consistent Ethic After 'Webster,'" p. 245.

⁵¹ John Coleman, *An American Strategic Theology* (New York: Paulist Press, 1982). The exact citation is found on p. 259, but throughout the volume there is wise advice on the manner of how the church should engage the social order.

5. Creation and an Environmental Ethic

¹ John Paul II, "Peace With God the Creator, Peace With All of Creation," *Origins* 19 (1989): 465–468.

² Ian Barbour, *Religion in an Age of Science*, The Gifford Lectures, vol. 1 (San Francisco: Harper and Row, 1990); Paul Santmire, *The Travail of Nature: The Ambiguous Ecological Promise of Christian Theology* (Philadelphia: Fortress Press, 1985); Joseph Sittler, *Essays on Nature and Grace* (Philadelphia: Fortress Press, 1972).

³ Lynn White, "The Historical Roots of the Ecological Crisis," *Science* 155 (1967): 1203–1207.

⁴ Matthew Fox, *Creation Spirituality* (San Francisco: Harper, 1991).

⁵ Anne Lonergan and Caroline Richards, eds., *Thomas Berry and the New Cosmology* (Mystic: Twenty-Third Publications, 1988). This volume includes two representative essays of Berry's as well as a number of brief responses to his work by sympathetic critics.

⁶ Richard McCormick, "Does Religious Faith Add to Ethical Perception?" in John Haughey, ed., *Personal Values in Public Policy* (New York: Paulist Press, 1979), pp. 155–173 at 169.

⁷ Charles Murphy, *At Home on Earth: Foundations for a Catholic Ethic of the Environment* (New York: Crossroad Publishing Company, 1989), p. 30.

⁸ *Scientific American* 261 (1989): 172.

⁹ Lester Thurow, *The Zero-Sum Society* (New York: Basic Books, 1980), p. 105 as quoted by Murphy, *At Home on Earth*, p. xvii.

¹⁰ Murphy, *At Home on Earth*, p. 26.

[11] A review not only of Judaism's and Christianity's but the other major world religions' encounter with the environmental movement is Martin Palmer, "The Encounter of Religion and Conservation," pp. 50–62 in J. Ronald Engel and Joan Gibb Engel, eds., *Ethics of Environment and Development* (Tucson: University of Arizona Press, 1990), pp. 50–62.

[12] John Paul II, *Sollicitudo Rei Socialis*, 34.

[13] Drew Christiansen, "Ecology, Justice and Development," *Theological Studies* 51 (1990): 64–81. This is an excellent overview of recent literature in the field. We have relied upon it at several points throughout this chapter. In addition, the entire issue of *Scientific American* 261 (September 1989) provides an extremely valuable introduction and overview to ecological issues from the perspective of a variety of empirical disciplines. These two publications are warmly recommended to those interested in understanding the framework and issues in the environmental debate and a religious response.

[14] Charles Murphy argues, "Since human dominion over the creation is to be carried out on behalf of God and is accountable to him, the divine rule becomes the norm of human behavior in this regard. Understood in this way, to have dominion emerges as 'to care for,' not to manipulate and to exploit." *At Home on Earth*, p. 92.

[15] Martin Buber, *I and Thou*, trans. Walter Kaufman (New York: Charles Scribners' Sons, 1970).

[16] St. Augustine, *Confessions*.

[17] Augustine, *Confessions*, Bk. 9, 10, 25.

[18] The scientist Marston Bates once was asked by a student, "What good are butteflies?" Bates replied, "What good are you?" As Lazarus Macior comments, the two questions reflect the polarization of attitudes toward the value of nature. The student measured nature in terms of his physical needs. Bates saw humanity as part of a larger reality not encompassed by humanity's physical need. One view is thoroughgoingly anthropocentric. The other view could be either biocentric or theocentric. See Lazarus Macior, "A Sense of the Sacred in Creation and Natural Science," *Proceedings of the 13th Convention of the Fellowship of Catholic Scholars*, P.L. Williams, ed. (Pittston: Northeast Books, 1990), pp. 101–107 at 101.

[19] Martin Heidegger, *An Introduction to Metaphysics*, trans. Ralph Manheim (New Haven: Yale University Press, 1959), p. 1.

[20] In his brief volume on Francis, G.K. Chesteron nicely portrays the saint's vision. Describing the heavily fortified stone walls and houses of Assisi, Chesterton suggests that Francis saw his world turned upside down as he gazed at the city from across the Umbrian valley. Those

things which seemed most secure and safe due to their solidity and weight now hung most precariously over the abyss of non-being. Chesterton comments that Francis grasped the truth that creation is held in existence by God's loving and ongoing providence and that even what appears to be self-sufficient is, in fact, contingent upon God's creative action. In this way Chesterton artistically expresses the lesson of the doctrine of *creatio ex nihilo*. See G.K. Chesterton, *St. Francis of Assisi* (Garden City: Image Books, 1957), pp. 70–75.

[21] Jonathan Edwards, *Treatise on Religious Affections*, ed. John E. Smith, *The Works of Jonathan Edwards*, vol. 2, ed. Perry Miller (New Haven: Yale University Press, 1959), p. 197.

[22] Edwards, *Treatise on Religious Affections*, p. 205.

[23] Paul Ricoeur, "Toward a Hermeneutic of the Idea of Revelation," in Lewis Mudge, ed., *Essays on Biblical Interpretation* (Philadelphia: Fortress Press, 1980), pp. 73–118 at 117.

[24] Gerard Manley Hopkins, "Hurrahing in Harvest," in W.H. Gardner and N.H. Mackenzie, eds., *The Poems of Gerard Manley Hopkins*, 4th ed. (London: Oxford University Press, 1967), p. 70.

[25] John Paul II, *Sollicitudo Rei Socialis*, 34.

[26] Murphy, *At Home on Earth*, p. 93.

[27] Christiansen, "Ecology, Justice and Development," p. 79.

[28] John XXIII, *Mater et Magistra*, 65.

[29] John XXIII, *Pacem in Terris*, 11–27.

[30] John Paul II, "Peace with God the Creator," 9.

[31] John Paul II, "Address to the General Assembly of the United Nations Organization" (October 2, 1979), 13.

[32] On the idea of environmental bankruptcy, see Jim McNeill, "Strategies for Sustainable Economic Development," *Scientific American* 261 (1989): 155–165 at 157.

[33] There is a developing body of literature on animal rights and the rights of nature. We have found the essay of the German theologian Wolfgang Huber to be helpful in this regard. Huber suggests that the motive behind ascribing rights to nature is a noble one. "It rests on the insight that human action is a threat to non-human nature and so must be contained by the latter's interests." But, he maintains, this aim can be attained without ascribing rights to non-human nature. Huber's analysis of the logical difficulty with rights of nature is one we find persuasive. "It is enough to state that non-human nature has not only an instrumental or intrinsic value but also an inherent dignity. By *inherent dignity* I mean an integrity unrelated to any extraneous purpose." We believe that recov-

ery of the theme of companionship can assist in the deepening of human appreciation for the dignity of creation and the integrity of creatures. "Rights of Nature or Dignity of Nature?" in *The Annual of the Society of Christian Ethics,* ed. Diane Yeager (Washington, D.C.: Georgetown University Press, 1991), pp. 43–60 at 54.

[34] John Paul II, *Centesimus Annus,* 31, 37.

[35] John XXIII, *Pacem in Terris,* 132.

[36] John XXIII, *Pacem in Terris,* 54.

[37] John XXIII, *Pacem in Terris,* 135.

[38] William D. Ruckelshaus, "Toward a Sustainable World," *Scientific American* 261 (1989): 166–174.

[39] Leonardo Boff, *St. Francis, a Model for Human Liberation* (New York: Crossroad Publishing, 1982), p. 38.

[40] Boff, *St. Francis,* p. 39.

[41] Boff, *St. Francis,* p. 39.

[42] Boff, *St. Francis,* p. 35.

[43] Christiansen, "Ecology, Justice and Development," pp. 66–67, helpfully summarizes the conclusions of third world leaders at the 1989 U.N. General Assembly under these headings.

[44] "The newly industrialized states cannot, for example, be asked to apply restrictive environmental standards to their emerging industries unless the industrialized states first apply them within their own boundaries. At the same time, countries in the process of industrialization are not morally free to repeat the errors made in the past by others. . . ." John Paul II, "Peace with God the Creator," 10.

[45] McNeill, "Strategies for Sustainable Development," p. 157.

[46] "Some heavily indebted nations are destroying their natural heritage, at the price of irreparable ecological imbalances, in order to develop new products for export. In the face of such situations it would be wrong to assign responsibility to the poor alone for the negative environmental consequences of their actions." John Paul II, "Peace with God the Creator," 11.

[47] "Rural poverty and unjust land distribution in many countries, for example, have led to subsistence farming and to the exhaustion of the soil. Once their land yields no more, many farmers move on to clear new land, thus accelerating uncontrolled deforestation. . . ." John Paul II, "Peace with God the Creator," 11.

[48] It was in *Mater et Magistra* that John XXIII expanded the usual papal focus on Europe to embrace the agenda of the wider world. Although he did not write an encyclical on the topic it was Pius XII who set

the stage for this shift with his reflections on the emerging world order following World War II.

⁴⁹ Paul VI, *Progressio Populorum*, 34–36, 40–42.

⁵⁰ 1971 Synod, *Justitia in Mundo* (Washington, D.C.: United States Catholic Conference, 1972), p. 36.

⁵¹ Donal Dorr, *Option for the Poor* (Maryknoll: Orbis Books, 1983), pp. 180–182.

⁵² John Paul II, *Redemptor Hominis*, 16.

⁵³ John Paul II, *Sollicitudo Rei Socialis*, 26 and 34.

⁵⁴ William Clark, "Managing Planet Earth," *Scientific American* 261 (1989): 47–54 at 48, quoting the report of the World Commission on Environment and Development, *Our Common Future* (New York: Oxford University Press, 1987).

⁵⁵ Clark, "Managing Planet Earth," p. 48.

⁵⁶ John Paul II, *Centesimus Annus*, 37.

⁵⁷ Murphy, *At Home on Earth*, p. 95.

⁵⁸ Christiansen, "Ecology, Justice and Development," p. 74.

⁵⁹ "An education in ecological responsibility is urgent: responsibility for oneself, for others and for the earth. This education cannot be rooted in mere sentiment or empty wishes. Its purpose cannot be ideological or political. It must not be based on a rejection of the modern world or a vague desire to return to some 'paradise lost.' " John Paul II, "Peace with God the Creator," 13.

⁶⁰ In this paragraph we borrow ideas from J. Bryan Hehir, although he was not writing in the context of the environmental issue. See his articles, "Mobilizing opinion, curbing technology," *Commonweal* 110 (1983): 298 and 319; "SDI: new technologies but old questions," *Commonweal* 111 (1984): 552.

⁶¹ Parker Palmer, *The Active Life, A Spirituality of Work, Creativity, and Caring* (San Francisco: Harper and Row, 1990), p. 52.

⁶² Palmer, *The Active Life*, p. 53.

⁶³ Dante Alighieri, *The Divine Comedy*. "Paradiso" (Canto 33 Line 145) 3:145.

6. Incarnation and Patriotism

¹ Oliver O'Donovan, "The Loss of a Sense of Place," *Irish Theological Quarterly* 55 (1989): 39–58 at 46.

² "We are not dealing here with the 'abstract' man, but the real, 'concrete,' 'historical' man." John Paul II, *Redemptor Hominis*, 13.

³ *Summa theologiae* II-II, q.26, a.6.

⁴ *Summa theologiae* II-II, q.26, a.6, *ad primum*.

⁵ *Summa theologiae* II-II, q.26, a.7.

[6] *Summa theologiae* II-II, q.26, a.7.

[7] The paragraphs above draw upon the analysis of Enda McDonagh, *Gift and Call* (St. Meinrad: Abbey Press, 1975), ch. 2.

[8] Pius XI, *Quadragesimo Anno*, 79, is the classic locus for the principle of subsidiarity.

[9] A recent exposition of the importance of intermediate organizations in the life of any society is found in John Paul II, *Centesimus Annus*, 49.

[10] Andrew Greeley, *No Bigger Than Necessary*, pp. 8–9.

[11] Paul Waddell, *Friendship and the Moral Life* (Notre Dame: University of Notre Dame Press, 1989), p. 81.

[12] Michael Ignatieff, *The Needs of Strangers*, p. 29.

[13] Greeley, *No Bigger Than Necessary*, p. 112.

[14] Alasdair MacIntyre, "Is Patriotism a Virtue?" The Lindley Lecture (Lawrence: University of Kansas, 1984), p. 16.

[15] MacIntyre, "Is Patriotism a Virtue?" p. 16.

[16] MacIntyre, "Is Patriotism a Virtue?" p. 4.

[17] Aristotle, *Nichomachean Ethics*, 1106b–1107a.

[18] Giambattista Vico, *The New Science of Giambattista Vico*, 3rd ed., trans. by Thomas Goddard Bergin and Max Harold Fisch (Ithaca: Cornell University Press, 1948), see esp. Book 4.

[19] *Oeuvres complètes de J. de Maistre*, 14 vols. and index (Paris/Lyons, 1884–1887), 1:74, quoted in Isaiah Berlin, "Joseph de Maistre and the Origins of Fascism," in Henry Hardy, ed., *The Crooked Timber of Humanity: Chapters in the History of Ideas* (New York: Alfred A. Knopf, 1991), p. 100.

[20] H. Richard Niebuhr, *Radical Monotheism and Western Culture, With Supplementary Essays* (New York: Harper and Row, 1943), p. 11.

[21] Niebuhr, *Radical Monotheism*, p. 27. Niebuhr also designated humanism a form of henotheism. Thus he did not regard the universal goals of humanity embraced by the *philosophes* as an acceptable or even a real alternative to nationalism. "The religion of humanism, starting as protest against the doubtful assurance and the partial loyalties of closed societies, ends with an enlarged but yet dubious and partial closed-society faith. It remains a kind of henotheism" (p. 35).

[22] Robert Goodin reports that the example originates with William Godwin in a book published in 1793. See Robert Goodin, "What Is So Special about Our Fellow Countrymen?" *Ethics* 98 (1988): 663–686 at 665 n.5.

[23] We omit here the additional complication of cases of familial favoritism which are unacceptable. This issue will be remarked upon later in the chapter.

²⁴ Goodin writes, "Within the conventional wisdom about international relations, nation-states are conceptualized as ongoing mutual-benefit societies." See "What Is So Special about Our Fellow Countrymen?" p. 675.

²⁵ David Miller, "The Ethical Significance of Nationality," *Ethics* 98 (1988): 647–662 at 651.

²⁶ Miller, "The Ethical Significance of Nationality," p. 652.

²⁷ The example is drawn from Goodin, "What Is So Special about Our Fellow Countrymen?" p. 678.

²⁸ Goodin, "What Is So Special about Our Fellow Countrymen?" p. 678.

²⁹ Miller, "The Ethical Significance of Nationality," p. 652.

³⁰ Gilbert K. Chesterton, "The Reality of Nationalism," in Lawrence Clipper, ed., *The Collected Works of G.K. Chesterton* XXIX (San Francisco: Ignatius Press, 1988), pp. 284–288 at 287.

³¹ Miller, "The Ethical Significance of Nationality," p. 656.

³² Richard Sennett, *The Fall of Public Man* (New York: Alfred Knopf, 1977), p. 259, as quoted by Parker Palmer, *The Company of Strangers* (New York: Crossroad Publishing, 1986), p. 49.

³³ Palmer, *The Company of Strangers*, pp. 120–121.

³⁴ Miller, "The Ethical Significance of Nationality," p. 654.

³⁵ Paul Gomberg, "Patriotism Is like Racism," *Ethics* 98 (1988): 144–150 at 144. Another definition of moral universalism is "the doctrine that all persons ought to be treated with equal and impartial positive consideration for their respective goods or interests." Alan Gewirth, "Ethical Universalism and Particularism," *The Journal of Philosophy* 85 (1988): 283–302 at 283.

³⁶ Gewirth, "Ethical Universalism and Particularism," p. 283.

³⁷ Miller, "The Ethical Significance of Nationality," p. 647.

³⁸ Miller, "The Ethical Significance of Nationality," p. 649. The author notes that this approach is very similar to what is attained by use of the "original position" of John Rawls. It is the kind of agency that one finds behind the "veil of ignorance."

³⁹ The emphasis on human rights in Catholic social teaching has been analyzed by a number of authors. A good overview of the teaching is John Langan, "Human Rights in Roman Catholicism," in Charles Curran and Richard McCormick, eds., *Readings in Moral Theology*, v. 5 (New York: Paulist Press, 1986), pp. 110–129.

⁴⁰ O'Donovan, "The Loss of a Sense of Place," p. 56.

⁴¹ Alasdair MacIntyre, "Is Patriotism a Virtue?" p. 5.

⁴² O'Donovan, "The Loss of a Sense of Place," 54.

⁴³ O'Donovan, "The Loss of a Sense of Place," p. 53.

⁴⁴ The chief competitor to human rights as a universalist moral theory is utilitarianism.

⁴⁵ Goodin, "What Is So Special about Our Fellow Countrymen?" p. 678.

⁴⁶ Excerpts of Sumner's essay, "The Conquest of the United States by Spain," were printed in *The Washington Post* (June 9, 1991), sec. D, p. 5.

⁴⁷ William Graham Sumner, "The Conquest of the United States by Spain."

⁴⁸ Sumner, "The Conquest of the United States by Spain."

⁴⁹ G.K. Chesterton, "A Denunciation of Patriotism," as quoted in Michael Finch, *G.K. Chesterton* (San Francisco: Harper and Row, 1986), p. 89.

⁵⁰ Chesterton, "A Denunciation of Patriotism," Finch, p. 89.

⁵¹ Chesterton, "A Denunciation of Patriotism," Finch, p. 89.

⁵² Chesterton, "A Denunciation of Patriotism," Finch, pp. 90–91.

⁵³ Chesterton, "A Denunciation of Patriotism," Finch, p. 89.

7. The Communion of Saints and an Ethic of Solidarity

¹ William Wordsworth, *The Prelude: A Parallel Text,* ed. by J.C. Maxwell (New Haven: Yale University Press, 1971), 11: 108–109, p. 441.

² Immanuel Kant, "What Is Enlightenment?" trans. by Lewis White Beck, in Immanuel Kant, *On History,* ed. by Lewis White Beck (Indianapolis: The Library of Liberal Arts, Bobbs-Merrill, 1963), p. 3.

³ Immanuel Kant, "Idea for a Universal History from a Cosmopolitan Point of View," trans. by Lewis White Beck, in Kant, *On History,* p. 17.

⁴ Kant, "Idea for a Universal History," p. 21.

⁵ J. Hector St. John de Crèvecoeur, *Letters from an American Farmer* (New York: E.P. Dutton, 1957), pp. 39–40.

⁶ Archibald MacLeish, "America Was Promises," in *New and Collected Poems, 1917–1976* (Boston: Houghton Mifflin, 1976), p. 323.

⁷ Ralph Waldo Emerson, "The American Scholar: An Oration delivered before the Phi Beta Kappa Society, At Cambridge, August 31, 1837," *Ralph Waldo Emerson: Essays and Lectures* (New York: The Library of America, 1983), pp. 53–71 at 57.

⁸ Emerson, "The American Scholar," p. 57.

⁹ Thomas Jefferson, "Letter to James Madison, January 30, 1787," in Merrill D. Peterson, ed., *The Portable Thomas Jefferson* (New York: Viking Press, 1975), pp. 416ff.

[10] Jefferson, "Letter to James Madison, December 20, 1787," in *The Portable Jefferson*, p. 431.

[11] Jefferson proposed this plan and the figures by which he had determined nineteen years as the acceptable limit to Madison in a letter of September 6, 1789, and still advanced the idea in a letter of July 12, 1816; see *The Portable Jefferson*, pp. 444–451 and 552–561.

[12] Jefferson, "Letter to James Madison, September 6, 1789," *The Portable Jefferson*, p. 449.

[13] Jefferson, "Letter to Samuel Kercheval, July 12, 1816," *The Portable Jefferson*, p. 560.

[14] Jefferson, "Letter to Major John Cartwright, June 5, 1824," *The Portable Jefferson*, p. 580.

[15] See the Fourth Eclogue, 11, 4–5:

> *Ultima Cumaei venit iam carminis aetas;*
> *Magnus ab integro saeclorum nascitur ordo.*

[16] Abraham Lincoln, "First Inaugural Address," in Don P. Fehrenbacher, ed., *Abraham Lincoln: Speeches and Writings*, 2 vols. (New York: The Library of America, 1989), 2: 224. It is interesting to note that in this speech Lincoln rejected the idea which Jefferson had held that governments should be reconstituted in every generation: "I hold, that in contemplation of universal law, and of the Constitution, the Union of these States is perpetual. Perpetuity is implied, if not expressed, in the fundamental law of all national governments. It is safe to assert that no government proper, ever had a provision in its organic law for its own termination," 2: 217.

[17] Abraham Lincoln, "Address Delivered at the Dedication of the Cemetery at Gettysburg, November 19, 1863," *Abraham Lincoln: Speeches and Writings*, 2: 536.

[18] Edmund Burke, *Reflections on the Revolution in France and on the Proceedings in Certain Societies in London Relative to the Event*, ed. by Conor Cruise O'Brien (London: Penguin Books, 1969), pp. 194f.

[19] Burke, *Reflections on the Revolution in France*, p. 119.

[20] Burke, *Reflections on the Revolution in France*, p. 119.

[21] Gilbert Keith Chesterton, *Orthodoxy* (Garden City: Doubleday, 1936), p. 48.

[22] G.K. Chesterton, *The Catholic Church and Conversion* (New York: Macmillan, 1926), p. 93.

[23] Virgil Michel, "Natural and Supernatural Society," *Orate Fratres* 10 (1935–36): 243–47, 293–96, 338–342, 394–98, 434–438 at 437.

[24] Michel, "Natural and Supernatural Society," p. 436.

[25] Michel, "Natural and Supernatural Society," p. 436.

[26] Philip Murnion, "Catholic Social Spirituality," *Church* 7 (1991): 11–15 at 12.

[27] Murnion, "Catholic Social Spirituality," p. 12.

[28] Fred Kammer, *Doing Faithjustice* (New York: Paulist Press, 1991), p. 56.

[29] Donal Dorr, "Solidarity and Integral Human Development," in Gregory Baum and Robert Ellsberg, eds., *The Logic of Solidarity* (Maryknoll: Orbis Books, 1989), pp. 143–154 at 153.

[30] Murnion, "Catholic Social Spirituality," p. 15.

[31] We borrow the expression "deep theory" from Drew Christiansen who, in turn, borrowed it from Ronald Dworkin, *Taking Rights Seriously* (Cambridge: Harvard University Press, 1977). Christiansen's essay on the role of solidarity and relative egalitarianism in Catholic social teaching has informed a good deal of this chapter. See Drew Christiansen, "On Relative Equality."

[32] Christiansen, "On Relative Equality," p. 668.

[33] National Conference of Catholic Bishops, "Economic Justice for All," 14.

[34] John Paul II, *Centesimus Annus,* 38 and passim.

[35] Michael Schuck, *That They Be One* (Washington, D.C.: Georgetown University Press, 1991), p. 187, quoting Raymond Plant, "Community: Concept, Conception, and Ideology," *Politics and Society* 8 (1978): 79–107 at 105.

[36] Robert Reich, "Secession of the Successful," *New York Times Magazine,* sec. 6 (January 20, 1991): 16–17, 42–45.

[37] John Kenneth Galbraith, *The Affluent Society,* 3rd ed. (New York: New American Library, 1976).

[38] Reich, "Secession of the Successful," p. 42.

[39] Reich, "Secession of the Successful," p. 42.

[40] Reich, "Secession of the Successful," p. 43.

[41] Reich, "Secession of the Successful," p. 43.

[42] Franz Hinkelanmert, "Crisis of Socialism and the North-South Fight," *Blueprint for Social Justice* 45 (December 1991): 3.

[43] It ought to be admitted that some of John XXIII's writing contained elements of an optimism about the inevitability of moral solidarity due to empirical interdependence. Taken as a whole, however, the basis for recognition of solidarity in Catholic social teaching is not self-interest, however enlightened, but a theory of justice founded upon an understanding of humanity's essential relatedness.

[44] Gregory Baum, "Structures of Sin," in *Logic of Solidarity,* pp. 110–126 at 121–122.

[45] John Paul II acted in just this way when he called for a preferential

solidarity with labor in *Laborem Exercens.* See John Paul II, *Laborem Exercens,* 8.

[46] NCCB, "Economic Justice for All," 77.

[47] Christiansen, "On Relative Equality," p. 652.

[48] Christiansen, "On Relative Equality," p. 653.

[49] Christiansen, "On Relative Equality," p. 653.

[50] John XXIII, *Mater et Magistra,* 157–159; Paul VI, *Progressio Populorum,* 9, 44; John Paul II, *Sollicitudo Rei Socialis,* 14.

[51] An instructive historical tracing of the development of this method in Catholic social thought and the emergence of inequality as the social question of the modern era may be found in Christiansen, "On Relative Equality," pp. 656–660.

[52] Raymond Flynn, "Operation 'Domestic Order,' " *Commonweal* 118 (1991): 251–256 at 252.

[53] Flynn, "Operation 'Domestic Order,' " p. 253.

[54] National Conference of Catholic Bishops, "Putting Children and Families First: A Challenge for Our Church, Nation and World," *Origins* 21 (1991): 393–404 at 393.

[55] NCCB, "Putting Children First," p. 395.

[56] NCCB, "Putting Children First," p. 395.

[57] Daniel Patrick Moynihan, "Social Justice in the Next Century," *America* 165 (1991): 132–137 at 134–135.

[58] John D. Rockefeller, "Preface," in *Beyond Rhetoric: A New American Agenda for Children and Families* (Washington, D.C.: Government Printing Office, 1991) as quoted in Moynihan, "Social Justice in the Next Century," p. 135.

[59] Moynihan, "Social Justice in the Next Century," p. 136.

[60] George Will, "Stressed Out in America," *Washington Post* (January 16, 1992), p. A27. Will goes on to note that if one wonders why this difference in government spending the answer is readily available. "Those over 65 have a voting rate 50 percent higher than those 18–34. . . . It is an old story: The squeaking wheels get the grease. The elderly write better letters than infants write."

[61] Paul Taylor, " 'Dow Jones of the National Soul' Sours," *Washington Post* (January 16, 1992), p. A25. The Index of Social Indicators is compiled by Marc Miringoff of Fordham University and is based on seventeen categories such as infant mortality, children in poverty, unemployment, and health insurance coverage. It relies mostly on government reported data for its statistics.

[62] Oral remarks made by Ms. Nancy Alexander, Director of Issues at Bread for the World, during a panel discussion on "Putting Children and Families First" at a meeting sponsored by the U.S. Catholic Confer-

ence's Department of Social Development and World Peace, "Catholic Social Ministry in the Nineties: Traditional Values, Contemporary Challenges" (Washington, D.C.: March 2, 1992).

[63] NCCB, "Putting Children First," p. 396.

[64] Hollenbach, *Justice, Peace, and Human Rights* (New York: Crossroad Publishing, 1988), p. 83.

[65] Bellah, et al., *The Good Society* (New York: Alfred Knopf, 1991), p. 274.

[66] Paul VI, *Progressio Populorum*, 17.

[67] Bellah, et al., *The Good Society*, p. 278.

[68] Bellah, et al., *The Good Society*, p. 282.

[69] This analysis of Paul VI's teaching draws on Christiansen, "On Relative Equality," pp. 663–664.

[70] Donal Dorr, "Solidarity and Integral Human Development," pp. 144–146.

[71] This of course is a major theme in Bellah, et al., *Habits of the Heart*. Chapter four on love and marriage is perhaps the clearest illustration of how our crimped language of individualism disables people in expressing their best perceptions.

Epilogue

[1] Milbank, *Theology and Social Theory*, pp. 282ff.

[2] *On the Genealogy of Morals*, I, 13, trans. Walter Kaufmann and R.J. Hollingdale, in Friedrich Nietzsche, *On the Genealogy of Morals and Ecce Homo* (New York: Vintage Books, 1967), pp. 44f.

[3] Milbank, *Theology and Social Theory*, p. 283.

[4] Milbank, *Theology and Social Theory*, p. 288.

[5] Milbank, *Theology and Social Theory*, p. 434.

[6] Friedrich Nietzsche, *The Gay Science*, trans. Walter Kaufmann (New York: Vintage Books, 1974), pp. 181f.

[7] Friedrich Nietzsche, *Untimely Meditations*, trans. R.J. Hollingdale (Cambridge: Cambridge University Press, 1983).

[8] Friedrich Nietzsche, *Thus Spoke Zarathustra: A Book for All and None*, trans. Walter Kaufmann (New York: Viking Press, 1966), p. 145.

[9] In the second edition Nietzsche added a fourth book in which various figures come to visit Zarathustra on his mountain. It is noteworthy that in the course of Zarathustra's transformation/transfiguration into the Overman, his eagle brings for his repast two lambs which he has snatched, *Thus Spoke Zarathustra*, p. 216. Presumably the Overman can be fully a "bird of prey."

[10] Nicholas Lash, *Easter in Ordinary*, p. 59.